LONDON RECORD SOCIETY
PUBLICATIONS

VOLUME IX
FOR THE YEAR 1973

THE
SPANISH COMPANY

BY

PAULINE CROFT

LONDON RECORD SOCIETY

1973

© *London Record Society*

SBN 9009 5206 7

Bodleian Library MS. Rawlinson C.178 appears by permission of the Keeper of Western Manuscripts. Transcripts of Crown-copyright records in the Public Record Office appear by permission of the Controller of H.M. Stationery Office

THIS VOLUME IS PUBLISHED WITH THE HELP OF A
GRANT FROM THE TWENTY-SEVEN FOUNDATION

Printed in Great Britain by
W & J MACKAY LIMITED, CHATHAM

CONTENTS

ABBREVIATIONS   vi

INTRODUCTION   vii
    i. The first Spanish Company, 1530–1585   vii
    ii. The revival of the Company, 1604–1606   xxix
    iii. The documents   li

REGISTER BOOK, 1604–6   1

BOOK OF OATHS, ACTS AND ORDINANCES   74

CHARTER OF 1605   95

ADDITIONAL DOCUMENTS   114
    i. Articles of trade, 1604   114
    ii. Petition to the lord treasurer, 1604   116
    iii. Letter from Sir Charles Cornwallis, 1605   117
    iv. Petition to the privy council, 1606   118
    v. Opinions concerning the charters, 1606   123

INDEX   125

NOTE ON THE LONDON RECORD SOCIETY   143

ABBREVIATIONS

A.G.S.	Archivo General de Simancas
A.P.C.	*Acts of the Privy Council of England 1558–1621*, ed. J. R. Dasent *et al*. Vols. 7–[39]. London, 1890–1930.
B.M.	British Museum
Cott.	British Museum, Cotton MS.
Cott. Vesp.	British Museum, Cotton MS. Vespasian
H.M.C.	Historical Manuscripts Commission
Harl.	British Museum, Harley MS.
Lansd.	British Museum, Lansdowne MS.
P.C.C.	Public Record Office, wills proved in the Prerogative Court of Canterbury
P.R.O.	Public Record Office
S.P.	Public Record Office, State Papers

INTRODUCTION

i. The first Spanish Company, 1530–1585

The origins of the Spanish Company are to be found not in England but in the organisation built up by English merchants in the early sixteenth century for their own welfare and protection in the Iberian peninsula. In this there was nothing unusual for both the Merchant Staplers and the Merchant Adventurers had established their headquarters in their mart towns rather than in London. The English merchants trading to Spain and Portugal did not possess any staple towns comparable to Calais or Antwerp; but the chief focus of English commerce was the coastline of Andalusia, the area to which the majority of English cargoes were shipped, and it was in the Andalusian ports of Seville, San Lucar de Barrameda, Puerto de Santa Maria and Cadiz that the majority of English merchants and factors congregated.

San Lucar, at the mouth of the Guadalquivir, was the natural seaport of inland Seville, where larger vessels unloaded their cargoes for shipment up the river in barges. As an exempt seigneurial port belonging to the dukes of Medina Sidonia, San Lucar levied its own customs duties which were far lighter than the exactions of the crown of Spain. The duchy had for many years pursued a policy of encouraging foreign merchants to trade and settle in the port, and in 1517 Don Alonso Perez de Guzman, duke of Medina Sidonia, granted to the English merchants resident in San Lucar their earliest corporate privileges, confirming the position of their leader as the 'consul and judge', and bestowing on them 'a piece of ground in the street down below the waterside' on which they might at their own expense erect a chapel dedicated to St. George.[1]

This grant, usually referred to in later petitions as 'the privilege of St. George' formed the basis on which the English community or 'brotherhood of St. George' as it was subsequently known, proceeded to establish itself. The complex of buildings around the chapel, which formed the main centre, eventually grew to include eight houses for the nation to lodge in, a house for the consul himself, and a riverside area adjacent to the chapel which was used as a quay; in addition the brotherhood owned a local vineyard and some other property in the nearby coastal hamlet of Chipiona.[2] With its religious and community functions it resembled many other *cofradías*

---

1. According to the preamble to the privileges of 1517, the English had received numerous earlier concessions dating back to the 13th century. The form of these grants, if they existed, is unclear. Gordon Connell-Smith, *Forerunners of Drake* (1954), 81–90.
2. English College, Valladolid, MSS. San Lucar de Barrameda, Miscelanea I, 'Donacion por el consul y mercaderes ingleses', 29 Apr. 1591.

maintained by foreign merchants in Spain, the largest and most famous being that of the wealthy Flemings of Seville.[1]

In England no attempt was made to organise the merchants trading to the peninsula until September 1530. By this time, Anglo-Spanish diplomatic relations were deteriorating rapidly, while religious changes in England were making the merchants into objects of suspicion within Spain itself. In response to petitions for assistance from some of the leading traders, Henry VIII incorporated them under the title of the Andalusia Company.[2] The powers and scope of the company were, however, very small. It incorporated only those who traded to the south coast, in particular to San Lucar, Seville, Cadiz and Puerto de Santa Maria. The residents of these ports, including the Welsh and Irish, were empowered to meet annually in order to elect a consul or consuls and twelve assistants for their own better government. The charter expressed the wish that the advice and consent of the London merchants, together with that of two representatives of Bristol and two of Southampton, should be sought beforehand, but no mechanism was instituted to ensure that this was done. The company had no organisation in England, its chief official being the consul or governor resident in the house adjacent to the chapel in San Lucar.[3] The Andalusia Company, in short, was not a true company in the sense in which the word later came to be employed; it was merely an attempt to strengthen the brotherhood of St. George by confirming in England most of the privileges already granted to it in Spain.

By 1538 the company was internally divided, with many of the merchants refusing to pay the imposts levied by the consul and his assistants on English trade. At the request of the English ambassador, Charles V confirmed the grant of 1530 in a document that was to become one of the chief safeguards of the merchants' corporate rights and liberties in Spain itself.[4] It did not succeed in preserving the Andalusia Company, however, and although the election of consuls at San Lucar was sporadically maintained, by the end of the reign of Henry VIII the company no longer had any real existence.

The following three decades were difficult ones for all branches of English commerce. A major European depression, the collapse of the credit of the great powers, the dislocation of the Antwerp trade and the debasement of the English coinage combined to undermine steady trade. In addition the merchants trading to Spain and Portugal encountered further difficulties of their own. Between 1550 and 1559, the great transatlantic commerce of Seville experienced a recession which affected the whole of the Spanish economy; meanwhile the Elizabethan settlement of religion, by ranking England alongside the protestant powers of Europe, brought Englishmen increasingly under the scrutiny of the Inquisition. A revision of customs duties in both England and Spain placed extra burdens upon trade, and in 1561 Philip II in his attempts to strengthen Spanish naval resources revived

1. A. Girard, 'Les étrangers dans la vie économique d'Espagne aux 16e et 17e siècles', *Annales*, v (1933), 567–78.
2. Connell-Smith, *Forerunners of Drake*, 91.
3. The charter is printed in *Select Charters of Trading Companies 1530–1707*, ed. C. T. Carr (Selden Soc., xxviii, 1913), 1–3.
4. Connell-Smith, *Forerunners of Drake*, 91.

earlier legislation prohibiting the loading of goods in foreign vessels if Spanish ones were available.[1]

More problems of a political nature followed. In 1563 Spain imposed a temporary embargo on English imports, largely as a result of the havoc caused by English privateers who were hovering off the Spanish coastline.[2] At the end of the same year a further embargo was instituted, arising not from events in Spain itself but as a result of the steady deterioration of Anglo-Netherlands relations.[3] At the same time the old Anglo-Portuguese alliance was increasingly strained by English expansion southward into Guinea, Barbary and other areas claimed by the Portuguese crown.[4]

Despite the failure of the incorporation of 1530, the idea of a company remained alive throughout the troubled early years of Elizabeth's reign. Various tentative schemes were put forward, usually based on the desire not only to obtain additional security for the merchants themselves but also to exclude the 'unskilful', the retailers or part-time traders who dabbled in Anglo-Iberian commerce. One early group of anonymous petitioners requested a new grant no longer confined to Andalusia but embracing the whole country, including the ports within the 'Strait of Morocco'. They claimed that such an incorporation would enable them to act in unison to defend themselves, particularly against the new customs levied by Philip II. They hoped to bring pressure on the king by confining all English trade to San Lucar, thereby depriving him of revenue from other ports. Moreover the English merchants argued that they would be in a better position to obtain justice in the Spanish courts if they were a company, not merely a collection of individuals. The envisaged incorporation was a modest one; its advocates merely requested that besides the consul at San Lucar, they might elect a consul and assistants in London 'to congregate themselves and punish offenders, with authority to send for them wheresoever they shall be within the queen's majesty's dominions'.[5] Another suggestion, equally limited, was that the office of consul in Spain should be revived and given extra powers.[6]

Nothing came of these plans, and in 1568 there occurred the worst breakdown that had as yet taken place in Anglo-Iberian relations. The anger of Sebastian I at English intrusions into the Portuguese sphere of influence in Africa came to a head with the seizure of William Winter's ship off Guinea. Portugal was closed to English merchants, and although illicit commerce gradually grew up, the ports were not to be reopened legally until 1576.[7] At first the dispute was more of an inconvenience than a disaster; the trade between London and Portugal was at most only a tenth

1. S.P. 70/26 nos. 155, 176.
2. S.P. 70/58 no. 859.
3. R. B. Wernham, *Before the Armada: the Growth of English Foreign Policy 1485–1588* (1966), 282; S.P. 70/66 no. 1291; S.P. 70/67 no. 38.
4. *Cal. S.P. Spanish, Elizabeth*, i, 218, 419; V. M. Shillington and A. B. W. Chapman, *The Commercial Relations of England and Portugal* [1907], 139–40.
5. S.P. 12/20 no. 65. The spelling in quotations from MS. sources has been modernised throughout the introduction.
6. Cott. Vesp. C. xiii f. 305.
7. Draft treaties were produced in 1571 and 1572 but negotiations continued until 1576 (Shillington and Chapman, *Commercial Relations*, 144–5).

of the total trade to the peninsula and the new contacts with Barbary were already more valuable than the fairly static Portuguese trade.[1] Moreover, through Spanish border ports such as Ayamonte, Bayona in Galicia and Vigo it was still possible to reach Portuguese markets. By an unhappy coincidence, however, the end of the year was also to see the closure of these and all other Spanish ports, thereby sealing the whole of the peninsula against legitimate trade with England.

The seizure of the duke of Alva's payships in December 1568 brought England, the Netherlands and Spain into acute conflict.[2] Despite the provocation, Philip II hesitated for a while before taking retaliatory measures. A temporary embargo was imposed in Seville and on the north coast, but only when it became clear that Elizabeth did not intend to return the money, nor enter into negotiations, were the embargo-orders made permanent and universal.[3] As in the case of Portugal, the growth of illicit trade helped to lessen the impact of the stoppage, but the announcement of the official reopening of the ports in April 1573, as the first move towards reconciliation, was warmly welcomed in London. The proclamation not only revived legitimate trade; it also put fresh life into the idea of forming a new Spanish company.

During the embargo the London merchants trading to Spain and Portugal had been forced to act in unison on several occasions. They had sought licences to continue an irregular trade to the Isles of Bayona, either directly or through the Channel Islands, and to St. Jean de Luz in south-west France. Together the leading merchants had formed committees to assess and sell off Spanish and Portuguese goods sequestered in England, and to distribute among their fellows the money thereby recouped as compensation for their losses in the peninsula.[4] In dealing with these matters they once again began to feel the need of some form of corporate organisation. In comparison with the Merchant Staplers or the Merchant Adventurers, they had no authorised representatives or standard channels of communication; transacting any sort of joint business was therefore slower, more complex and less reliable.

In May 1573, the merchants trading to Spain and Portugal had been due to receive a dividend of £8,000 from the sale of confiscated goods. The collection of this sum from the commissioners and its division were causing so much trouble that a deputation waited on the earl of Leicester at his London house to seek his help in solving the problem. They requested him to ask Burghley if they might nominate their own officers, as distinct from the commissioners chosen by the crown, who would 'receive for the whole company and make to every man payment according to his due share'. As they pointed out, the Merchant Adventurers and the Merchant Staplers already had such officers, which they lacked only because they were not a recognised company. The earl, who had many carefully cultivated contacts

1. T. S. Willan, 'English Trade with Morocco' in *Studies in Elizabethan Foreign Trade* (Manchester, 1959), 109.
2. For a detailed narrative of the incident see Conyers Read, 'Queen Elizabeth's seizure of the duke of Alva's payships', *Jour. Modern History*, v (1933), 443-6.
3. A.G.S. Estado legajo 565, 25 Nov. 1575; P.R.O., High Court of Admiralty 13/17 f. 124v; S.P. 70/106 no. 194.
4. Cott. Vesp. C. xiii f. 318; S.P. 12/85 nos. 29, 30; Lansd. 110 (66).

in the City, was broadly sympathetic to their plea. 'For my part', he wrote to Burghley, 'I cannot perceive their request unreasonable', but he added that he left the matter to the secretary's further consideration. Returning from the country in July, Leicester again took up the merchants' cause and sent Thomas Wilford, the future president of the company, over to Burghley to discuss the problem.[1]

Friends such as the royal favourite were valuable at court, but without support in the City the protagonists of incorporation would have made little headway. They were extremely fortunate at this juncture to have the active co-operation of John Mershe of the Merchant Adventurers. A former common sergeant of the City of London, Mershe had also served several terms as governor of the Merchant Adventurers, leading them in their running battle against interlopers. In addition, he was a former warden and influential member of the Mercers Company, the foremost of the livery companies, and had friendly relations with a large number of government servants and courtiers. On many occasions he had acted unobtrusively as the link between the City interests and the crown.[2]

During the stoppage Mershe had had numerous dealings with the Spanish merchants, for besides acting as a commissioner for sales he had headed the committee authorised to oversee the regulation of the clandestine trade to Guernsey and thence to Spain.[3] In May 1571, he and the merchant Thomas Aldersey had submitted a report to Burghley on John Frampton's claim to compensation for injuries received in Spain,[4] while in December of that year he had signed the petition drawn up to urge the reopening of the Portugal trade, 'not as a merchant trading Portugal but understanding their minds and the necessity of the matter'.[5] These incidents brought Mershe face to face with the inconveniences arising from the lack of incorporation in the Spanish trade, and as a result he urged the merchants to become a regulated company. His claim to have been the instigator of the whole movement was perhaps a little sweeping, in view of the attempts made earlier by at least some of the Spanish merchants themselves to raise the issue.[6] Still, Mershe's influence, at a time when the other schemes were fading into the background, may well have been decisive.

Another well-known City figure who gave the plan his qualified support was Peter Osborne, one of Burghley's most trusted economic advisers and a former merchant of wide experience who now held the post of lord

1. Harl. 6691 ff. 43, 50.

2. G. D. Ramsay, *John Isham, Mercer and Merchant Adventurer* (Northants. Record Soc., xxi, 1962), pp. liv–lx; O. de Smedt, *De Engelse Natie te Antwerpen in de 16e eeuw* (Antwerp, 1950–4), ii, 90; for Mershe's correspondence with Cecil see *Relations politiques des Pays-Bas et de l'Angleterre sous le règne de Philippe II*, ed. K. de Letten-hove (Brussels, 1882–1900), v, 141, 145, 153, 157, 163.

3. Lansd. 110 (66); Cott. Vesp. C. xiii f. 318v.

4. S.P. 12/78 no. 5. The Bristol factor John Frampton, taken prisoner in 1559 in Seville, was probably the best-known English victim of the Inquisition; the ramifications of his case dragged on for nearly twenty years. For his subsequent fame as a translator and publisher of Spanish works, see L. C. Wroth, 'An Elizabethan merchant and man of letters: John Frampton', *Huntington Library Quarterly*, xvii (1954), 299–314.

5. Cott. Nero B.i. f. 190.

6. S.P. 15/24 no. 94.

treasurer's remembrancer in the exchequer. Osborne, with remarkable foresight, felt that the proposed company would meet with trouble unless it made every effort to avoid conflicts with the Merchant Adventurers. Moreover, in his opinion some guarantee was needed to prevent London and Bristol from drawing even more of the Spanish trade to themselves, at the expense of the smaller outports.[1]

The plan of incorporation under discussion by November 1574 was more ambitious than anything so far. It envisaged 'a body politic by the name of consuls, assistants and fellowship of merchants trading Spain and Portugal', including both London and the outports, which would unite the merchants in England and nominate a consul or governor for them in Spain. Interlopers were to be punished, retailers and artificers excluded, and the company would have power to make binding ordinances for the conduct of trade.[2]

After 1573, the movement for incorporation was slowly gathering speed, but at the same time it was generating opposition. The Iberian trade by now was prosperous and expanding; as the memory of the stoppage faded, the need for corporate action seemed less urgent, while the advantages of company membership might prove inadequate to compensate for the internal regulations and financial exactions which would inevitably be imposed. Above all, the new company by the terms of its proposed charter intended to restrict membership to those merchants not free of another society, who had traded to Spain and Portugal since 1569.[3]

The chief opponents of Mershe's plans for a Spanish company were a group of his fellow Merchant Adventurers, led by Aldermen Thomas Pullyson, Thomas Starkey and Anthony Gamage. They protested that the restriction clause would exclude them, as their vigorous trade between London and Spain was composed largely of re-exports from Flanders, Hamburg and Emden, imported into England during the course of their commerce as Merchant Adventurers. They alleged that if they were not permitted to trade in this way then Flemings, Spaniards and Frenchmen would replace them, 'without bringing any of the same into this realm, to the great hindrance of the navigation . . . and the great diminishing of her majesty's customs'.[4]

The opposition continued until February 1577, but Mershe had in the meantime persuaded the privy council that the grant of a charter would be in the national interest. Summoning several leading Spanish merchants such as Sir James Hawes and Alderman Edward Osborne, the council asked them to send for the recalcitrants 'and plainly declare unto them that unless they shall be contented to do as others do, order shall be taken that they shall not be suffered to traffic into Spain'. Hawes and his colleagues were also asked to certify to the council the names of the opponents and the reasons for their actions.[5]

1. S.P. 12/105 no. 3.
2. S.P. 12/99 no. 8.
3. The charter of 1577 is printed by Shillington and Chapman, *Commercial Relations*. Unfortunately they failed to allow for old-style dating and mistranscribed the names of several merchants.
4. S.P. 12/99 no. 9.
5. *A.P.C.*, ix, 282.

After further hearings the councillors delivered their verdict in April 1577. The twenty-four Merchant Adventurers who had been excluded were each to be admitted as full members for the fee of £5. Since the two formal documents intended to receive the royal seal had already been drawn up, they were also to bear the cost of making out the new copies which would include their own names. The antagonists 'acknowledged themselves contented and willing to stand to perform and observe this their lordships' order' whereupon they were all dismissed 'and willed to behave themselves as dutiful subjects and good friends and neighbours both in their trade into Spain and other actions'.[1]

The council's next action was less agreeable to the Spanish merchants. A month later the privy councillors decided that for the better government of the company, a 'principal officer' should reside in Spain in addition to the governor in London.[2] This would consolidate the position of the old brotherhood of St. George as part of the new company, for the nominee would act as consul at San Lucar and administer the property of the brotherhood. The idea was a valuable one, but the councillors' choice for the post was disastrous. Roger Bodenham, an English catholic trader resident in Seville with a Spanish wife and family, had acted as an informant for Burghley for many years, and to the council he seemed the obvious candidate; but he was disliked by a large majority of the community abroad and Mershe tried strenuously to have him removed.[3] Mershe's judgment was to be vindicated for Bodenham proved useless as consul, and his negligence was to be a major factor in the subsequent disintegration of the brotherhood.

The charter finally granted on 8 July 1577 was of vastly greater scope than that of 1530 or even the most ample recommendations of 1574. The area of jurisdiction was extended to include the whole Iberian coastline from Fuenterrabia to Barcelona. The president of the company, together with forty assistants, of whom at least ten were to dwell outside London, controlled all business transacted in England. In addition the merchants were empowered to elect a governor and six assistants in Spain, who would in effect act within the framework of the brotherhood of St. George. The company was granted all the usual powers of a corporate body including that of punishing interlopers. Mershe, now knighted, was named in the charter as the first president; among the London assistants were such influential figures as Sir James Hawes, probably the merchant trading to the peninsula on the largest scale,[4] Edward Osborne who was already supporting the exploration of the Levant,[5] and Richard Saltonstall. Of the thirty men appointed by the charter, seven were past or future lord mayors of London. Also included were Pullyson and Starkey, the protesters of 1574, together

1. *A.P.C.*, ix, 331.
2. *A.P.C.*, ix, 254.
3. S.P. 70/132 no. 973; S.P. 70/131 no. 896; S.P. 94/2 ff.41–2; S.P. 94/1 f.190; S.P. 94/2 f.3.
4. In 1576, Hawes was much the largest London exporter of goods other than broadcloth to Spain (P.R.O., King's Remembrancer Exchequer E 190/6/4). He also maintained an extensive network of partners and factors within the peninsula itself (A.G.S., Guerra Antigua 88 ff. 16, 32, 38).
5. R. Hakluyt, *The Principall Navigations . . . of the English Nation*, ed. W. Raleigh (Glasgow, 1903–5), v, 168.

with William Hewett, John Heydon and other Merchant Adventurers who had been brought before the privy council in the winter of 1577. Among the usual honorary members named at the head of the list were Walsingham, Leicester and the pro-Spanish Sir James Crofts, along with the diplomat Sir Henry Cobham, not long back from Madrid, Admiral William Winter, and Sir Thomas Gresham, the most venerable member of the City hierarchy.[1]

The new company seemed to have good prospects of success. Backed by a large number of leading merchants, with powerful support from the privy council, it had managed to overcome and then to conciliate its opponents. Yet events were quickly to show that this appearance of solidarity concealed serious weaknesses. Within eighteen months of the company's foundation it found itself at odds with the Merchant Adventurers, the outports and the government itself. The renewal of conflicts with the Merchant Adventurers would perhaps have been avoided had Sir John Mershe lived a little longer. His death early in 1579[2] left the company without anyone of sufficient stature or experience to mediate in such disputes.

Thomas Wilford, Mershe's successor as president and the dominant figure in the Spanish Company for the rest of its existence, was not an obvious choice. The son of an obscure family,[3] he had worked earlier as a factor in Portugal alongside his brother William, but in 1559 when returning to the continent after a visit to England he had been taken captive by the French. His trade was never on a large scale and was conducted largely with northern Portugal and the coast of Galicia, where he maintained an agent named George Kerwyn. Although a member of the Merchant Tailors Company he was not particularly active in its affairs, and he never became an alderman. However, he served as chamberlain of the City and in this influential office he may well have had the opportunity to amass a substantial private fortune.[4]

Wilford's position as a medium-scale trader may perhaps be compared with that of some of the early seventeenth-century governors of the Merchant Adventurers, who had practically retired from active commerce but were elected mainly for their prestige with the government.[5] Wilford had, if not prestige, a number of extremely useful contacts. He was known to Leicester, who had used him in his negotiations with Burghley in 1574; he had worked with Mershe in setting up the company and was rewarded with an assistantship. Above all, Wilford had admirable connections by marriage. Through his wife, a daughter of Sir James Hawes, he was linked

1. P.R.O., Patent Rolls 19 Eliz. pt. 8.
2. P.C.C. 2 Bakon.
3. P.R.O., H.C.A. 13/8 ff. 2–7, 166, 187. Wilford does not seem to be connected with the well-known Wilford or Wilsford family of Ileden in Kent which produced his namesake and contemporary Sir Thomas Wilford, soldier and intelligencer (*The Oxinden Letters 1607–42*, ed. Dorothy Gardiner, 1933). It seems more likely that he was related to Nicholas Wilford of Bilbao, a substantial merchant resident there in 1527 (*Letters and Papers Henry VIII*, iv (2), nos. 1362–3).
4. P.R.O., E 190/2/1; A. B. Beaven, *The Aldermen of the City of London* (1908–13), ii, 137; C. M. Clode, *The Early History of the Guild of Merchant Tailors* (1888), ii, 252.
5. Astrid Friis, *Alderman Cockayne's Project and the Cloth Trade* (Copenhagen, 1927), 80–3.

with some of the most powerful Iberian merchants including the future privateer Sir John Watts. It seems probable that his election to the presidency was largely due to the influence of Hawes who intended Wilford to ensure that his own extensive trade should be in no way prejudiced by any future regulations that the company might impose.[1]

The conflict with the Merchant Adventurers in 1579, just after Wilford's election, was essentially a recurrence in a slightly different form of the issue which had arisen in the winter of 1577. A body of opinion within the Merchant Adventurers now complained of the activities of various of their brethren, who as members of both companies were shipping Hamburg and Eastland goods directly to Spain and Portugal without unloading them at an English port. This lessened the sale of similar goods to the Spanish merchants in England, while the offenders could also afford to sell off their English goods in Germany at lower prices, since they drew an additional profit from their trade to Spain; other traders were thus undercut. These complaints were aggravated by a narrow outlook redolent of secretiveness and suspicious jealousy. It was feared that, 'since no man can serve two masters', the members trading to Spain would put that branch of their commerce first, and not vote in general courts in accordance with the interests of the Merchant Adventurers. This would breed disruption: 'we shall have opinions, sects, divisions, brawls and suspicions amongst us as if it were to begin hell on earth', argued the others. Moreover, an offender could easily evade any fine or imposition, 'for when we shall look for him in our mart towns, he will be gone into Spain or Eastland'. Above all, the culprits would join 'in portable dealings with unfree men, and their servants are made partakers of the secrets of the commodities and reckonings of our company, whilst they make their portable provisions for Spain and other countries'. The fear that the company's carefully guarded 'secrets' would be revealed seems to have been at the root of much of the hostility; although these were left undefined, the reference to commodities indicates some form of price fixing.[2]

The leaders of the Spanish Company must have been perturbed by this revival of opposition among the Merchant Adventurers when they had hoped that the matter had already been settled. But there was little they could do about it, since officially at least it was an internal dispute within another company. Meanwhile a more ominous threat had arisen. Again, it concerned the re-export of foreign goods to the peninsula, but this time the cause of contention lay in the nature of the goods themselves.

The export of English hides, skins, tallow and related commodities had long been forbidden in order to conserve home supplies. Now, however, 'certain informers' were arguing that these statutes also applied to foreign goods of a similar nature, so that once they had been imported it was illegal to ship them out again to Spain or Portugal. In addition, they extended the list of prohibited exports to include 'shaven latten, virginall wire, thimbles of latten and other things wrought with copper or latten,

1. S.P. 94/1 ff. 41–2. It is of course possible that the name of Sir James Hawes in the port-books covers a partnership of which Wilford was a member, which would explain the paucity of references to Wilford's individual trade.
2. *Tudor Economic Documents*, ed. R. H. Tawney and Eileen Power (1924), ii, 53–8.

or andirons tongs fireshovels and such like having any tipping or mixture of brass or latten', all of which were classed as gunmetal and confined to England.[1]

Wilford retaliated by presenting a petition to the privy council, which argued that since Richard II's reign English merchants had re-exported spices without paying any extra duties, a precedent subsequently invoked by Edward IV to cover leather and metals. He therefore asked that these time-honoured forms of the re-export trade might continue without any hindrance. The councillors, who had no intention of allowing a lucrative branch of commerce to be obstructed, especially as they had just openly lent their support to the company in charge of it, obligingly required the attorney-general and the solicitor-general to join together 'to devise such articles as they shall think meet for a grant to be passed from her majesty for the better authorising of the same unto them'.[2]

During the course of this dispute the hostility between the Spanish Company and the Merchant Adventurers had withered away with the rise of a new object of joint suspicion. Three months after they had been at odds they found themselves acting in concert to block the foundation of the proposed new Eastland Company, led by Alderman Thomas Pullyson, a member of both the older incorporations.[3]

The details of this incident are unclear, but it apparently concerned the exclusion of the Adventurers and Iberian merchants alike from the new company on the grounds that they were not 'mere merchants' within the definition of the term. At first it looked as if the dispute might be settled quickly, for the privy council was informed of a *rapprochement* in July 1579,[4] but these hopes proved illusory and the quarrel dragged on for over a year despite the close links between all the merchants concerned. The master of the rolls and the attorney-general were instructed to hold hearings on the issue, and in July 1580 their letters were submitted to the councillors. The council then ruled that the Eastland Company's definition of a 'mere merchant' was 'rather a cavil in effect than of moment to debar any merchant of the said companies of Merchant Adventurers and Spanish merchants from being admitted in their said company, paying the ordinary fine appointed'.[5] The Eastland Company would not accept this verdict but continued to argue that any member of another regulated trading company was not a 'mere merchant' within the meaning of their charter. Angered by this, the privy council again summoned the combatants in August, and informed the Eastland Company that when their plea for a charter had been granted, the council had only intended the words 'mere merchants' to debar those who were also artificers or retailers. The verdict of July was reiterated: those Merchant Adventurers or members of the Spanish Company who had traded to the east country since 1568 were to be admitted into the Eastland Company on payment of £10. Moreover, the dispute had taken so long that the time originally allowed in the charter for submitting

1. Lansd. 110 (75).
2. *A.P.C.*, xi, 77.
3. *The Acts and Ordinances of the Eastland Company*, ed. Maud Sellers (1906), p. xi.
4. *A.P.C.*, xi, 205.
5. *A.P.C.*, xi, 428; xii, 110.

requests for membership had by now nearly expired. The council therefore extended it from 17 August to 10 October.[1]

These differences with the Merchant Adventurers and the Eastland Company were not in themselves insoluble, although they illustrate the importance attached by the London merchants to the re-export trade with Spain. The dispute with the outports, which was in progress at the same time, was of much greater importance in that it brought to the fore a problem that was to dog the Spanish Company throughout the years of its brief existence.

The move towards the foundation of a regulated company had been the work of the Londoners, who of course handled the bulk of the trade. Nevertheless the interests of the outports had been taken into account to a far greater extent than in 1530. Two assistants each were appointed for Bristol, Exeter, Southampton and Hull, along with the well-known merchant John Barker who became assistant for Ipswich although like many other Ipswich men he did much of his trade through London. Besides the assistants, four large contingents of outport merchants were listed among the founder-members; seventy-four from Bristol, twenty-nine from Exeter, twenty-six from Southampton and fourteen from Hull, making a total of 173 members out of the overall number of 389.[2]

The outports named in the charter were not the only ones which traded to Spain and Portugal. Nearly every harbour in the west country sent at least one ship a year to the peninsula, for few of the major trade routes were as diffuse as that between England and Spain. In an attempt to cope with the problem, the company gradually recognised other towns as members, and by the outbreak of war the 'privileged ports' included Barnstaple, King's Lynn, Newcastle, Plymouth and Chester. The number of outport assistants also increased; by 1585 Exeter had sixteen, Plymouth twelve and Barnstaple six.[3] Despite this expansion, however, it seems likely that in many of the outports the recognised freemen of the company were in a minority. Yarmouth immediately protested against the incorporation of the company in 1577,[4] and thereafter Yarmouth men continued their trade to the peninsula without troubling to apply for membership. They traded to most of the other monopoly areas with an equal lack of concern,[5] and although they appear to have been the only outport merchants to make a formal protest, they cannot have been the only ones to adopt this casual approach.

Yarmouth's attitude was not encouraging, but it could be disregarded provided that the major outports acknowledged the new incorporation. It was fortunate for the Spanish Company that the merchants of both Bristol and Exeter already possessed some degree of monopoly organisation within their respective ports. The Merchant Adventurers of Exeter were chiefly concerned with France but in 1566 they had also reserved to themselves

1. *A.P.C.*, xii, 146–50.
2. P.R.O., Patent Rolls 19 Eliz. pt. 8.
3. See below, **10, 299.**
4. Lansd. 78 (70).
5. N. J. Williams, 'The Maritime Trade of the East Anglian Ports 1550–90' (unpublished Oxford D.Phil. thesis, 1952), 151–66.

all trade to Spain and Portugal. Some time before August 1577 they received an invitation to join the company. After sending a deputation of two members up to London to discuss the question, they accepted, and from then on the Exeter branch of the Spanish Company met in the same hall as the Merchant Adventurers of Exeter since for all practical purposes they were the same group of people. A copy of the charter also seems to have been kept on permanent display there.[1] In Bristol the situation was rather different for the attempt to establish the Merchant Venturers in the first decade of Elizabeth's reign had proved abortive.[2] There are no traces of negotiations parallel to those at Exeter, and although a large number of Bristol men became members, at least one of them continued to retail goods as well as to trade.[3] Wilford appealed to the privy council to punish such a violation of the charter, but long-distance control of this type cannot have been very satisfactory. Although evidence is scanty, it is possible that a number of incidents such as this one preceded the open break between Bristol and the company that was to occur in 1605.

The city which was to give the Spanish Company most trouble, however, was the relatively remote and unimportant town of Chester. In 1554 the Chester Merchant Venturers had been granted a charter by Queen Mary which gave them a monopoly of all trade to the continent, besides excluding retailers and all followers of manual occupations. The latter provision seems to have been disregarded almost from the beginning; the Chester Merchant Adventurers became a fairly comprehensive body despite some early disputes with the town corporation, and the charter was confirmed in 1559.[4] Shortly after the incorporation of the Spanish Company, president Mershe asked the Merchant Venturers to confer with him over the question of membership. Like their fellows in Exeter they were then established as an outport branch, with a deputy and assistants chosen from among the leading merchants of the town.[5]

The Iberian merchants of Chester soon made themselves unpopular at home by insisting that all those who traded to Spain and Portugal should join the company, on the grounds that the charter of 1554 allowing them to trade without restrictions had been superseded by the new charter of the Spanish Company. At the same time they tried to prevent those Merchant Adventurers who both traded abroad and retailed goods from doing so, ordering them to choose one activity and abandon the other.[6] Although technically the dispute lay between the Spanish Company and the Chester Merchant Venturers it soon degenerated into a faction fight among the

---

1. W. Cotton, *An Elizabethan Guild of the City of Exeter* (Exeter, 1873), 144–5; below, **300**.

2. The Merchant Venturers had been incorporated in 1552, but when a bill of confirmation was presented to parliament in 1566, strong opposition was aroused in Bristol itself which resulted in the repeal of the charter in 1571 (*Records relating to the Society of Merchant Venturers of Bristol in the 17th century*, ed. P. McGrath (Bristol Record Soc., xvii, 1952), pp. i–xiii).

3. *A.P.C.*, x, 408–9.

4. D. M. Woodward, 'The Foreign Trade of Chester in the reign of Elizabeth I' (unpublished Manchester M.A. thesis, 1965), 139–46.

5. *The Liverpool Town Books*, ed. J. A. Twemlow (Liverpool, 1918–33), ii, 360–1.

6. S.P. 15/25 no. 77.

latter who were divided into the 'mere merchants' and the merchant retailers. More accurately the first group comprised the large-scale merchants whose prosperity was based entirely on commerce, the second the smaller traders whose less ample resources forced them to supplement their income by practising an additional craft or occupation. To add to the confusion, Eric Massey, the Spanish Company deputy in Chester, had meanwhile been attempting without much success to enforce the company monopoly over the merchants of Liverpool, one of the subsidiary havens of Chester.[1] The Liverpool merchants, angered by this interference, sided with the 'merchant retailers' in Chester, and invoked the assistance of a powerful local magnate, the earl of Derby, who took the matter up in London.

At last in November 1581 the privy council intervened, ordering the lord chief justice and the master of the rolls to hear the conflicting arguments put forward by Wilford, acting for the company, and some of the merchants of Chester and Liverpool.[2] The law lords concluded that the Spanish Company had acted beyond its powers in attempting to prevent the retailers from trading, since in the small outports there were not enough mere merchants to maintain the trade.[3] The privy council thereupon permitted the merchant retailers to continue their commerce and informed the earl of Derby of its decision.[4]

This was not the end of the matter, for in September 1582 the privy council was forced to repeat the whole process as the quarrel had not abated. It summoned the Chester merchants to London and reiterated its orders that the branch of the Spanish Company within the town should not stop the retailers from trading.[5] Again the settlement was short-lived for in 1584 the 'mere merchants being members of the Spanish Company' obtained from the queen a licence to export 10,000 dickers of calfskins a year. The retailers complained that this was another ploy to monopolise the trade, while the mere merchants argued that as the grant had been awarded 'in respect of their losses sustained by the French' as a result of privateering, the retailers who had suffered no such injuries were not entitled to participate. If they were to share in the transport of calfskins, the mere merchants asked that they in compensation should be allowed to retail.[6] Finally in July 1589 the councillors adopted the mere merchants' suggestion and in an attempt to obtain a lasting solution they ordered that henceforth all retailers might trade freely and take advantage of the licence, provided that the merchants could retail goods if they wished.[7] By now the cessation of commerce following the outbreak of war had rendered the conflict pointless, and at last it ended.

The altercation over the powers of the Spanish Company in Chester was not a headlong clash between the Londoners and the outport merchants

1. *Liverpool Town Books*, ii, 358–9, 361–4.
2. *A.P.C.*, xiii, 255.
3. *Liverpool Town Books*, ii, 403–5.
4. *A.P.C.*, xiii, 207.
5. R. H. Morris, *Chester in the Plantagenet and Tudor Reigns* (Chester, 1894), 464–5.
6. S.P. 12/129 nos. 52–3. The calendar assigns these documents to 1579 but as the first one deals with the calfskin licence they cannot have been written before 1584.
7. *A.P.C.*, xvii, 371–4.

of the type that was to occur in 1605. Moreover, its continuation into 1589, after the company had ceased to hold its courts, reinforces the impression that it was essentially a conflict between two groups within Chester. Then, too, Massey by his bullying arrogance had needlessly inflamed the situation. Nevertheless the privy council by its decision not to enforce the company monopoly had grievously weakened the chances of any effective control over the outports when the war came to an end. The significance of the affair must have made an impact in many places other than Chester itself.

However, conflicts between the company and the outports were not so widespread as to preclude all co-operation between them. Each provincial deputy and treasurer was expected to make an annual visit to the capital to render the accounts of membership fees and fines; they also attended the annual elections which took place in the general court on Ascension day or shortly after.[1] Besides being responsible to the central administration for its own affairs, each major outport controlled the smaller havens of its division or stretch of coastline allotted to it, which roughly followed the divisions of the customs system. The details of Chester's intervention at Liverpool suggest that at least some of the head ports made a genuine effort to organise the smaller ones. Similar contacts are apparent later at Exeter where in 1587 and 1588 the merchants on receipt of instructions from Wilford sent out letters to the towns of their division asking them to list the goods and property they had lost in Spain and Portugal on the out-break of war. They were requested to return the lists to the merchants of Exeter, who would forward them all to London where a general register was being compiled in order to press for compensation.[2]

The degree of control exercised by the company over its most distant branch, the former brotherhood of St. George, is hard to estimate. The London merchants were apparently eager to maintain those good relations with the dukes of Medina Sidonia which had contributed so much to the emergence of the company itself, and there survive some sketchy indications of financial matters transacted between the company and the duke through John Barker of Ipswich.[3] If the duke was friendly, however, other Spanish authorities were not. In later years the merchants asserted that they had sent over to Andalusia a copy of the letters patent of 1577, 'fair limmed and set forth in the best sort we could devise' in order to strengthen the position of the merchant community there. They had subsequently learned that 'they of the Inquisition got it and in despiteful manner did burn it'; if the story is true, it seems likely that this was another of those formal English documents to which the Inquisition objected on the grounds that it named Elizabeth as 'defender of the faith'.[4]

The consulate at San Lucar had had a precarious existence since the

1. Auditing was probably also dealt with on the election day as this would minimise the number of journeys up to London (see below, **11, 314**). Even the Bristol deputies travelled to London in the early stages of the company's existence, despite their opposition in later years: in 1583 John Barker the Bristol treasurer claimed £6 13s. 4d. 'for my charges to London twice being assistant general' (*Records relating to Merchant Venturers*, 82).
2. Cotton, *An Elizabethan Guild*, 143–4.
3. B.M., Additional Charter 1053.
4. S.P. 9/7 p. 41: Madrid, Archivo Historico Nacional, Inquisicion 2946, 6 Apr. 1577.

demise of the Andalusia Company, but its memory was by no means extinguished, for the last consul to serve had only left Spain in 1570.[1] Bodenham as the new consul-governor could easily have transformed the post into a valuable agency for the protection of merchants within the peninsula and the transmission of news and advice to London. To assist him in this he had a number of useful contacts in England and Spain as well as his own lengthy personal experience in the Iberian and other trades.[2] All this went for nothing as a result partly of his own prickly character, partly of the circumstances of his appointment, and above all of his own attitude to his commission. Throughout the years of his consulate, until he returned to England in 1586, he regarded himself as responsible to the privy council, not the company; he disliked the merchants and was in turn disliked by them, for he seems to have performed no useful services for the trading community. He informed on those merchants who shipped prohibited goods such as corn and ordnance, whilst participating in these trades himself; and both he and his family steered an ambiguous course through the muddy waters of Anglo-Spanish intelligence and espionage.[3]

Although Bodenham was not a good choice, allowance must be made for the additional difficulties that arose in the contacts between the new company in London and the older brotherhood at San Lucar. The years after 1577 saw rising diplomatic tension; as a result English residents in many Spanish ports both north and south experienced harassment and unpopularity. Moreover the brotherhood itself was in an increasingly anomalous position. Openly catholic at its foundation in 1517, it now comprised not one religious group but two or three, for among the English community in Andalusia there were those who had spent most of their lives in Spain, who wished to continue in the old ways; those who had come out more recently from England, who desired to express their reformed convictions; and those, perhaps a majority, who adopted a position of judicious conformity, catholic in Spain and protestant in England.[4] In this delicate situation the chapel with its usual services posed a real dilemma as the community tried to conciliate its own members and to maintain amicable relations with the local authorities. Not surprisingly, the major feast of the year, the festivities of St. George's day, fell into disuse although the chapel itself seems to have been maintained.[5] With all these problems to beset him any consul would have found himself in difficulties, and although Bodenham aggravated the situation he cannot be held wholly

1. Although the charter of 1530 empowered the merchants to hold annual elections for the post of consul, they appear to have been very infrequent. William Ostriche, elected in 1538, was succeeded by Hugh Tipton who continued in office until his departure from Andalusia in 1570 (S.P. 70/111 no. 577; Harl. 36 f. 26v).
2. Bodenham was married to a native of Seville; in addition he had a cousin who was waiting-woman to the countess of Feria, the former Jane Dormer who had married Philip II's ambassador to England. In England his kinsman Sir James Crofts held office in the royal household, while his son William Bodenham was in touch with many foreign envoys in London (S.P. 70/74 no. 579; S.P. 94/2 f. 9; A.G.S., Estado 561, 31 Aug. 1574). For Bodenham's Levant, New World and Barbary trades see Hakluyt, ed. Raleigh, v, 71, ix, 359; S.P. 70/133 no. 973.
3. S.P. 94/1 ff. 190, 158; S.P. 94/2 f. 1; Harl. 295 f. 174; S.P. 94/2 f. 9.
4. Hakluyt, ed. Raleigh, xii, 33–4; Bodleian Libr., MSS. Wood F. 30–32 f. 86.
5. Cotton Galba C. i f. 214; S.P. 94/2 ff. 106–16.

responsible for it. At no time, however, was his presence in Andalusia of any help to the merchants in London.

By its charter, the company had been granted a monopoly which was legally enforceable, and in the early stages at least of the company's existence the privy council upheld the incorporation which it had granted. In its turn, the council found the company a convenient organisation through which to do business. Pleas for preferential treatment or special concessions made by merchants and shipowners were passed on to the president as were commands to bestow charitable benefactions on mariners' widows or those who had fallen foul of civil or religious authority in Spain.[1] Similarly, mercantile disputes which came before the council could be delegated to the company for hearing and settlement if one or both of the participants were freemen.[2] By this means the councillors lessened the burden of the endless private requests made to them and at the same time increased the company's control over business connected with the Iberian trade.

One aspect of that business which needed frequent attention from council and company alike was the general problem of safeguarding English interests in Spain and Portugal. With the situation in the Netherlands growing daily more intractable, a direct conflict between England and Spain appeared more and more likely. A few months after the foundation of the Spanish Company Don John of Austria was urging Philip II to embark on a war of commercial attrition against England and the rebels.[3] At the same time the king himself was once more trying to revive the Spanish navigation laws, although their operation was suspended for two years to allow time for building the much-needed extra tonnage. Letters from Elizabeth, reminding him of the compromise which had eventually been reached in 1561 whereby the English had been exempted, persuaded Philip to delay until 1580[4] but by that year Anglo-Spanish relations had deteriorated further; the loading restrictions, the uneasy state of Ireland and above all the great fleet that was gathering in Spanish harbours all made the council anxious to ensure that English vessels should not be caught in a surprise embargo of the type occasionally used to replenish Spanish naval strength. Early in the year a licensing system was imposed on voyages to unsafe areas; this was then lifted for all regions except the peninsula, and the company was left to handle much of the day-to-day administration of the revised scheme.[5] Fresh orders were sent out in April, disregarding the merchants' complaints, for the air was thick with unconfirmed rumours about the impending invasion of Portugal.[6] The stoppages continued until the autumn when it gradually became clear that the need for foodstuffs in Andalusia, together with the absence of Spanish shipping to take off exports, had made the implementation of the threats a practical impossi-

1. S.P. 12/131 no. 61; *A.P.C.*, xii, 300, 183, 327.
2. *A.P.C.*, xi, 213.
3. A.G.S., Estado 572, 15 Nov. 1577.
4. A.G.S., Estado 832, 5 Aug. 1577; *ibid.* 832, *c.* 1579; *Colección de Documentos Inéditos para la Historia de Espãna* (Madrid, 1842–95), ed. M. F. Navarrete *et al.*, xci, 529; A.G.S., Estado 832, Dec. 1579.
5. *A.P.C.*, xi, 416, 404.
6. *Cal. S.P. Spanish*, iii, 19–24; *A.P.C.*, xi, 451.

bility.[1] Nevertheless the council had decided on a mild measure of retaliation and the company received notice that henceforth all Spanish goods should come out of Spain in English bottoms.[2] In all these manoeuvres the company, willingly or otherwise, found itself increasingly being used as a political tool by the English government. Its vulnerability was to prove two-sided, for in the crisis that arose over Drake the delicate position of the Spanish Company was to be exploited by a master hand.

In November 1577, Drake had slipped away to sea almost unnoticed, and it was not until he began to make his presence felt on the shores of the Pacific late in 1578 that the Spaniards started to watch his movements.[3] The reports and rumours of his activities were at first confused; it was not clear if the venture was merely an instance of individual freebooting or a portent of something more sinister, perhaps even an organised English attack on Spanish possessions in the New World. By August 1579 Mendoza, the Spanish ambassador in England, was receiving orders to keep alert for Drake's return. In September, news arrived from Seville of his raids on Spanish goods and territory. The Spanish Company, full of anxiety at the situation that was developing, waited on the privy councillors to impress upon them the real probability of retaliation by Philip II through the seizure of English property in Spain at a time of year when many ships were in the ports of Andalusia loading the annual vintage. The merchants were already paying high insurance premiums to guard their property against sequestration.[4]

The council returned a soothing but ambiguous answer. Many of its members were themselves shareholders in Drake's venture, as was the queen herself, and there was little hope that his deeds would be disavowed on his return. By February 1580, the company had realised that the councillors' vested interests were obstructing a fair hearing of the case. Vigorous protests were lodged but to little effect although the government was now restricting trade for rather different motives. Mendoza, advocating the issue of Spanish letters of mark to Drake's victims in the New World trade, reported with satisfaction that 'the merchants themselves make the greatest outcry over it, saying that because two or three of the principal courtiers send ships out to plunder in this way, their prosperity must be thus imperilled and the country ruined'.[5] In this situation, anxious to keep open some lines of communication that might enable them to stave off an embargo, the merchants cultivated the ambassador's favour and indicated their willingness to purvey information about the plunder. Mendoza was far too skilled a diplomat to let such a chance slip. Playing on their fears of confiscation he began to use them as a pressure group, and in August, just before Drake's return, he urged the company to press the council on the whole subject of English piracy, which had been an irritant to his

1. *A.P.C.*, xii, 274; A.G.S., Estado 834, 29 Sept. 1580; *A.P.C.*, xii, 212.
2. *A.P.C.*, xii, 114. The licensing system was re-imposed in similar circumstances the following year (*Cal. S.P. Spanish*, iii, 102; *A.P.C.*, xiii, 162–3; *Cal. S.P. Spanish*, iii, 155; *A.P.C.*, xiii, 190).
3. Archivo General de Indias, Seville, Patronato Real 266 (real armada) *passim*.
4. *Cal. S.P. Spanish*, ii, 697.
5. *Ibid.*, iii, 47.

master for years.[1] The arrival of the *Golden Hind* in Plymouth in September 1580, ballasted with silver taken from the *Cacafuego*, brought the clash between the merchants and the privy council into the open. Any hopes which the company had entertained of lessening the growing governmental animosity towards Spain were dashed by the news that in the same month 800 papal troops had with Philip II's permission sailed from La Coruña to the aid of the Irish rebels in Munster.

The Spanish merchants were not alone in their hostility to Drake, for there was a solid body of opinion in the City which held that such exploits did little except harm the numerous established trades which depended on the maintenance of good diplomatic relations between England and Spain. Stowe noted that 'many disliked it', while at court those who also opposed the belligerent protestantism of Walsingham and his circle argued earnestly for a restoration of the plunder to its rightful owners. Mendoza encouraged the fears that Spain would go to war over the affair but as long as Drake continued in the queen's favour the ambassador could do little to recover the pillaged goods.

The brunt of the losses had been borne by the members of the powerful *consulado* of Seville, which organised the New World trades from its head-quarters in the great port. The Seville merchants soon concluded that Mendoza was powerless to help them, and in August 1581 they decided to send over their own agent. They chose Pedro de Zubiaur, a native of Biscay who had traded with England for some twenty years and possessed a wide network of contacts.[2] The members of the *consulado* wrote to the English merchants requesting their co-operation in Zubiaur's mission with the implicit threat that if no compensation was forthcoming they must of necessity ask Philip to reimburse them out of English goods in Spain.[3] The ambassador was displeased when he heard the news; far from giving Zubiaur any help he insisted that all negotiations should still be carried on through the embassy.[4] Instead of being reinforced, Spanish pressure was thus divided.

Meanwhile Mendoza continued to use the Spanish Company to petition the privy council. In June he had agitated the merchants even further by telling them that any English aid to Dom Antonio, the Portuguese pretender who was now trying to raise support in London, would inevitably lead to war with Spain since the king was already incensed over the retention of Drake's plunder. They went first of all to Walsingham, but meeting with little response they hastily contacted their sympathisers on the privy council, thereby managing to delay the outfitting of the pretender's ships.[5] The ambassador again used these tactics to put pressure on the English government over Drake in November 1581, and in the following January he was

1. *Cal. S.P. Spanish*, iii, 47.
2. Madrid, Archivo Historico Nacional, 2947, 18 July 1580; P.R.O., H.C.A. 13/25 f. 62.
3. S.P. 94/1 ff. 230–1. The calendar only prints the English endorsement which describes the recipients as 'the governors of the Merchant Adventurers' but the original Spanish endorsement reads, 'To the illustrious president and company of the merchants of London trading to Spain'.
4. *Coleccion de Documentos*, xci, 531, 560–1.
5. *Cal. S.P. Spanish*, iii, 130.

able to extend his influence further afield by warning the Bristol merchants of the risk they ran in allowing Dom Antonio to fit out his vessels there.[1]

By now, however, Mendoza's hold over the company was beginning to weaken. No steps had been taken against English property in Spain although Drake's loot was still in English hands. The Spanish loading prohibitions had proved ineffective against English trade and were widely disregarded by the Spaniards themselves. Above all, in the developing conflict between the ambassador and Pedro de Zubiaur, the Spanish Company was whole-heartedly behind the latter. The two Spanish representatives were deeply at odds over the question of Drake. Zubiaur hoped only for some reason-able composition over the losses of the *consulado*, whereas Mendoza, anxious to salvage Spanish honour, insisted on the return of the whole of the booty, a political impossibility. Moreover, he hindered Zubiaur in his attempts to reach a settlement, and was suspected of having prevented any grant of assistance to the Seville merchant Pedro de Martinez, which might have staved off his bankruptcy. As several members of the London company had themselves broken when Martinez defaulted on his debts, feeling was running high. All in all, the merchants had become uniformly hostile to the ambassador, 'whose malice and deceiving mind', they informed Burghley, 'they have just occasion to fear'.[2] In future Mendoza would not be able to use them as a channel of Spanish diplomacy.

In addition to these problems the company also had to cope with the irritating activities of a professional monopolist named William Tipper. In the spring of 1578 Tipper had managed to drum up some influential support in the City for his petition for the grant of a patent for the hosting of strangers. How he had intended to put this into operation was not dis-closed, for the impracticability of the project was quickly made apparent by the floods of protests that prevented him from doing anything at all.[3] The opposition included the Merchant Adventurers and the Archduke Matthias, acting as spokesman for the merchant strangers, but in the end it was the Spanish Company which managed to buy Tipper off, in order to stop him from molesting the small number of Spanish and Portuguese merchants resident in London.[4] Foolishly the company failed to keep its half of the bargain, thereby laying up trouble for the future, for Tipper's next attempt to enrich himself through a patent was a direct attack on the merchants' trade. He requested the grant of a short-term monopoly on the import of cochineal.

Cochineal had been little used outside Spain until the mid-sixteenth century when its production in the New World greatly increased. Its superiority over the older kermes and lichen dyes was soon appreciated and by 1575 substantial amounts were being imported into England.[5] The mer-chants had no wish to lose this expanding trade and the company at once took the matter to the council, as it was of far more consequence than the

1. *Ibid.*, iii, 208–9.
2. H.M.C., *Salisbury MSS.*, ii, 515.
3. *A.P.C.*, x, 281.
4. *A.P.C.*, x, 378–9.
5. R. L. Lee, 'American cochineal in European commerce 1526–1625', *Jour. Modern Hist.*, xxiii (1951).

hosting patent had been. Wilford meanwhile made some devious moves to bring pressure on Tipper through one of his debtors named Munslow;[1] Tipper for his part drew up a lengthy reply to the objections raised against his proposal by the company. His chief argument was that under his handling the commerce in cochineal would be as well organised as the alum trade had been under the Pallavicini.[2] These protestations failed to convince the council. The plan to monopolise cochineal was stopped and its importation continued freely until the grant of a patent to Essex on his return from the Islands voyage in 1597.[3]

The members of the company at this time also came into conflict with the court. As leading importers of the immensely popular sherry-sack, many of them had dealings with the royal household which was a large-scale purchaser. The official in charge of such matters was the pro-Spanish Sir James Crofts who had been appointed controller in January 1570. At some point, perhaps shortly before Crofts proposed his reform of the household in December 1586, the leaders of the company entered into negotiations 'touching the service of her majesty's house with sack', during which they protested against the royal debts of at least £400 which were owed to fellow-members. If the money was repaid promptly, they offered to sell tuns of the best-quality sack to Crofts at £3 sterling below the market price. They also suggested an honorarium of £100 a year to any officer of the household who would agree 'to serve and to content the merchants' so that they might 'be free and not constrained to serve'.[4] Matters such as provision for the household were probably an irritant to busy City men, but despite their generous offer the matter was not settled, and it arose again in the reign of James I.[5]

One issue that concerned all the members of the company and not just the importers of sack was that of the facilities and organisation of the port of London. In 1564, in order to prevent fraud, a royal regulation had decreed that all cloth shipped outwards should go by water from Custom House quay to the vessels waiting to load, while all fine or haberdashery wares unloaded inwards should be brought to the same quay by lighter.[6] Early in 1582 George Needham, the queen's farmer of the quay, had informed the privy council that the regulations were being disregarded. When the councillors re-enforced them several of the London companies, particularly the Merchant Adventurers, the Eastland Company and the Spanish Company, pleaded that the whole system of restricted quays should be abolished, enabling any merchant to load or unload at any quay within the port.[7] They argued that the present arrangements were not only an

---

1. S.P. 12/157 no. 87.
2. Lansd. 122; S.P. 12/273 no. 69.
3. Lee, 'American cochineal in European commerce', follows the tentative dating of the calendar, assigning Tipper's petition to the years after the expiry of the Essex patent, but the document itself indicates that the conflict followed immediately after the hosting patent of 1578.
4. Lansd. 83 (64); A. P. Newton, 'Tudor reforms in the royal household', in *Tudor Studies presented to A. F. Pollard*, ed. R. W. Seton Watson (1924), 231–56.
5. See below, **482–6**.
6. Lansd. 171 f. 468.
7. Lansd. 35 f. 119.

impediment to commerce, but that Needham himself was also opposed to any improvement merely from personal malice, for 'he hath said that he will bridle the merchants before he hath done with them'. The Spanish and Eastland Companies further complained that the number of lighters Needham supplied was insufficient for ferrying their goods between the quay and the ships. The vessels, which 'do lie at Deptford or at Limehouse, or often times nearer, or most commonly at Blackwall' were kept waiting while the goods themselves were often spoilt by the weather as they lay piled on the quayside.[1]

Needham was at great pains to rebut their charges, and eventually Burghley appointed various of the officers of the customs, including Robert Dow and John Robinson, to hear the matter. In July 1582 they reported back, outlining the misunderstandings that had arisen and suggesting a compromise. They proposed that broadcloths and kerseys should be restricted to Custom House quay as before, but that all other wares including cottons, frizes, bays, lead and tin could be shipped from any quay at the merchants' pleasure. With regard to imports 'all manner of wares whatsoever to be brought in might be landed and taken up at all other quays at the appointment of the queen's majesty's farmer of her subsidies and customs inwards'. The arrangement could be tried until Christmas when any inconveniences in its operation should be reviewed and redressed.[2] As the issue did not revive, the plan presumably worked smoothly.

During the course of all these disputes the company continued to meet privately to deal with its internal business. The members gathered together in Pewterers' Hall in Lime Street, a fifteenth-century building to which was attached the pewterers' bowling-alley and a pleasant garden with a vine. They paid £6 a year for the use of the hall which was also hired out for dinners and weddings.[3] There is no complete record of the dates of their meetings but from the information which can be gleaned elsewhere it seems that a general court was held at least once a month. The court of assistants probably convened separately between each major gathering.

Of the many trade-regulations which the company must have enacted in its eight years of active life only two survive. One concerns the buying of fruit in Andalusia, the other the restraint on corn-ships' return cargoes, a rule which aroused the irritation of the company's old patron, the earl of Leicester, who feared it would affect the value of his sweet wine farm.[4] Both, apparently by coincidence, date from August 1580. On 17 August the company ruled that if any member should load fruit at Rota or Jerez, 'it should be lawful for them to do it, so that it were laden by any one of the commissioners elected for the buying of fruit'.[5] This reference may indicate some scheme whereby a company representative bought fruit in bulk, which he then sold off to other members and at the same time supervised its loading; it is unfortunate that no other information survives concerning it.

1. Lansd. 35 (37, 36).
2. Lansd. 35 (35).
3. C. Welch, *A History of the Company of Pewterers of the City of London* (1902), i, pp. vii–viii, 285.
4. Cott. Vesp. C. xiv f. 418.
5. S.P. 12/143 no. 9.

In many respects 1580 had been the crucial year in Anglo-Spanish relations and thereafter it could be argued that a war was ultimately inevitable. Cardinal Granvelle, who could recall more imperial days and who was now the chief architect of that return to an aggressive foreign policy which marked the Spanish outlook on Europe after 1580, was urging the strict enforcement of the navigation laws and the seizure of all English ships in Iberian ports.[1] The following two years however were surprisingly peaceful, and it was not until the crushing defeat of the French Terceira project that the deterioration of the political situation was once more apparent. Dom Antonio's commissions served only as a thin disguise for an increasing number of piratical ventures against peninsular shipping. In addition commercial groups in the City, including some members of the Spanish Company, were by now intent on opening up a direct trade to Brazil.[2] The early voyages, which were disastrous, did little to achieve this but succeeded in aggravating tension even further. More and more private merchants and shipowners were prepared for their part to take individual action for injuries sustained in the Spanish dominions; as privateering was the easiest method to hand, the high seas became increasingly dangerous.[3]

Ordinary trade meanwhile continued, but uneasily, and in dwindling volume. Several merchants prudently began to withdraw their factors and goods from the peninsula. Finally in the spring of 1585 events moved towards a climax. By March, news was reaching Stafford, the ambassador in Paris, that English and French ships were being impounded in Spain and Portugal for use in the growing armada. On 29 May, orders came down to the *corregidor* of Biscay to arrest all the larger ships of any nation which were then to join the fleet in Lisbon or Seville.[4] A fortnight later English ships on the Guadalquivir were stayed; some of them were attempting to take off such English goods as remained in Andalusia. Factors and sailors caught in the embargo were imprisoned, some of them later being handed over to the Inquisition.[5]

Arrests such as these were not technically a declaration of war, although they had made peaceful commerce impossible. Elizabeth reacted by ordering the issue of letters of mark and reprisal to all those merchants who could prove their losses, but it was still possible to hope for an early peace as talk of negotiations was common. The company did not immediately dissolve; it began to amass details of its members' sequestered property, and the secretary, Richard May, continued to receive letters from factors caught in Spain, apparently passing them on to the government since many of them contained naval and military information. May also noted the names of those who claimed the freedom after the discontinuation of general courts, which ceased sometime before February 1589.[6] But as the war wore on, the company inevitably broke up, apparently without any formal attempt to

1. *Cal. S.P. Spanish*, iii, 308.
2. K. R. Andrews, *Elizabethan Privateering* (Cambridge, 1964), 205.
3. S.P. 12/144 no. 22; S.P. 12/153 no. 73.
4. S.P. 94/1 f. 78.
5. S.P. 94/1 ff. 92–92v, 106; Madrid, Archivo Historico Nacional, 2948–50, 'la nao Manuela', *passim*.
6. Harl. 295 f. 180; and see below, **245**.

complete its business or settle its affairs. Neither the last treasurer, George Hanger, nor his immediate predecessor Sir John Watts, bothered to present any accounts. Already in May 1586 the privy council was complaining of the company's lethargy, for it had made no response to letters urging financial assistance for the wives of mariners imprisoned in Spain.[1] By the spring of armada year, it had ceased to function. Wilford took home with him the common seal and the court book, to wait for the return of peace.

ii. The revival of the Company, 1604–1606

As long as the war continued there was no hope of reviving the Spanish Company. Its members diversified their interests, some entering the Levant and other trades, some managing to keep in contact with the peninsula by devious means, sending their goods through the ports of France and Barbary or disguising their ships as neutral Scots or Irish vessels. Very many of them, probably the majority, were involved in the maritime war of reprisals against Spain, forming 'the weightiest element in the mass of merchant privateering promoters'.[2] Wilford himself seems to have been curiously inactive, although he was no more than middle-aged when war broke out. On two occasions he was asked by the privy council to arbitrate in commercial disputes, but otherwise his whereabouts and occupation are unknown.[3]

By 1600 however the prospects for a European settlement were growing brighter, and in February of that year the committee which had been deputed to confer with Verreyken, the envoy sent over by Archduke Albert, called before it some of the former members of the company. They were asked to furnish evidence of the privileges they had previously enjoyed in the peninsula and to indicate whether they had felt the need of further guarantees of security, or would need them in the light of any events which had occurred since their withdrawal. The merchants could recall all their old privileges but were hazy about the diplomatic arrangements which had provided the framework of their trade. 'Mr. Secretary Wilson when he was secretary', they informed the committee, 'was desirous to collect all the treaties and grants that had passed between the king of England, the king of Castile and the king of Portugal, which books if you can get the sight of will better satisfy you than we can'.[4] The talks held that summer came to nothing, but with the death of the queen in March 1603 the time seemed ripe for another attempt at a durable settlement. James I on his arrival in England took the initiative by ordering a suspension of hostilities, and to Philip III, his newly-inherited empire suffering from internal tensions, there seemed little reason to continue an expensive war against a nation now headed by a friendly monarch. In April 1603, English catholic merchants were granted free access to Spanish and Portuguese ports; a month later the religious

1. *A.P.C.*, xiv, 103.
2. Andrews, *Elizabethan Privateering*, 112.
3. *A.P.C.*, xxi, 351; xxii, 186.
4. S.P. 9/7 p. 34; Sir Henry Sidney, *Letters and Memorials of State*, ed. A. Collins (1746), ii, 172.

proviso was abolished.[1] The war had come to an end, and slowly trade began to resume its normal course.

The first moves which were made towards re-establishing the company cannot be determined with precision, for by the time of the opening meeting at Wilford's London house on 16 March 1604 certain measures had already been taken. Apart from Wilford himself, several notable merchants were present, including the great privateer Sir John Watts, his brother-in-law Sir Robert Lee, Alderman Robert Cobb who had also been an active privateer, and Alderman Andrew Banning who had formerly acted as Spanish factor for his more powerful brother Paul, the Levant and East India merchant. The meeting began by electing the lawyer Richard Langley as secretary, after he had agreed to divest himself of some of his other responsibilities in order to undertake the task. Langley then outlined the progress that had been made so far, for the letters patent of 1577 were about to be presented to the lord chancellor for the engrossing of a charter of confirmation. A committee was appointed to attend the chancellor on the matter, and before departing those present agreed to a levy of 20s. each on themselves and a large number of absentees, presumably former members, to defray costs.[2]

The overall situation was not encouraging. A number of major problems confronted the merchants, each requiring a speedy solution if their incorporation was to continue on a firm basis. First, the company needed swift and forceful support for its legal position, not merely a confirmation of its old privileges which might easily be overlooked in the new postwar situation. It was expected that the coming session of parliament would see a renewed onslaught on all patents and private monopolies, which might well be broadened to include the joint-stock and regulated companies. In the previous debate on monopolies in 1601 the commons had agreed to exclude corporations, but the issues were so closely connected and the hostility towards the London merchants so deep-rooted that the question was almost bound to arise once more. The situation was rendered all the more precarious as the first legal judgment on a private monopoly, delivered at the end of Elizabeth's reign, had ruled against it, an event which had led James I on his accession to suspend all the others until the privy council was able to scrutinise them.[3] Secondly, although the war was over, no formal peace treaty had been concluded, and as yet the negotiations showed little sign of starting in earnest. When they did, it was vital that the company should receive safeguards and privileges sufficient for its members to undertake their trade without harassment. Above all, it might be possible by diplomatic means to undo the disaster that had occurred during the war, the loss of the brotherhood at San Lucar with all its property and influence.

Within a few years of the seizures of 1585, only a few catholic Englishmen were left of the once-thriving community in Andalusia. On St. George's day 1591, eight of these merchant factors had met together to announce on

1. S.P. 94/9 f. 20.
2. See below, **3.**
3. W. Hyde Price, *The English Patents of Monopoly* (Cambridge, Mass., 1906), 22–4; Price, 'On the beginning of the cotton industry in England', *Quarterly Jour. Economics*, xx (1906), 610–13.

behalf of the whole brotherhood that in future their land, income and right to levy impositions would be devoted to the upkeep of a 'confraternity of English priests', ruled by the current superior of the Jesuits in Andalusia, to be called 'the chaplains of St. George'. The new confraternity would be a staging-post for the young seminarians returning secretly to England after their training abroad in the colleges of the counter-reformation. Moreover, the chaplains' future influence over the merchants would be great, for they were to vote in the election of the consul at San Lucar and in the event of his death they and not the traders would fix the date of the next election.[1] Giving their reasons for this drastic step of dubious legality, the factors instanced the heavy burden of maintenance and administration which they, as the remnant of the brotherhood, had borne since 1585. Their real reason however was concealed, and the chief mover in the affair was not mentioned in the official document handing over the property. Between 1589 and 1592, Father Robert Parsons had travelled the peninsula seeking support for his plans for the reconversion of England, and he had persuaded not only the factors but also the cardinal-archbishop of Seville and the duke of Medina Sidonia to agree to his scheme, whereby a new religious house would be established at San Lucar, already possessing considerable endowments and conveniently sited on a major sea-route. By the transfer, the brotherhood would be absorbed into the network of seminaries already established at Valladolid, Lisbon, Madrid and Seville.[2]

It was entirely predictable that these new arrangements would be furiously disputed by the absent protestant merchants, even before the advent of peace enabled them to return to Andalusia. Not only was the intention of the original founders of the brotherhood overriden and ignored; the new seminary outraged them by its very existence and by its power to levy taxes on trade at San Lucar for its support. In 1600 and again in 1603, the London merchants summoned before the council to give commercial information insisted on the return of their property and the restoration of the brotherhood to its original function. Without control over both it and the consulate, the position of the revived Spanish Company would be seriously undermined in the major Iberian market for English goods.[3]

As events turned out, parliament met before the diplomatic negotiations had even begun, and thus the first problem to be faced by the new Spanish Company was not the question of the brotherhood but the attack on commercial monopolies made by the commons. The debate on free trade proved to be the stormiest issue of the session, but by the time the two bills abolishing all trading companies were presented to the House in April, the charter of the company had already been confirmed by the lord chancellor.[4] The protagonists of free trade came mostly from the outports, whose representatives in the commons outnumbered those of London. In addition the M.P.s for the clothing towns could be relied on for support since their constituents had long suspected the Londoners of monopolising the profits of the cloth

---

1. English College, Valladolid, Miscelanea I, Donacion.
2. A. J. Loomie, *The Spanish Elizabethans* (New York, 1963), 196; English College, Valladolid, Miscelanea I, Rodrigo de Castro, Alonso de Guzman.
3. S.P. 9/7 p. 44.
4. See below, 7.

trade, returning little to the producers themselves.[1] Within the capital, the merchants were unable to unite in their own defence, for some of the lesser traders resented the great concentration of wealth and power that now lay in the hands of one small oligarchy which dominated all the major branches of commerce.[2] The opposition was not however composed solely of outport merchants and discontented Londoners. In these years the gentry themselves were deeply involved in the expansion of English trade. During the war, many of them had been active privateers; others had connived at the illicit shipment of surplus corn overseas, and in the west country they had been drawn into the new and thriving triangular trade whereby salted cod from the Newfoundland banks was sold in the Mediterranean in return for fruit and wines shipped back to England. All these motives were present as the first parliament of the new reign assembled, although they did not become fully apparent until the attack on the trading companies was re-newed two years later.[3] Nevertheless it was already clear in 1604 that the outports and their supporters were even less amenable to corporate control than they had been before the war. If the peace was about to create a boom in European trade, as many hoped, the provinces intended to participate in it without suffering the restrictions of London-oriented company member-ship and regulations.

The recent re-emergence of the Spanish Company must have been known to at least some outport M.P.s, for one of the members for Exeter was present at a general court held on 14 May 1604.[4] It does not seem likely, however, that the commons' attack was specifically directed against the company, and the argument that there was no open mention of it in the debates merely because 'it was difficult to attack a company that had been suspended for about eighteen years' seems an odd one.[5] On the contrary, nothing could have been easier than to oppose a fledgling corporation which was only just beginning to re-assert itself. An assault on the revival of such a long-defunct monopoly would have had far more chance of success than did those mounted against much wealthier and more tenacious bodies such as the Merchant Adventurers and the Muscovy Company. It is more prob-able that as yet the Spanish merchants were too obscure to attract direct parliamentary attention.

If the commons did not hound the company, the latter for its part played a negligible role in the free trade debates. No courts were held between 29 March and 1 May, over the early weeks of the parliamentary session, and when the members reconvened at Pewterers' Hall they proceeded to hold elections for the offices of president, treasurer and assistants without any mention of the controversy raging at Westminster. The next general

1. Friis, *Alderman Cockayne's Project*, 151–2.
2. *Commons Journals*, i, **218**.
3. See below, **477–8**. For the controversy over these debates see T. K. Rabb, 'Sir Edwyn Sandys and the Parliament of 1604', *American Hist. Rev.*, lxix (1963–4), 646–70, and R. Ashton, 'The parliamentary agitation for free trade in the opening years of the reign of James I', *Past and Present*, xxxviii (1967), 40–55. The history of the Spanish Company and the demands made on it in 1606 throw some new light on the issue.
4. See below, **24**.
5. Friis, *Alderman Cockayne's Project*, 156–7.

court on 8 June was equally untroubled. It is quite likely that some of the freemen had been called before Sandys' committee which was now hearing evidence, nor can anyone present have been unaware of the issues at stake, but again there was no reference to them in the proceedings.[1]

Meanwhile, impressed by the arguments formulated in the committee and presented by Sandys on 21 May, the commons sent the bill up to the lords after passing it almost unanimously. The lords called in their own witnesses so that they could give further consideration to the matter, and their initial hesitations were reinforced by the comments of Sir Edward Coke, the attorney-general, who praised the intention of the bill but criticised its drafting.[2] Before these differences between the two Houses could be ironed out, the session was abruptly terminated by James on 7 July.

The Spanish Company had survived its first threat although the victory was scarcely due to its members' efforts. Meanwhile a second set of problems had emerged with the beginning of negotiations for a formal peace treaty with Spain and the Spanish Netherlands. By May 1604, Archduke Albert had grown tired of the lethargy shown by James I and Philip III; seizing the initiative he sent three commissioners over to England to begin the talks without awaiting the arrival of the principal Spanish delegate, Velasco the constable of Castile.[3] The eighteen sessions held between 20 May and 6 July were crucial for the future of the company, which in contrast to its sluggish behaviour towards the commons made considerable efforts to put forward its viewpoint.

Wilford was the prime mover in this matter as he had been earlier in the re-establishment of the company itself. At the court of assistants on 24 May, he read out a series of articles which he had drawn up to offer to the privy council, setting out the trading conditions required from Spain if a durable peace was to be concluded.[4] They began by reviewing all the legal instruments already granted to the company, from the privileges accorded by the duke of Medina Sidonia in 1517 to the letters patent of Elizabeth. Then, they requested that all previous privileges enjoyed in Spain should be confirmed; that members should not be molested for offences committed against the king of Spain's subjects in wartime, nor prosecuted by any foreigner before a Spanish law-court for injuries arising over the same period; that the house and lands of the English brotherhood at San Lucar should be returned, and lastly, that the new taxes imposed since 1585, particularly the famous 'thirty per cent' should be abolished.[5]

Wilford's long memory also enabled him to recall all the disadvantages under which the English had laboured before 1585, and to ask for their

1. See below, **5–23**.
2. *Commons Journals*, i, 218–21; *Lords Journals*, i, 334–6.
3. For a detailed account of the negotiations see A. J. Loomie, 'Toleration and Diplomacy: the religious issue in Anglo-Spanish relations 1603–5', *Trans. American Philosophical Soc.*, new ser., liii (Philadelphia, 1963).
4. See below, **31**; Cott. Vesp. C. xiii f. 449; Harl. 295 f. 216; and see below, **705–22**.
5. In its attempts to curb Dutch trade the Spanish government in 1603 had imposed a 30% tax on all goods entering the peninsula. Only those originating in the ten loyal provinces ruled by the archdukes were exempt (S.P. 94/9 f. 117; *A Proclamation or Edict on the Opening of Trade*, 27 Feb. 1603 (Brussels, n.d.)).

removal. In an extremely comprehensive memorandum he dealt with such matters as the Spanish loading prohibitions and navigation laws, the trade to Barbary, the Inquisition, and the need for consuls with wide powers; in conclusion he envisaged an open period of six months after the outbreak of any future hostilities, for the purposes of transferring goods and winding up outstanding business. These articles represented the maximum claims of the English government and the Spanish Company, and were not intended as a realistic estimate of the gains the merchants might hope for from the treaty. They illustrate in a striking manner the extent to which the corporate memory of the company was vested in its elderly but still vigorous president, who had just been confirmed in office 'by full election of hands'. The memorandum provoked a lively discussion in court, but in the end, 'being several times read, and the conceits and opinions of every man heard', it was referred to a sub-committee which would present the case to the privy council.[1]

The company did not slacken in its efforts to influence the negotiations in every way available. At the next court, a gratuity was voted to Sir Daniel Dun and Sir Thomas Edmondes, 'employed by the lords about the articles of peace'. As the diplomatic sessions drew to a close in August, the company appointed a committee to attend on the privy council and on Velasco, who had finally arrived in England from Brussels. By this time Wilford had also drawn up a new charter, to be procured from Philip III in confirmation of the merchants' privileges in the peninsula; it was referred to the consideration of the committee already appointed to wait on Velasco, in the hope that his support might be forthcoming.

In mid-August 1604 the treaty of London was at last concluded. It restored all the rights and concessions enjoyed by the English in Spain before the war, but made no specific mention of either the brotherhood or the consulate.[2] If this was less than the company had hoped, at least it could look to the treaty for general support in making good its old claims. The merchants decided to publicise the terms and at the court held on 31 August it was decided that letters should be sent to the outports enclosing a copy of the treaty and a translation. A further committee was nominated, this time to consider what gifts should be bestowed on those who had laboured for the good of the company during the discussion and drafting of the articles of the peace. The names of the recipients are not noted but if they included members themselves, it would seem safe to assume that Wilford was one of them.

An issue which had already arisen even before the conclusion of the negotiations concerned the thorny question of certified cargoes. A wide variety of goods both English and foreign which were shipped to Spain could easily be confused with similar products manufactured in the rebel United Provinces and thus barred from the peninsula. To avoid clashes with the customs-officers the treaty had stipulated that such goods should be registered in their town of origin and sealed with the seal of their place of shipment. The company hoped that this procedure could be simplified, perhaps by the use of one universal seal instead of those of the various ports.

1. See below, **31**.
2. T. Rymer, *Foedera* (2nd ed., 1704–20), xvi, 589–91.

On 23 August, the court of assistants set up a committee to consider 'what seal or certificate is required by the article to be for our goods to pass into Spain without danger or trouble'. A fortnight later, having formulated their plans, they wrote to Dorset the lord treasurer to enquire if a certificate from the president or deputy, sealed with the company seal, would be an acceptable substitute for the sealing envisaged in the articles of the peace. Dorset referred the question to Dun and Edmondes, commending the proposal, while in court Wilford exhibited the seal he had had made for the purpose. Despite these efforts the traders in Spain were to experience considerable difficulty in making the customs-officers accept these or any other certificates as clearance for dubious goods.

The company seemed well on the way to organising itself when a new and unexpected obstacle emerged. The attack on the charter which had failed to materialize during the last session of parliament was suddenly mounted from a different quarter. Like other trading bodies the company reserved its freedom for the 'mere merchants', excluding shopkeepers and retailers. The opening of the Spanish market had attracted a large number of speculative traders who ventured an occasional cargo while continuing their main line of business elsewhere. The company had already requested the government to forbid the customers to take entries for goods exported by such undesirables, but without much effect.[1] The retailers, shopkeepers and some others excluded from the company now banded together to 'disable and discredit the power of the charter' on the grounds that it was 'not sufficiently authorised and warranted by law, for that their charter granted by the late queen became void by non-user during the long time of the continuance of the war, which doth therefore dissolve the said corporation'.[2] The merchants, taken aback, were apparently too confused to respond; placing the matter before the government they ceased to hold their courts, and for four months between September 1604 and January 1605, the Spanish Company was once more in abeyance. Fortunately, the privy council was unsympathetic towards the opposition, holding 'the foresaid allegation of non-user in this case to be a strict interpretation, considering that there was no default in the merchants but that the wars were the occasion thereof.' Nevertheless, to clarify the position a distinguished committee was appointed to consider the legal problem.[3] Reassured by this, the company resumed its assemblies on 30 January, although the attendance was poor.

The lawyers completed their work with speed, reporting ten days later that they had found two defects in the charter. First, the title of incorporation, 'Per Nomen Presidentis Assistentium et Societatis Mercatorum Hispanie et Portugalie' was inadequate, since 'it should have been named of England or some part thereof, trading into Spain and Portugal'. Secondly, the company was obliged by the charter to hold an annual election for president, which they had neglected to do for some eighteen years. They also found fault with the charter of confirmation on the same grounds, for it had been granted to the president, assistants and society at a time when

1. Cott. Nero B.i f. 296.
2. S.P. 14/12 no. 41; and see below, **96**.
3. *Ibid.*

there was no legally-elected president. The committee recommended that a revised charter should be drawn up, omitting nothing that would facilitate a well-ordered trade.[1] On receiving this report, Salisbury immediately ordered the attorney-general to draw up a new charter, 'whereunto hereafter no just exception need be taken', since the king was well-disposed towards the Spanish Company.[2] At the next general court, the company appointed a committee headed by Wilford to consider what extra legal powers might be needed, at the same time authorising the treasurer to take up a loan of £100 to be disbursed if necessary in procuring the charter with all speed. A draft was read out at an assembly on 18 March, and two days later the company sent a deputation to wait on the attorney-general at his country home, hoping thereby to expedite matters. Finally, on 12 June, the new charter was exhibited to the members. Proudly and carefully described as 'containing five skins of vellum', it was read out in open court and the officers of the company sworn in afresh.[3]

The new constitution differed substantially from that of 1577. Memories of the commons' assault were still fresh, and in the hope of avoiding future conflicts with the outports no less than 310 merchants from fifteen manufacturing and trading centres were named as founder-members of the company. Despite the numerical preponderance of the provinces, administrative power was to remain firmly in the capital. It was decreed that out of the total number of sixty-one assistants at least thirty were to reside outside London, and although technically this was a minimum number which could be exceeded, in practice it became a maximum. The charter appointed as assistants thirty London merchants, thirty outport merchants, and the secretary Richard Langley, who as a Londoner himself would inevitably vote for the London interest.[4]

Elections for the posts of president and assistants would in future be held annually on the Monday before the feast of the Ascension or within twenty days after it, but the company was free to call courts for business at any time. It was granted all the usual powers of a commercial company in fining interlopers and other delinquents, and in addition a letter from its officers to the barons of the exchequer would cause the latter to send out writs to the customers forbidding them to accept any goods being shipped to Spain or Portugal by non-members. Stressing the value of ordered commerce and the danger that inexpert merchants would quickly antagonise the king of Spain, the charter empowered the president and assistants to appoint consuls abroad to govern all the subjects of James I, including the Scots and Irish, who traded to the peninsula. Still with an eye to placating the outports, the government had ensured that the rules governing membership would not become over-exclusive. In addition to the large numbers named in the charter, anyone listed in the grant of 1577 was eligible for the freedom as were his sons or apprentices and all those admitted after 1577.

The charter of 1605 serves to demonstrate the government's new approach

1. See below, **103.**
2. S.P. 14/14 no. 21.
3. See below, **129–31.**
4. See below, **663–5.**

to trading companies, which distinguishes those established in the early seventeenth century from those of Elizabeth's reign. Both the king and Salisbury retained a belief in the value of company organisation as the best method of advancing trade and safeguarding English interests. But the parliamentary attack on monopolies had made them wary of lending their support to exclusive oligarchies which could easily become bodies for the restriction of trade rather than its advancement. The Spanish Company was therefore to be open to all merchants with a legitimate interest in peninsular commerce. Exactly the same outlook can be discerned in the new charter received by the Levant Company in December 1605, which carefully described the company not as a monopoly but an association whose reasonable terms and conditions were intended solely for the good of the trade itself.[1]

By June 1605 the Spanish merchants at last seemed firmly established, and could continue their business without fear of being undermined by the opposition. They had not been idle while waiting for their new charter, although their courts had been less frequent than before. In March, they had acted on Salisbury's suggestion that they should make contact with Sir Charles Cornwallis, the newly-appointed ambassador to the court of Philip III. This was to be the beginning of a not entirely happy association, typified perhaps by the company's initial confusion of the ambassador with his elder brother the recusant Sir William Cornwallis.[2] Salisbury had originally asked the company to inform Cornwallis about the merchants' former legal position in Spain, and to notify him of any complaints sent home by the residents there. They decided to draw up, for the ambassador's benefit, a collection of the privileges granted to them previously, and on the initiative of John Dorrington, one of the assistants, steps were also taken to procure a copy of the grants made to the English by the former kings of Portugal.[3]

Cornwallis then left London as a member of the entourage accompanying the earl of Nottingham on his journey to Valladolid to ratify the treaty, and the company heard nothing from him until 6 July. His first letters caused so much anxiety that they were deferred for consultation until the next general court, when a committee was appointed to consider what form the reply should take. In the absence of any copy of the letters it is impossible to reconstruct the incident in full, but this much seems clear. The company received one letter from Cornwallis, together with another from Nicholas Ouseley, who as a former servant of the late Sir James Hawes had taken his freedom of the company on 23 August 1604. After a shady wartime career as a naval officer, illicit trader, spy and dealer in the exchanging of prisoners, Ouseley himself, originally a factor in Spain, had reappeared on the scene as the ambassador's 'Secretary for Merchants' causes'.[4] The tone of Cornwallis's own letter was apparently so unhelpful that the company debated if it would be worth while to disregard him and visit Tassis, the resident Spanish ambassador in London, 'to desire his favour for the

1. M. Epstein, *The Early History of the Levant Company* (1908), 59, 154.
2. For the Cornwallis family see A. Simpson, *The Wealth of the Gentry* (Cambridge, 1963), 142–78.
3. See below, **116–17**.
4. P.R.O., H.C.A. 13/33 f. 28v; Cott. Vesp. C. xiii f. 393; S.P. 94/2 f. 191; A.G.S., Guerra Antigua 88 *passim*.

confirmation and enlarging of our ancient liberties in Spain'. However, on 13 August the company agreed to make a bargain with Ouseley. From the terms of this letter it emerges that Cornwallis had condoned an attempt by his secretary to procure money from the merchants. He had written to the company in favour of Ouseley, who had then 'volunteered' his assistance in procuring a new grant which would confirm all the old liberties at San Lucar de Barrameda formerly enjoyed by the brotherhood. In the light of the implicit threat by the ambassador that he would do nothing of his own volition to help them, the merchants had little option but to accept Ouseley's offer. They agreed to give £50 to his wife, who resided in England, in addition to a grant of 1,200 ducats to Ouseley himself, a third of which would be paid at once and the rest after the promised confirmation of their privileges had been obtained.[1]

By applying pressure in this way, Cornwallis had probably hoped to pass on to the company most of the expense of retaining Ouseley in Spain to deal with commercial cases. There was after all no reason why he should bear all the costs of employing a secretary solely on the merchants' behalf especially at a time when the embassy was overwhelmed by such business.[2] Unfortunately the means employed had aroused so much distrust in London that from then on the attitude of the company to the embassy was one of undisguised hostility. A further clash occurred in August after the arrival of letters concerning the arrangements made by the ambassador with regard to Rowland Mailart, who was acting as English consul in Lisbon when Cornwallis arrived in Spain. At Mailart's request the ambassador had confirmed him in his post, on the understanding that he would resign should the Spanish Company ever object to his behaviour. Instead of the thanks he had expected for his tact, Cornwallis received a sharp rebuff. The merchants had already been pressured by others to accept strangers as their consuls, and they were anxious to discourage any further infringements of their powers in this sphere. They refused to accept Mailart, even though this meant leaving the English community in Lisbon without leadership until the company made its own elections.[3]

Goaded by Cornwallis's move, the merchants acted quickly to demonstrate their authority. A week after their rejection of Mailart, a general court met to consider the appointment of consuls. The successful candidate for the key post of San Lucar-Seville was Hugh Bourman, a member of the well-known Anglo-Spanish family,[4] and it was hoped that the presence of a reliable company official in Spain would provide more room for manoeuvre. Late in September a court of assistants decided that Bourman should take with him a duplicate of the charter under the great seal, together with two messages, one to Ouseley and the other to Cornwallis. Bourman was also to ascertain whether any progress had been made in obtaining the confirmation; if not, a letter 'signifying the company's dislike' would be delivered. Cornwallis too was entreated to procure the

---

1. See below, **251**.
2. Cornwallis was later to complain that mercantile affairs arose round him 'like hydra's heads' (S.P. 94/16 f. 130).
3. See below, **295–6**.
4. See below, **151**.

confirmation with the bait that the promised gratuity would be conferred 'where his lordship shall appoint'.

When the next general court assembled, however, some progress had been made in obtaining the support of James I. A deputation led by Wilford had waited on the king in the country, obtaining a royal letter to Cornwallis instructing him to press the king of Spain for 'allowance of our ancient privileges and liberties and enlargement thereof'. Thus armed, the merchants felt able to break the terms of the bargain made with Ouseley, on the grounds that his services had become 'needless and unnecessary'. During this time Cornwallis had been growing increasingly irate. He complained repeatedly that the company did not bother to inform him of important matters; he was angered by the treatment of Mailart, which had undermined his authority in Spain, while the dismissal of Ouseley roused him to fury.[1] In December, a letter from him was read out at a court of assistants, 'intimating that he expected better allowance to be made to Mr. Nicholas Ouseley'. Replies were formulated by the merchants but the matter was cut short when the charter once again came under fire in parliament. No confirmation of the pre-war privileges was ever obtained in Spain; Ouseley never received his money, and some three years later he and the ambassador parted company after an acrimonious quarrel, sharpened perhaps by the knowledge of each other's complicity in this previous episode.[2]

As soon as the company had received the new charter of 31 May, it had begun to consider another facet of its internal government, the question of oaths and ordinances.[3] The ones in use dated from Elizabeth's reign and some were no longer suitable or necessary. A committee including two outport deputies was asked in June to meet at Merchant Tailors' Hall—the only occasion on which the company strayed from Pewterers' Hall—to revise the oaths in accordance with the new charter, and after three meetings the members presented a report to the general court on 12 July. The committee recommended that most of the ordinances should continue in their present form, although some slightly emended versions were offered which were intensively discussed. They reveal a good deal about the internal organisation of the company. The members usually met in a general court, at which at least thirteen assistants had to be present to form a quorum. Courts of assistants, excluding the generality, were less common but fairly frequent; meetings held in the form of a general court but without the requisite thirteen assistants were known as assemblies, as were the gatherings during the periods in which the legal status of the company was uncertain. All these meetings were held in the presence of Wilford himself or of John Newton, who had been elected deputy in July 1605, perhaps in view of Wilford's advancing age.

1. Cornwallis's irritation was probably due in some degree to the fact that Ouseley had just carried out part of his bargain. On 10 Dec. 1605 he was issued with a copy of the confirmation of 1538, from the archives at Simancas, countersigned by the royal archivist, Antonio de Ayala. Had the company known of this it might have acted differently (A.G.S., Estado 844, 10 Dec. 1605).
2. Cott. Vesp. C. xiii f. 393; S.P. 94/16 f. 188.
3. See below, **510–638**. The ordinances revised by the committee are those entered between **510** and **588**; those which follow were added by the company between Aug. 1605 and Jan. 1606.

Although courts were held regularly the merchants did not assemble at the same place and time every week. In consequence, some traders capable of the freedom complained to the privy council that they were unable to join the company since they did not know where to seek it out. It was decided to remedy this by holding a general court every Wednesday morning, from seven to eleven in summer and from eight to eleven in winter. Members who gathered at these bleak hours must have been glad that they had previously increased the comforts of Pewterers' Hall by buying for their own use a carpet and a dozen cushions.[1]

Every effort was made to ensure that courts were smooth and well ordered. Bad or offensive language was fined, as were talking after the president had commanded silence or interrupting another speaker. If a matter was debated which concerned an individual member, he, his relatives and partners left the court, but other members who did this without cause were fined for disrespect. Moreover, as company business was considered confidential, members who revealed any aspect of it outside court could lose their freedom. The seating of members was arranged in a careful hierarchy, with fines for presuming to sit in a more exalted position. General courts were publicised by the beadle, who contacted freemen and kept a note of absentees. The functions of other officials such as the president, the treasurer and the secretary were all carefully defined, and appropriate oaths were set out for them in the new ordinances.

Besides ordering the conduct of company administration, the acts and ordinances dealt with numerous miscellaneous problems. Clauses of the charter were expanded to allow greater precision, as in the act on retailing; the status and behaviour of non-members such as the factors and apprentices in Spain were closely regulated in the best interests of the company. Members were forbidden to enter into partnerships with those who were not free, and were ordered to notify the secretary if they had already linked themselves to outsiders in this way.

Both the acts and ordinances and the court book devote much space to the admission of freemen. During the short period of its existence the Spanish Company spent more time on this aspect of its business than on any other. Admissions, which took place at the beginning of each session after the reading of the minutes, were divided into the four main categories of patrimony, service, redemption, and 'ancient trade' for those who had participated in peninsular commerce before the incorporation. Applications were made in advance to the secretary, and at first were scrutinised by a special committee.

Some pleas for the freedom were of a more complex nature. Exchange memberships were on occasion arranged with the Merchant Adventurers and the Eastland Company. As members of other trading companies were admitted on slightly different terms, the Spanish Company was careful to check the aspirants' claims. In September 1605, a point was raised about the ambiguous position of the East India Company, which had wound up its joint stock after the first voyage and whose ships had not yet returned from the second. It was decided that in effect 'the said East India Company is dissolved and not to be any longer accounted a company'; former

1. See below, **206, 183**.

members must therefore be admitted under the oath for those without any other affiliation.[1]

Some petitioners offered their services in exchange for their freedom, rather than pay redemptioners' fees. Among the successful ones were John Sozar, who promised to translate any Spanish documents coming into the hands of the company, and Richard Candler, mercer, 'being the clerk for policies of assurance'. Candler's former master had served Sir Thomas Gresham, an honorary member of the pre-war company. In addition he offered the use of a room in his house at the Royal Exchange, in which the assistants could 'meet together at any convenient times upon any sudden business for the company'. He received his freedom gratis but it was limited to Candler alone, any future claims by his sons or servants being explicitly disallowed.[2]

There were also those who attempted to avoid paying fees by applying pressure from eminent patrons. This placed the company in difficulties since a refusal might entail the loss of support from powerful persons such as Dorset or Salisbury. Sir Thomas Flemying, chief baron of the exchequer, was particularly importunate. In June 1605 he wrote to ask that the freedom should be conferred without charge on several traders in Southampton, some of whom were also retailers and some officers of the customs. The company sent a deputation to inform Flemying 'how dangerous a precedent it were and how inconvenient for the company to yield to his lordship's request' but in October he renewed his efforts. This time John Long of Southampton was admitted at his behest, without paying the entrance fee of £10.[3] These aspects of the Jacobean system of patronage were a financial drawback and an interference in the internal regulations of the company.

Despite the attacks that had been made on the company during the early stages of its revival, there was no shortage of applicants for the freedom. Between March 1604 and January 1606, no less than 149 new members were admitted in addition to those named in the charter. Once more, however, the problem of 1604 was all too apparent, for only twenty-six of the newcomers were outport men. Support for the company was still essentially metropolitan, and the disastrous results of this imbalance soon became clear.

It has already been noted that although the outport merchants were amply represented in the charter the Londoners retained their constitutional control. As before, each of the privileged ports headed a section of the coastline, with the deputy and assistants handling all company business in the area. But from the beginning, the outports showed little interest in the attempt to re-establish the company. The letters sent out in March 1604 notifying them of its revival elicited only three replies, from Bristol, Exeter and Chester. Similarly, at the elections on 14 May 1604 assistants were chosen for Bristol, Exeter, Plymouth and Chester, but none of those elected were present in court. When during the following year the elections came

1. See below, **342–3**.
2. See below, **275**. It is possible that the secretary misunderstood Candler's claim. The latter may have served Gresham himself, for one Richard Candler or Candeler was his factor in 1560 (J. W. Burgon, *The Life and Times of Sir Thomas Gresham* (1893), i, 106–7).
3. Flemying sat as M.P. for Southampton from 1597 until his appointment as lord chief baron of the exchequer in 1604 (*D.N.B.*).

round again, the same procedure was followed; assistants were nominated for twelve of the outports, then letters were sent out informing them of their election.[1] These arbitrary dealings did not please the merchants concerned, several of whom wrote back to indicate their unwillingness to fulfil the duties of their office. The company nevertheless proceeded to set up a committee of Londoners to consider what powers the deputies should have for the administration of their districts. Their report was read, considered and approved at a general court in August, where it was agreed that it should be entered as an act of the company and copies distributed to the outports. By this time, however, it was clear that some more positive action would have to be taken to encourage the outports to participate. One or two deputies had by now attended an occasional session of the court, but the majority had still made no reply to the earlier letters. Accordingly it was decided that John Newton, the deputy president, and Arthur Jaxon, one of the assistants, should ride round all the ports for which deputies had been elected, 'for the swearing of the several deputies and to settle government and give direction in every of the said places'.[2] Before Newton and Jaxon could begin their journey, the problem of the outports suddenly took on a much more ominous complexion.

The general court of 21 August was attended by no less than four outport deputies. Three of these—Richard Dochester of Exeter, James Bagg of Plymouth, and Nicholas Downe of Barnstaple—had come up to London to take their oaths of office.[3] In addition, they presented a strongly-worded petition, which after its initial hearing was referred to the committee formerly appointed to consider the deputies' powers, now revived and enlarged. On the afternoon of the same day, after the general court had ended, the committee convened to consider the petition. The demands of the western deputies, as they were later known, aimed to break the dominance of London. They began modestly enough by asking that Exeter and Plymouth might have as many assistants as had had before—sixteen and twelve respectively—while those representing Barnstaple should be increased from six to eight. In addition they wanted a copy of the new charter to be kept at Exeter. They went on, however, to request that the outport courts over which the deputies presided might have power to pass regulations binding on the company, and that they should not be forced to come up to London either to be sworn in or to take their freedom, since it was 'so great a journey and needless charge'. Moreover all the fines collected should remain within the division instead of being handed over to the treasurer in London. Last and most explosive, they demanded that the regulations passed in London should not bind them, 'unless they may stand with the good of our country and the consent of our several courts there'.

The committee made no significant concessions. They agreed to increase the number of assistants and to send a copy of the new charter down to Exeter. In addition apprentices could from henceforth be indentured or granted their freedom by their local deputy, and the outports were to be

1. See below, **22–3, 159–63.**
2. See below, **249.**
3. James Bagg was one of the five outport merchants on the commons' free trade committee of 1604 (Rabb, 'Sir Edwyn Sandys', 665).

allowed to make regulations for their own trade, provided they obtained prior consent from London. In all other matters, however, the old customs were to prevail. Deputies, assistants and redemptioners must continue to journey up to London, all cash collected was to be handed over to the London treasurer, and the acts made in the general court would be as binding as before.

The whole episode boded ill for the expedition of Newton and Jaxon which was about to begin. Their draft commission was ratified at the end of August and by mid-September they had left London for Bristol. The merchant community there had so far offered no opposition to the company; their members were well represented in the charter and their deputy, the well-known local philanthropist John Whitson, had been present at three courts.[1] Once in Bristol, however, it was revealed that this quiescence did not mean compliance. The merchants would have nothing to do with the company if membership entailed any limitations on their own freedom. The two envoys were compelled to report that 'the merchants of Bristol pretend to stand and govern themselves and refuse to submit to the orders and government of the society'. By 12 October, the two Londoners had returned, having achieved nothing apart from demonstrating the powerlessness of the company in the outports. Some business relating to the west country still came up before the court but the problem as a whole was shelved. There was nothing more to be done, and in December 1605 the Bristol merchants quietly seceded from the Spanish Company before embarking on their own programme of internal reform and corporate organisation.[2] With Bristol gone, the company could never have established any real degree of control over the outports, even if it had been able to assert itself more effectively in the rest of them. The failure of Newton and Jaxon's mission was probably the most significant defeat suffered by the Spanish merchants, for it foretold all too clearly that revival of outport opposition which was ultimately to prove fatal to the company as a corporate body.

Before the extent of the collapse of its authority in the outports was fully known, the company embarked on its last and most ambitious venture, the establishment of a wide network of consuls around the coast of the Iberian peninsula. On Friday 6 September 1605 a general court was called specifically to elect suitable persons for the office. After some discussion it was agreed to set up nine consulships, one each for Biscay, Bayona in Galicia, Lisbon, San Lucar and Seville, Malaga, Valencia, the Canaries, the Azores, and 'Matheres', which may be Madeira. Most of these places

1. Whitson himself was proud of his association with the company for he had its arms sculpted on the mantelpiece of his mansion in St. Nicholas Street, along with those of the crown and the city of Bristol (P. McGrath, 'The wills of Bristol merchants in the Great Orphan Books', *Trans. Bristol and Glos. Archaeol. Soc.*, lxviii (1949)).
2. In May 1605 the Bristol merchants met in their common hall to elect their own officers, at what appears to have been their first corporate session for many years. In Dec. 1605 the common council of the city agreed that the merchants should 'exempt themselves from the company and government of the merchants adventurers of London trading into Spain and Portugal', forming instead a company of merchant adventurers of Bristol, in effect a re-born Merchant Venturers such as had briefly existed in the 16th century (Merchant Venturers Hall, Bristol, Book of the Charters of the Society of Merchant Venturers I f. 33; *Records relating to the Merchant Venturers*, 3–5).

had never had consuls before, and in the event the company was unable to fill more than the first five, deciding that for Valencia and the rest they would 'take further time to make enquiry and to inform themselves of fit and worthy men'. In the ensuing election, three names were proposed for each post and the successful candidate chosen by show of hands. James Wych, son of one of the assistants, was appointed for Biscay where he was already resident, Francis Lambert for Bayona, and Hugh Lea, defeated in the Bayona election, for Lisbon. Of the more important southern consulships, Hugh Bourman was chosen for the joint post of Seville–San Lucar and Humphrey Wootton for the expanding port of Malaga. The company at the same general court also set up a committee headed by the president, to meet four days later in order to confer with as many of the consuls 'as are now remaining about London' on the subject of emoluments.

Reporting back to the next general court on 13 September, the committee, which had taken two days to come to an agreement among its members, recommended a generous system of payment consisting of a declining scale of annual fees, related to the importance of the port served. Seville–San Lucar was rated at £200 a year, Lisbon at £150, whilst the rest were only to receive £40. In addition there was to be a levy of one or two ducats on each ship unloading within the consul's coastal division. Moreover, impositions were also to be collected in England, where the committee had decided on a rate of 3s. 4d. for every unit of cargo worth £100. After the reading of this comprehensive report the court found itself deeply divided. Some thought the scale of payment would prove an excessive burden on the finances of the company; others, less realistic, wished that the consuls' allowances might be 'as great in substance', but at the same time strongly opposed the proposal 'that the same should be made by such certain yearly fee from the body of the company'. The dispute raged for four more general courts, with 'much time spent and little concluded', until finally although no agreement had been reached it was decided to send Bourman to Seville with £50 as the first instalment of his annual fee. Swallowing its pride, the company also asked Cornwallis to obtain some confirmation of the consul's position.[1]

The unsettled dispute over emoluments did not prevent the company from pressing on with its scheme for the consulates. On 8 November the consuls' commissions were read out, together with an explanation of their precise territorial limits, and on 2 January 1606 an advance of £50 was also agreed for Hugh Lea the consul of Lisbon. By now however the very existence of the company was in doubt, and with its abolition the grandiose plan to re-establish the consular system came to an abrupt end, leaving those consuls who were already in Spain in a position of some difficulty. In vain they and Cornwallis struggled to establish their authority in the eyes of the Spanish court; without official backing from England it proved impossible to win acceptance from either the English residents in Spain or the native Spaniards.[2]

The renewed assault that took place in November 1605 came once more from parliament. The protagonists of free trade in 1604 had been robbed of

1. See below, **344–406, 409**.
2. A.G.S., Estado 2512, 27 Feb. 1606; S.P. 94/13 f. 106.

success by the sudden ending of the session, but they were still determined to see the matter through. As soon as the lower house began its sittings on 5 November 1605, Sir George Somers the M.P. for Lyme Regis raised the issue. This time the Spanish Company was a more obvious target, for it was better known and had received its last charter at a time when the commons were unable to scrutinise it, a circumstance which they found highly suspicious. A committee was at once chosen to consider 'the inconveniences or mischiefs in trade and traffic growing by reason of the late patent of incorporation'.[1]

The members of the company, then in the midst of electing their consuls, were alarmed to hear that the committee was sitting in the hall of the Middle Temple with the explicit intention of drawing up a bill against their charter. Wilford, Newton and Langley went together to enquire 'in what points they did except against our charter', and received an uncompromising answer. The committee asked first if the company would allow complete free trade in fish, in order that 'all manner of persons that shall adventure to the sea to take fish, may carry their fish freely for those countries and there sell it at their will and pleasure'. Secondly they wished to know if the company would allow all gentlemen, yeomen, farmers 'and all others of what quality soever to carry corn into Spain and Portugal and to make their return in merchandise from thence at their will and pleasure'. Wilford at once called a general court to discuss these demands, but it was clear that to concede them would be tantamount to abandoning the charter. They decided not to give any consent to the committee's proposals, preferring instead to risk the decision of parliament on the validity of their incorporation.

The questions posed by the M.P.s reveal the roots of the renewed agitation. The triangular trade in Newfoundland fish was going from strength to strength, and the fishermen of towns such as Dartmouth had no desire to curb their booming commerce by submitting it to the regulations of the Spanish Company.[2] The M.P.s for the west country, in arguing for a free trade in fish, could point not only to their constituents' interests but also to the safety of the realm, for the Newfoundland trade was a powerful impetus to shipbuilding and to the training of seamen.[3] Furthermore, the areas in which the fishermen traded were the best market in Europe for corn, which despite numerous prohibitions was exported from the outports to the great profit of the farming gentry; the M.P.s were thus defending their own private commercial interests.

As November wore on, it became increasingly clear that there was little hope of saving the charter. The Spanish Company had had the misfortune to interpose its insecure monopoly in the path of two new and powerful economic interests which were now uniting against it in a parliament already hostile to all trading companies. In Somers himself, many of the strands of opposition were made visible; as a west-country gentleman sitting for an

---

1. *Commons Journals*, i, 256, 261.
2. For the growth of the triangular fishing trade in Dartmouth see P. Russell, *Dartmouth* (1950), 63–72.
3. See below, **756–7**. Such arguments were to become a commonplace of parliamentary debate in the early 17th century (see *Commons Journals*, i, 874).

outport constituency, promoter of the Virginia Company and future re-discoverer of the Bermudas, the company must have been anathema to him on every count.

Although the instability of their position was apparent, the merchants continued their sessions, discussing the consulships and reviving the old dispute with the royal household over composition for wines and spices. They also drew up an account of the wrongs suffered by English merchants and factors in Spain, which was presented to the privy council in the form of a petition for redress.[1] Lastly they tried to gather support by a little judicious bribery. On 2 January 1606 the treasurer was authorised to purchase a piece of plate worth £30, to be presented as a new year gift to 'such a person as the company have in private acquainted Mr. President, Mr. Treasurer and Mr. Secretary they mean to confer and bestow the same upon'. The attempt to disguise the identity of the recipient rouses the suspicion that it was intended for James I himself. If the plate was ever presented it had no effect, for the court of assistants which discussed the gift was the last meeting which the company was to hold.

The bill for free trade into Spain, Portugal and France went through the lower house with little opposition and was specially commended by the commons to the lords. As in 1604, the lords showed less enthusiasm for the project than the commons had done. They summoned more merchants as witnesses and in April the committees reported that the draft was 'so general and imperfect' that a conference would be necessary. Some points such as the fishing trade were still causing difficulty. However, the amendments were read and the commons signified to the upper chamber that the bill had been received 'with great applause'.[2] It passed into law at the end of the session and although subsequently legislation was carried to safeguard the local monopoly of the Merchant Adventurers of Exeter,[3] the Spanish Company was henceforth abolished.

Several factors had contributed to its downfall. Pre-eminent among them was the hostility of the outports as expressed by M.P.s such as Somers. He and his fellows cared little for free trade as a theory; their real concern was with the prosperity of their local ports which faced increasing difficulties as the wealth and power of the London mercantile oligarchy increased. When a monopoly actively favoured the outport interest, the opposition of the commons faded away, as in 1607 with the act safeguarding the Exeter Merchant Adventurers; and in areas in which the outports could not in any case compete, such as the East India trade, the dominance of London was ignored. Outport merchants with their modest resources could participate only in those trades which posed no problems of distance and required relatively little capital, and of these the commerce with France, Spain and Portugal was at once the most lucrative and long-established. When London attempted to organise such a trade in its own interests, conflict was inevitable.

It would be inaccurate to assume that the outport merchants were unanimous in opposing the charter. Some were willing to seek the freedom

1. See below, **733–51**.
2. *Lords Journals*, i, 393, 405, 412.
3. *Commons Journals*, i, 275.

of the company in order to continue their trade without infringing the monopoly.[1] Yet even those who were prepared to accept such regulation often found themselves genuinely unable to abide by the terms of their admission as mere merchants, for the amount of trade they undertook was not sufficient to support them. In the outports, very many merchants were also shopkeepers and retailers, and the exclusiveness of Londoners who had no need to supplement their income by such undertakings found little response in the provinces. Lastly, the natural inclination of the gentry M.P.s to fight against the dominance of London and defend their constituents' welfare was sharpened by their own private interests in the corn and fishing trades.

The outport attack was formidable, but its success might have been less overwhelming had the company been able to muster strong support within commercial circles. Despite the large number of its freemen, it was unable to do so. When suing for the new charter in March 1605 Wilford had found that the idea of re-incorporation did not appeal even to those who had been members of the pre-war company. 'I find not our people', he reported to Salisbury, 'much affected to pray any new charter, in respect they must give way to all that will adventure, alleging that they shall be at charges, and cannot tell how to raise the same, and shall be brought in question every parliament'.[2] These dissensions, notorious among the London merchants, were even discussed by the residents in Spain who watched anxiously to see what would befall.[3] Even as the new charter was being drawn up, a war of petitions continued to rage between the protagonists and the opponents of incorporation, each citing the hackneyed arguments always used to defend or attack trading monopolies. On the one hand it was claimed that a company would keep up the prices of English goods, promote order in the trade, and enable the merchants to defend themselves more effectively. The opposition insisted that on the contrary, monopolies led to a decline in trade and hence in customs revenue, enriched the few at the expense of many and conferred no benefits despite all the rules and regulations.[4]

The lack of widespread support also manifested itself in the low rate of attendance at company courts. Several could not be held for lack of a quorum of assistants; on two occasions, persistent non-attenders were discharged and replaced, but the complaints continued. Few of the leading merchants named in the charter as freemen played any part in administering the company, and too much work devolved on a small number of relatively undistinguished people, especially Wilford and Newton. Wilford, who died the year after the company was dissolved,[5] must have been an elderly man

1. Among those who took the freedom of the company after the charter was granted were merchants from Ipswich, Yarmouth, Lynn, Norwich, Wells (in Norfolk), Walsingham, Southampton, Plymouth, Rye, Dorchester, Bridgwater, Topsham, Poole and 'Culleton' in Devon (see below, **489** n). The most difficult journey was probably that of Abraham Beavoir of Guernsey, the longest, that of John Mockett of Weymouth who twice came up to London in his attempts to prove his eligibility.
2. H.M.C., *Salisbury MSS.*, xvii, 80.
3. S.P. 94/11 f. 38.
4. S.P. 14/12 no. 63; S.P. 14/21 no. 2.
5. P.C.C. 61 Windebanck. Wilford made his will in Feb. 1607 when he was already 'sick in body', and it was proved on 30 June.

by 1607 although he was amazingly energetic in his attempts to restore the company to a stable position. Problems such as these were not of course unique to the Spanish merchants, for other, more durable bodies also suffered from them;[1] but in a struggling company under constant attack they assumed more serious proportions.

In comparing the Spanish Company with its contemporaries several other weaknesses become apparent. With its sixty-one assistants, or even the thirty-one Londoners, the governing body was significantly larger and less easily organised than were those of the Merchant Adventurers, Levant or Eastland Companies.[2] Its finances were unsound, and at the last of its courts the treasurer had to inform the assembly that the company was in debt and would need to resort to loans. This situation was largely due to the substantial fees voted to officers in September 1605 at a time when income was derived almost entirely from entry fines; in contrast, the Levant Company with its much greater resources made no regular payments for over a decade after the grant of its new charter in December 1605.[3]

Even more important than administrative matters such as these was the fact that the company had very little essential business to transact. Unlike the Merchant Adventurers, who defended their monopoly by stressing the need for skilled manipulation of their market, the Spanish Company did not stint its members or lay down the prices of commodities. Unlike the Levant and Eastland Companies, it did not regulate shipping, draw up charter-parties or deal with paperwork such as toll-bills. Perhaps most damaging of all, it had little to offer. As long as the brotherhood of St. George at San Lucar had functioned, together with its appended consular system, the London company had been able to provide some measure of protection in Spain. By 1604 the brotherhood had been taken over by the English priests, an event which the company was unable to undo, and it failed to turn its attention to the question of consuls until the autumn of 1605. During the course of its short existence it was apparent that its free-men received very little in return for their membership fees, although the rules of the company such as that prohibiting partnerships with non-members could seriously inconvenience their trade. Sir John Popham the lord chief justice had commented that whatever reasons merchants might give for incorporation, 'they ever have it in their private ends'. To many London merchants it seemed as if those private ends were little served by a Spanish company.[4]

One last question remains to be answered. All successful trading companies, whether regulated or joint-stock, were dependent on a nucleus of members whose interests were vitally identified with the continuing existence of the company, whatever other branches of trade they might pursue. It is not clear if the Spanish Company possessed such a nucleus; on the contrary it seems likely that many of its most influential freemen were

1. Epstein, *Levant Company*, 101.
2. The Merchant Adventurers had 24 assistants, the Levant Company 18, and the Eastland Company 25 (Friis, *Alderman Cockayne's Project*, 80; Epstein, *Levant Company*, 62; R. W. K. Hinton, *The Eastland Trade and the Common Weal in the 17th Century* (Cambridge, 1959), 56).
3. Epstein, *Levant Company*, 70–1.
4. H.M.C., *Salisbury MSS.*, xvii, 418–19.

principally interested in other areas of commerce. These included the Levant, Muscovy, the Eastland and the Low Countries. The connection with the Levant and Adriatic trades is both the most natural and most easily traceable of these links. It was to be expected that many Spanish merchants, following the example of Richard Staper, would enter the expanding Mediterranean trade. They soon found that its central feature, the purchase of currants from Zante, was dependent on trade with Spain for it was largely financed by the dollars and pieces of eight picked up en route at ports such as Lisbon, Cadiz, Malaga and Alicante.[1] A third of the charter members of the revived Levant Company of 1605 were also members of the Spanish Company,[2] and the proportion would probably have been higher had not the latter been abolished soon after the incorporation of the former.

The absence of other contemporary charters or complete lists of freemen makes it more difficult to assess with precision the contacts that existed with other areas. Nevertheless the evidence, although fragmentary, is highly suggestive. The re-export trade to Spain was flourishing in the first half of the seventeenth century, and before the conclusion of the peace in 1604 Wilford had listed the goods brought into London, 'returned in exchange of English cloth from Russia, Eastland, Stade, Hamburg and other parts of Germany as also out of France, most vendible in Spain and needful for the West Indies'.[3] They included wax, tallow, hemp, cordage, copper, flax, linen cloth and canvas 'of all sorts and in great quantity', German ironmongery, haberdashery and battery. When trade resumed in the last quarter of 1604 such goods formed over half of the total non-broadcloth export to Spain.[4]

Several Merchant Adventurers and Eastland men took their freedom of Spain and Portugal, and of the fifteen Eastland merchants trading to other areas in 1606 nine, including Sir Stephen Soame and the former assistants John Highlord and Arthur Jaxon, had been members of the Spanish Company.[5] The direct export trade, which left no records, may well have been even greater in its extent and involved more freemen. Wilford in 1605 expressed his dislike of this direct trade conducted by Merchant Adventurers, Eastland and Muscovy merchants, for it undercut the business of those who had formerly bought these commodities after their import into England, then re-shipped them for Spain and Portugal. He admitted with regret that some freemen had 'coloured' such goods, acting as agents for others.[6] These agents cannot be identified, but others took no trouble to

---

1. A. C. Wood, *A History of the Levant Company* (1935), 43.
2. Epstein, *Levant Company*, 158–60.
3. S.P. 14/11 no. 17; S.P. 14/8 nos. 35, 36.
4. P.R.O., E 190/12/2. For quantitative tables of re-exports see J. P. Croft, 'English Trade with Peninsular Spain 1558–1625' (unpublished Oxford D.Phil. thesis, 1969), 513–16. They declined over the decade following 1604.
5. Friis, *Alderman Cockayne's Project*, 232–3. Cockayne himself, an active assistant of the Spanish Company and subsequently the most famous of all Eastland merchants, does not appear to have been trading to the peninsula in 1606, although in the last quarter of 1604 he was one of the three Eastland merchants then re-shipping Baltic goods to Spain. The others were Arthur Jaxon and William Greenwell.
6. H.M.C., *Salisbury MSS.*, xvii, 79–80.

conceal themselves and their trade. The powerful Wych family was deeply involved; Richard Wych the elder, an assistant of the company, shipped Muscovy and Eastland goods direct to San Sebastian and Pasages where they were received by his son James, elected as company consul for the area. The ships anchored in the Downs to take on letters but their cargoes were never customed in England.[1] All in all, there is every indication that many influential Spanish merchants were not solely committed to peninsular trade and could not be expected to give the company their fullest support. Many of them may secretly have welcomed its abolition, which freed their already complex commerce from at least one set of regulations.

Despite the widespread lack of enthusiasm which had contributed towards the demise of the company, a measure of support for incorporation continued to exist after 1606. Cornwallis, putting aside his irritation with the merchants, argued repeatedly that only the existence of a regulated company could prevent the constant confusions and inconveniences that arose in the early stages of re-establishing English trade in Spain.[2] His own attempts to build up a consular system in the peninsula convinced him that the task was impossible without organised backing in London. Such views were not confined to the ambassador. In 1617 and 1619, the Londoners complained of the 'abuses and notorious disorders' which hindered their commerce. Yelverton the attorney-general recommended that they alone should be incorporated, excluding the outport merchants who would be left free to carry on their business as before.[3] The privy council nevertheless felt obliged to notify the west-country towns of this proposal, whereupon a storm of protest arose; they considered that such an incorporation would be 'full of inconveniences and very prejudicial' although they did not trouble to spell out the problems involved. The dispute was referred to a committee consisting of Lake, Greville and Coke, who reported that they disagreed with Yelverton, preferring to let the act of 1606 stand unchanged.[4]

The London merchants, disregarding the rebuff, tried again in April 1619. On this occasion the councillors asked them to propose a solution to their own problems, whereupon six merchants of whom at least three had been active in the old company formed a deliberative committee.[5] Not unexpectedly they recommended that no better course of redress could be found than to revive the Spanish charter. The inconveniences of monopoly which had been stressed in 1606 were overshadowed by those which subsequently arose from the abolition of the company; 'the trade and the dependencies thereof', they argued, 'were then in happy condition in comparison of the later and present miserable estate of the same'. Incorporation would enable them to exclude the 'tobacco sellers, grocers, vintners, dyers and other engrossers of double trade that eat out the mere and orderly merchants'.[6] Again, the attempt failed; but the incident indicates that there were

1. S.P. 94/12 f. 128; S.P. 94/13 f. 46.
2. S.P. 94/13 f. 106.
3. S.P. 14/92 no. 72.
4. *A.P.C.*, xxxv, 292–3, 342, 349–50, 353.
5. *A.P.C.*, xxxvi, 431–2. The members were Morris Abbott, Nicholas Leate, Robert Bell, Richard Wych, Edward James and Lawrence Greene (S.P. 94/112 no. 13).
6. *A.P.C.*, xxxvii, 116–17; S.P. 94/112 no. 13.

still some merchants anxious for the return of regulated trade, even though Wilford, largely responsible for the revival of 1604, was long since dead.

The chequered history of the Spanish Company is in many ways a commentary more on the fluctuations of economic opinion in the sixteenth and seventeenth centuries than on the fortunes of the trade itself. Originally the members of the Andalusia Company had banded together in self-defence when conditions in Spain grew difficult, only to fall apart quickly through lack of harmony. There was always a need for some form of united action by the English residents in the peninsula to ward off the varied harassments which threatened their position; if the central organisation of the Spanish merchants had been situated abroad, as was that of the Merchant Adventurers, much of the later friction might have been avoided. But there was little real desire for a London-based company and no useful rôle for it to fill. In the heyday of regulated companies under Elizabeth this anomaly was easily concealed, for it seemed natural that all the major trade-routes should be subject to some form of incorporation. When at the end of the century opinion turned against monopolies of every sort, the lack of support in London, the opposition of the outports, and the numerous inconveniences involved inevitably became more and more apparent. From then on, the days of the Spanish Company were numbered.

iii. The Documents

The documents calendared here contain between them most of the information which still survives concerning the revived Spanish Company of 1604–6. The Register Book, now in the British Museum, is a folio volume written in a large, clear hand, with only a few corrections. Its first entry is for 16 March 1604, the last for 2 January 1606. The Book of Oaths, Acts and Ordinances from the Rawlinson Collection in the Bodleian Library was written on 30 August 1605 with some subsequent additions covering the period between then and the dissolution of the company; the last act relates to an issue first raised at the general court of 6 November 1605. The charter printed here is a copy of the original enrolment, and is now among the State Papers Domestic in the Public Record Office. All three documents are in the same legible hand and it seems likely that they are all the work of Richard Langley, the lawyer who was appointed secretary to the company at its first meeting. The section entitled 'Additional Documents' contains some correspondence and other material to which reference was made in the Register Book.

After the dissolution of the first Spanish Company on the outbreak of war, Thomas Wilford the president kept the records at his home, and it is possible that he or Langley took both them and the later records into similar safekeeping after 1606. Thereafter, unfortunately, the early records disappeared completely, and nothing is known of the whereabouts of the documents assembled here until they re-emerge as items in the great national collections. The British Museum purchased the Register Book in December 1833 from the bookseller Thomas Thorpe the elder of 38 Bedford Street, Covent Garden; some time earlier, before his death in 1755, the bibliophile

Richard Rawlinson had acquired the Book of Oaths, Acts and Ordinances for the vast collection which he left to the Bodleian Library. It may perhaps have come through the City connections of his father, the one-time Lord Mayor Sir Thomas Rawlinson, but this cannot be firmly established.

In calendaring the documents, the aim has been to eliminate common form while retaining everything of significance. Christian names have generally been modernised but the original spelling of surnames has been followed, although suspension marks at the end of names have been ignored. Scribal corrections are given in footnotes only if they contain any material of interest. The Register Book and the Book of Oaths also contain in the margins brief notes made by the original scribe on the contents of paragraphs. These too have been omitted unless they add to the information given in the text: they are then noted in footnotes. The original spelling has been retained in quotations within the calendar; short quotations being enclosed within single quotation marks and longer ones appearing in a smaller type size.

REGISTER BOOK, 1604–1606

(B.M., Add. MS. 9365)

1. [p. 1] *An assembly held at the dwelling house of Mr. Thomas Wilford the last president on Friday 16 March 1604 in the presence of Thomas Wilford and the following:*

2. Sir Robert Lee, alderman, Sir John Watts, alderman, George Hanger, George Collymere, Robert Cobb, Arthur Jaxon, Andrew Banning, John Dorrington.

3. The persons named above and other English merchants of the society, being free of Spain and Portugal entreated Richard Langley, 'the Solicitour of the Cities lawe causes', to ascertain how the company might procure from the king a confirmation of the charters and liberties previously granted by the king's ancestors to the English merchants trading to Spain and Portugal. They also asked Langley to become the secretary of the company, which he dowbted he should not be hable to dischardg by reason of other ymployments unlesse he gave over some other place or office which he enioyed. Yett neverthelesse he thought himself so much bound to the said woorshipfull parsons for their love and good opynyon conceyved of him that he would dischardg himself of some other [p. 2] ymployments and accept of their loving and kinde offer.

He then informed the company that the old charter was shortly to be presented to the lord chancellor, who would give orders for the drawing up of a new charter of confirmation which would soon receive the great seal. It was therefore agreed that a committee consisting of Sir John Watts, Paul Banning, Thomas Wilford, John Harby, George Hanger, Richard Weech, John Dorrington, Roger Howe and Laurence Greene, or any six of them, accompanied by Richard Langley, should attend the chancellor on the matter of the charter. In addition it was agreed to levy 20s. apiece on the following persons, to cover the charges thereby incurred:

4. Sir Robert Lee, Sir John Watts, Paul Banning, Richard Staper, John Harby, George Hanger, George Collymere, Richard Weech, Robert Cobb, William Gore, John Dorrington, William Towreson, Francis Barnes, John Bate, Arthur Jaxon, Roger Howe, Joseph Jaxon, Thomas Bostock, Edward James, William Cokayne, Laurence Greene, William Stone, Andrew Banning, Jeffrey Kerby, Robert Bowyer, Thomas Allabaster, Leonard Parker, Robert Jenny, William Jennings.

5. [p. 3] *A court held at the house of Thomas Wilford, president, on Thursday 29 March 1604, in the presence of Mr. Wilford and the following:*

1

6. Sir Robert Lee, Sir William Romeney, Robert Chamberlen, Richard Staper, John Newman, George Hanger, John Hawes, Richard Weech, William Cokayne, John Dorrington, John Bate, John Highlord, Nevill Davies, Robert Bowyer, Andrew Banning, Robert Cobb, George Collymere, Roger Howe.

7. At this court, 'the charter of our Soveraigne Lord King James purporting a confirmation of the Companies former charters and liberties was openly shewed to the company under the greate seale of England'. The charge for renewing it came to £26 7s. 4d., 'as by a particuler bill thereof under the hand of one of the Clarcks of the Chauncery appeared'. The sum was disbursed by Richard Langley, employed by the company to procure the same confirmation.

8. Thomas Burgh, former servant and apprentice to George Hanger, 'did humbly desire that he may be admitted into the freedome of this company'. It was agreed that he should 'produce and shewe furth his Indenture whereby he claymeth the same'.

9. [p. 4] Those present at the last assembly explained that they had employed Richard Langley to pursue the confirmation of the charter, and had moved him to take on the office of company secretary.

It hath nowe pleased all the woorshipfull parsons here assembled to signifie their generall likinge and consente and approbation of the said Richard Langley. But they cannott determyne of any perfect or absolute graunt, nor agree upon any certen fee untill a generall court and a greater assembly to allowe of the same.

10. It was also thought very fit to send letters to the privileged ports, namely Bristol, Exeter, Hull, Barnstaple, Southampton, King's Lynn ('Lyne'), Newcastle-upon-Tyne, Plymouth, Ipswich and Chester ('Westchester'), informing them that the king had ratified the charter of the company. Thomas Wilford and Richard Langley were asked to see that letters were sent out from the company as a whole but signed by Mr. Wilford as president. He was also asked to take some of the assistants and Langley with him, if he thought it convenient, 'and to take sound advise of some lerned Counsailour of good experience and Judgment upon the said letters patents of confirmation so passed and graunted by the king's moast Excellent Majestie as aforesaid'.

11. As Thomas Wilford was the last president to be elected, 'and never yett displaced, they all agree that he shall contynue in the said place'. The following persons were thought 'very fitt and sufficient men [p. 5] out of which the Assistentz should be elected on th'election day being yerely the Munday before the Assentionday'. They were Sir John Spencer, Sir Robert Lee, Sir Richard Goddard, Sir John Watts, Sir Thomas Smyth, Sir Thomas Cambell, Sir William Romney, Richard Staper, John Highlord, Paul Banning, Robert Dow, Thomas Bramley, William Cokayne, Robert Hawes, John Hall, Francis Barnes, Roger How, Robert Chamberlen, Thomas Forman, John Newman, George Collymere, Nicholas Stile, Oliver Stile, Nicholas Ling,

Richard Gore, Robert Bowyer, Thomas Allabaster, Richard Weech, Arthur Jaxon, George Hanger, Robert Cobb, John Dorrington, John Bate, and John Harby.

12. '*A Generall Courte holden at Pewterers hall on Munday in the afternoon before the Ascention day, the 14th day of May, Anno Domini 1604 . . . being also th'election day appointed by the letters patents.*'

13. The following worshipful members of the company were present: Thomas Wilford the last president, Sir Thomas Pullyson, Sir Robert Lee and Sir John Watts, William Cokayne, John Hawes, George Collymere, George Hanger, Robert Cobb, Robert Bowyer, John Bate, Robert Savage, Nicholas Peele, William [p. 6] Stone, John Brooke, Nevill Davis, William Jennyngs, Allen Thompson, George Samuell, 'and dyvers others who were sonnes and servaunts to freemen, and may laufully be admytted into the freedome by patrymony or service'.

14. Since the king by his letters patent had confirmed the charters and liberties previously granted to this society of merchants trading to Spain and Portugal, the letters patent were read out in English to the whole assembly.

15. Then three letters were read out, from the merchants of Bristol, Chester and Exeter respectively. They were in reply to the letters recently sent out advising them of the confirmation of the charters and liberties of the company, in accordance with the orders of the last court.

16. Thomas Wilford the last president, Sir Robert Lee and Sir John Watts were nominated as candidates for the office of president in the coming year. 'And by full election by hands the said Mr. Thomas Wilford was freelie chosen againe with such fees and commodities as he did formerlie enioy, and in open Court this day tooke his oath accordinglie for the due execution of the said place.'

17. The company decided not to elect a deputy president 'untill further occasion should require'.

18. [p. 7] William Cockayne, Roger Howe and Richard Weech were then nominated as candidates in the election of the treasurer for the coming year. Roger Howe was elected, 'but by reason of his absence, his oath is deferred, and allowance of his sueties untill an other Court'.

19. Divers members of the company were nominated as assistants[1] for the coming year, and the following were elected from among them:

20. Sir Thomas Pullison, Sir Robert Lee, alderman, Sir John Watts, alderman, Sir Thomas Cambell, alderman, Sir William Romeny, alderman, Richard Staper, Robert Chamberlen, William Cockayne, John Newman,

1. Margin note, 'The election of the 30 Assistentz for London'.

3

John Highlord, John Hawes, George Collymere, Richard Weech, George Hanger, Robert Cobb, John Harby, Andrew Bannyng, Thomas Allabaster, Nicholas Lyng, Robert Bowyer, Francis Barnes, Arthur Jaxon, John Dorrington, John Bate, Robert Savage, Edward James, William Toureson, Lawrence Greene, Nicholas Peele, William Jennyngs.

21. Of these thirty persons only thirteen were present, namely Sir Thomas Pullison, Sir Robert Lee, Sir John Watts, Mr. Cokaynes, Mr. Hawes, Mr. Collymere, Mr. Bowyer, Mr. Hanger, Mr. Cobb, Mr. Bate, Mr. Savage, Mr. Peele and Mr. Jennyngs. The above 'tooke their oathes accordinglie and the residue are to take their othes at some other tyme'.

22. [p. 8] 'And Concerning the ten assistants, to be chosen out of the Cuntry,[1] to make upp the nomber of fortie for the Citty of London, according to the letters patents, there were only chosen at this Court these fyve following viz.'

23. John Hopkyns and John Barker for Bristol, Thomas Walker for Exeter, James Bagg for Plymouth, Fulck Aldersey for Chester. The nomination of the other five was deferred until the company should receive letters from the port towns.

24. Also present at this court were John Howell and Henry Sweete of Exeter, 'which said Mr. Howell is one of the present Burgesses of the parliament for Exetour, but not free of this Company.[2] But the said Mr. Sweet is a free Marchaunt of Spayne and Portingale'.

25. As the last secretary and beadle were both dead, two names were put forward 'for order sake and according to Custome', for each post.[3] Richard Langley and George Samnell stood for secretary; Richard Colman and Thomas Wilford the younger stood for the post of beadle. By general consent and show of hands, Richard Langley was freely chosen as secretary, and Richard Coleman was elected beadle. Each was to hold his office with the fees, allowances and duties [p. 9] belonging to it, as were formerly paid to Richard Maye, secretary, and George Turner, beadle. Thereupon in open court each took the oath proper to his office.

26. 'John ApJohn the comon Cryer of this Cittie attending upon my Lord Maior', was elected as the officer of the company 'to commytt disobedient brothers that shall offend, Contrary to the orders of the company, with such fee as formerlie hath byn allowed'.

1. As provided for under the charter of 1577.
2. See above, pp. xxxi–xxxiii. As one of the port-town burgesses Howell would have been eligible to sit on Sandys' committee for free trade, as well as on less controversial committees considering other measures of commercial reform (*Commons Journals*, i, 183, 199, 209, 218, 232, 243).
3. For the late secretary, Richard May, see above, p. xxvii. He cannot be firmly identified with Richard May, merchant tailor, whose son and apprentice both took the freedom of the company, since the latter is not noted as 'deceased' in the usual fashion of such entries (see below, **75, 90**).

4

27. *A court of assistants held at Pewterers' Hall on Thursday 24 May 1604 in the presence of Thomas Wilford, president, Roger Howe, treasurer, and the following assistants:*

28. Sir Robert Lee, alderman, Sir John Watts, alderman, John Highlord, John Hawes, George Collymere, George Hanger, Robert Cobb, Andrew Bannyng, Nicholas Lyng, John Dorrington, John Bate, Robert Savage, William Jennyngs.

29. Mr. Bannyng, Mr. Lyng and Mr. Dorrington, who were absent from the last general court at which they were chosen as assistants, 'did receive and take the oath in that Case made and provyded'.

30. [p. 10] Roger Howe, elected treasurer at the same court, took the usual oath 'for the due and lawfull Execution of the said office. But the allowance of Suerties is deferred untill an other Court'.

31. The president then submitted to the court for its consideration 'certen articles by him drawne to be offered to the Lords of the Counsaill on the behalf of the Company, to be required at the hands of the king of Spayne, yf a peace shalbe Concluded upon betweene our most Gratious soveraigne Lord the king, and the said king of Spaine'. The articles were read several times, 'and the Conceipts and opynions of every man heard', but eventually their detailed consideration was left to the president, the treasurer, Sir John Watts, Sir William Romeny, Mr. Cockayne, Mr. Weech, Mr. Hanger, Mr. Harby, Mr. Jaxon and Mr. Dorrington. They were also asked to present the articles to the lords of the privy council.

32. It was also ordered 'that all such persons as challendge the freedome of this Company shall sett down their Clayme in wryting, and delyver it to the Secretary, whoe shall present the said Claymes at the next court after he hath received the same'.

33. Andrew Bannyng and John Bate took their oaths as freemen by ancient trade, each paying 6s. 8d. to the treasurer to the use of the company.

34. [p. 11] '*A Generall Court entended at Pewterers' Hall the 8th of June 1604.* Unto which Court there only resorted Mr. Presedent, Mr. Treasurer, Sir Thomas Pullison, Sir Robert Lee, Mr. Cockayne, Mr. Hawes, Mr. Hanger, Mr. Cobb, Mr. Ling, Mr. Jaxon, Mr. Dorrington, Mr. Bate, Mr. Savage and Mr. Peele, (being of the assistents), and only Mr. John Hall, Mr. Nevill Davis, and Mr. Jeffrey Davis of the generallytie. So as for want of sufficyent apparance the said generall Court could not be held.' Nevertheless as Mr. Hanger the last treasurer was present he was asked to prepare his accounts and present them at the next general court. He was also asked to make an immediate payment from the money still in his hands towards the charges of renewing the company charter, and for a gratuity for Sir Daniel Dunne and Sir Thomas Edmonds, 'who are ymployed by the lords about the

5

articles of peace'. Mr. Hanger promised to pay to Roger Howe, his successor as treasurer, the sum of £20 provided he received a receipt for the payment, 'that he be not afterwards required the same by others, and soe dryven to make double payment thereof'. It was agreed that such a receipt should be provided for him.

35. [p. 12] *A general court held at Pewterers' Hall on the morning of Friday 20 August 1604, in the presence of Thomas Wilford, president, Roger Howe, treasurer, and the following assistants:*

36. Sir Thomas Pullison, Sir Robert Lee, Sir John Watts, Mr. Stapers, Mr. Chamberlen, Mr. Highelord, Mr. Collymere, Mr. Weech, Mr. Harby, Mr. Cobb, Mr. Bannyng, Mr. Lyng, Mr. Dorrington, Mr. Savage, Mr. James, Mr. Peele, Mr. Jennyngs, and divers of the generality.

37. The minutes of the last general court and also of the last court of assistants were read and confirmed.

38. The following were then admitted into the freedom of the society by service; Nicholas Farrar, skinner, formerly servant to John Harby, skinner, Edward James, merchant tailor, formerly servant to John James, and Thomas Altham son of Thomas Altham, clockworker, free of this company and also servant to William Jennyngs. They took the oath of freemen by ancient trade, each paying 6s. 8d. to the treasurer.

39. Richard Staper, Robert Chamberlen, John Highlord, Richard Weech, John Harbie and Edward James, 'who were lately elected to be of the assistents, did also receive the oath in that Case ordayned'.

40. [p. 13] It was ordered that the president, the treasurer, Sir John Watts, Sir William Romeny, Mr. Staper, Mr. Cockayne, Mr. Weech, Mr. Allabaster, Mr. Jaxon, and Mr. Dorrington, 'shall attend the Lords, against the Cunstable of Casteele shall come over'.[1] They or any six of them were authorised

to treat and conclude of matters for the benefitt of the Companie, and to disburse money for the necessary affaires, and good of the Company. And that which they or any sixe of them shall doe the Company will allowe.

41. The draft of a charter drawn up by the president was read out in court, 'to be procured from the king of Spayne unto this Company'. The matter was referred for the consideration of the members of the committee named above.

42. It was agreed that the treasurer should borrow £100 at interest for six months, as payment for the charges involved in the renewal of the company charter, for officers' fees, and other items of company business. All those present at the court faithfully promised,

1. See above, pp. xxxiii–xxxiv.

that if Mr. Treasurer before th'expiration of the said 6 monethes, shall not receive to th'use of the said Companie, by fynes for freemen, and other laufull meanes, soe much money as shall paie the said one hundreth pownds, and interest and all other chardges that he shall disburse for the good of the Company, that then they and everie of them share, and share lyke would satisfy and [p. 14] pay so much laufull englishe money a peece as in the whole should amount to the said £100 and interest.

To ensure this it was agreed that a copy of the order or a document to the same effect should be drawn up and kept by the treasurer, to which all the above should put their names.

43. It was ordered that James Weech, formerly apprenticed to Sir Richard Saltingstall, and John Aspshawe formerly apprenticed to Simon Bourman, both of whom were now beyond the seas but lawfully able to claim their freedoms, 'shall not be ympeached for trading untill they returne into England'.

44. Sir Roger James, alderman of London, resorted to the court asking to be made free of the company by redemption.

And this assembly supposing that he had given over, either being a Retailour or Artificer were Content to accept of his Woorship into the said freedome. But first they advysed hym to heare redd the oath of a freeman by Redemption. After the reading whereof, he refused to be sworne thereunto, and soe departed, and surceased his suyte.

45. [p. 15] *A court of assistants held at Pewterers' Hall, 23 August 1604, in the presence of Thomas Wilford, president, Roger Howe, treasurer, and the following assistants:*

46. Sir Thomas Pullison, Mr. Stapers, Mr. Chamberlen, Mr. Cokayne, Mr. Cullymore, Mr. Weech, Mr. Cobb, Mr. Andrew Bannyng, Mr. Lyng, Mr. Jaxon, Mr. Dorrington, Mr. Savage, Mr. James, Mr. Greene, Mr. Peele, Mr. Jennyngs.

47. John Mokett of Weymouth came to the court to request the freedom of the company, 'alleadging that he hath ben an auncient merchant trading Spayne. But he was aunswered that he must be referred to Southampton where his clayme should be examined'.

48. It was ordered and agreed that a committee should be constituted, to 'meete togeather and appoynt all such persons to be warned before them as either clayme their freedome by Patrymony or service, or desyre to be admitted by redemption, and to conferr with them and examyne their claymes and understand their suite and to make report att the next court'.[1]

49. Lawrence Greene, grocer, former servant to the late alderman Robert Brooke, was admitted to the freedom of the company by service, taking the

1. Margin note, 'Committees to examyn the claymes and requests of such as desire the freedome, vide page 23', i.e. **79.**

oath of a freeman by ancient trade and paying 6s. 8d. to the treasurer. Afterwards he was also sworn in as an assistant.

50. [p. 16] Nicholas Oseley, clothworker, former servant to Sir James Hawes, was admitted to the freedom by service, taking the oath of a freeman by ancient trade.[1]

51. *A general court held at Pewterers' Hall on the morning of Friday 31 August 1604, in the presence of Thomas Wilford, president, Roger Howe, treasurer, and the following assistants:*

52. Mr. Stapers, Mr. Chamberlen, Mr. Newman, Mr. Collymer, Mr. Cobb, Mr. Harby, Mr. Bowyer, Mr. Jackson, Mr. Dorrington, Mr. Bate, Mr. James, Mr. Greene, Mr. Peele, Mr. Jennyngs.

53. William Towerson son of William Towerson, skinner, and John Hall and Humphrey Hall sons of John Hall, draper, were admitted into the freedom by patrimony.

54. The following ten persons were admitted into the freedom by service: Ralph Edmunds by service with Sir Thomas Pullyson, draper, 'being also recommended by letter from Don John de Taxis one of the Ambassadors of the king of Spayne', Thomas Seracold by service with John Newton, mercer, John Worsupp and Francis Taylor by service with Robert Cobb, girdler, William Evans by service with the late alderman John Moore, skinner, Leonard Harwood by service with William Mascall, mercer, Gawen Walcott by service with John Hall, draper, Robert Angell by service with Augustine Fowlks, grocer, Thomas Southake by service with Alderman William Massam, grocer, and John Ramridge by service with William Barker, mercer. The three previously made free by patrimony together with the ten made free by service [p. 17] paid 6s. 8d. each to the treasurer and took the oath appointed for freemen by ancient trade.

55. Two more persons were admitted into the freedom by service. The first was William Speight, former servant of Alderman Sir Robert Lee, merchant tailor, who paid £10 to the treasurer as his master Sir Robert Lee had done on his admission. The second was William Cater, servant to John Dent, salter, who paid £5 to the treasurer as his master had done on his admission. Then, George Benson, merchant tailor, a mere merchant and not free of any other company of merchants, was admitted into the freedom by redemption and paid £10 to the treasurer for the same. The three new members took the oath appointed for freemen received by redemption.

56. John Newman, Arthur Jaxon and William Towerson, 'lately elected to be of the Assistents, did receave the oath in that case ordeyned'.

57. The assistants and generality present at this court were pleased of their free good will and bownty (withowt any suite made for the same) to

1. See above, pp. xxxvii–xxxix.

graunt unto Richard Langley their Secretary the freedome of this company, to have and enioy for him selff his Children and servants in as large and beneficiall manner as any auncyent merchant or other freeman whatsoever for which extraordinary favor the said Richard Langley did acknowledge himselff much bownd to the company.

He then took the oath appointed for freemen by ancient trade, which was administered to him in open court by the president, and paid 6s. 8d. to the treasurer.

58. [p. 18] Richard Colman the beadle was also granted his freedom without his making any prior suit for it, 'to have and enioye onely during so long tyme as he shall contynewe officer unto the company'. He was admitted and sworn in accordingly.

59. It was ordered and agreed that every person admitted into the freedom by patrimony or service should pay 12d. to the secretary and 6d. to the beadle. Those admitted by redemption should pay 2s. to the secretary and 12d. to the beadle. In addition, the secretary was empowered to collect 12d. for the enrolment of each indenture, any former orders to the contrary notwithstanding.

60. Forasmuch as during the tyme of the breach betweene our late Soveraigne Lady Queene Elizabeth and the king of Spain dyvers persons of this company being withowt hope of any peace or reconsiliation did omytt owt of their apprentices Indentures the words 'Marchant of Spayne and Portyngale', so as by the stricknes of an auncyent order noe such persons can clayme the benefitt of their freedome of Spayne and Portyngale by any such servyce, yt is neverthelesse (upon full and deliberate consideration) att this court concluded and agreed that all such persons as were bound to any freeman of this company att any tyme sithence the yere of our Lord God one thowsand fyve hundreth eightie fyve untill this present daye shall and may be dispensed withall and be admitted into the freedome notwithstanding the omitting of the said words, soe as they make just prooff of their service, and also make their clayme before the feast of Christmas next ensewing, and so as the Indenture of every apprentice already bound be inrolled with the Secretary before the said feast of Christmas next.

61. [p. 19] It was also agreed that all indentures made after the date of this court should observe the ancient order for the inserting of the words 'merchant of Spain and Portugal'. Every indenture which omitted the words should be regarded as void concerning the freedom of the company.

62. A letter was read out from the duke of Lennox 'for the preferring of a Consull in Spayne', but the company took further time to consider the matter.[1]

1. Ludovick Stuart, 2nd duke of Lennox (1574–1624). Son of the favourite, Esme Stuart, he accompanied James I to England on his accession and was one of the five Scots then added to the privy council, where he always showed a particular interest in foreign affairs. In Sept. 1605 he obtained his notorious patent for the sealing of the new draperies, which was heatedly attacked in the parliament of 1606 (Price, *English Patents of Monopoly*, 27; Sir Robert Douglas, *The Peerage of Scotland* (2nd ed. rev. J. P. Wood, Edinburgh, 1813), ii, 100).

9

63. It was agreed that letters should at once be written 'unto the Cuntry to the severall dyvisions and ports', each containing a copy of the articles of the peace together with a translation of them into English.

64. It was agreed to set up a committee of the following members or any six of them, namely the president, the treasurer, Sir John Watts, Sir William Romeney, Mr. Staper, Mr. Cokayne, Mr. Weech, Mr. Allabaster, Mr. Jaxon and Mr. Dorrington. They were to consider

the paynes and travell of such as have ben ymployed for the good of the Company, towching the Articles concluded upon in the treaty of peace betweene England and Spayne. And what they or any sixe of them shall thinck fitt to bestowe upon them, this court will allowe.

65. A further committee consisting of the following members or any five of them was also set up, namely the president, the treasurer, Mr. Dorrington, Mr. Jaxon, Mr. Bates, Mr. James, Mr. Nevill Davys and Mr. Bostock. They were

entreated to consider what seale or certificate is required by the Article to be for our goods to passe into Spayne withowt danger or trowble. And to procure letters from my Lord Treasurer that none but freemen of this company maye be admitted to enter their goods to be sent into Spayne or Portingale.

66. It was agreed that if Mr. Hanger the last treasurer did not bring in his account within fourteen days of [p. 20] due warning, 'that then he shalbe comytted by Mr. President for his contempt'.

67. It was also agreed that every indenture of apprenticeship already made to any freeman of the company must be enrolled with the secretary within the following year. Every indenture made thereafter must be enrolled with the secretary within a year of its being made, 'upon payne that the master of every such apprentice shall forfeit to the use of the company for every such Indenture which shall not be enrowled as aforesaid the some of Tenn shillings'.

68. *A general court held at Pewterers' Hall on the morning of Friday 7 September 1604 in the presence of the president, the treasurer, and the following assistants:*

69. Sir Thomas Pullison, Sir William Romeney, Robert Chamberlen, John Newman, George Collymere, Richard Weech, George Hanger, Robert Cobb, Andrew Bannyng, Nicholas Lyng, Robert Bowyer, John Dorrington, John Bate, Robert Savage, Edward James, William Towerson.

70. After the reading and confirmation of the acts of the last general court the proceedings were as follows:

71. Sir William Romeney, alderman of London, 'who was elected one of the assistants did att this court receave the oath in that case provyded'.

72. [p. 21] George Hanger the former treasurer brought in his account, whereupon eight auditors were appointed to examine it. They were Richard Weech, Robert Cobb, Andrew Bannyng, John Bate, Edward James and William Towerson from among the assistants, and Mr. Castlyn and Mr. Cletherowe of the generality. At least five of them were to 'subscribe their names thereunto according to the auncyent orders of this company'.

73. It was agreed that Sir John Watts, who preceded Mr. Hanger as treasurer, 'and never yett accoumpted', should be warned to present his account to a general court with all convenient speed.

74. The following six persons were admitted into the freedom of the company by patrimony: John Newman the younger son of John Newman, grocer, Phillip Smyth son of Phillip Smyth, haberdasher, Nathaniel Martyn son of Sir Richard Martyn, goldsmith, Christopher Cletherowe son of Henry Cletherowe, ironmonger, Simon Lawrence son of Simon Lawrence, grocer, and Richard Shorter, merchant tailor, son of William Shorter, draper. Each paid 6s. 8d. to the treasurer for the use of the company, and took the oath of a freeman by ancient trade.

75. The following eleven persons were made free by service: Nicholas Buckeridg by service with John Newman, grocer, William Woder by service with Thomas Bramley, haberdasher, Nicholas Smyth, by service with Jerrard Gore the elder, merchant tailor, William Wastell, grocer, by service with Andrew Bannyng, Jeffrey Kerby, grocer, by service with Paul Bannyng, Gyles Parslowe, grocer, by service with Francis [p. 22] Bowyer, Alderman Leonard Parker, haberdasher, by service with William Welden, William Stone, skinner, by service with William Towreson, John Sherrington by service with Robert Cobb, girdler, William Adderley, merchant tailor, by service with Richard Maye, and William Aldington by service with Roger Howe, mercer. They each paid 6s. 8d. to the treasurer to the use of the company and took the oath of freemen by ancient trade.

76. 'And John Suracold alias Seracold who hath ben an auncyent merchant and was long remayning in Spayne is admitted into the freedome by reason he is named in the charter or patent graunted by the late Queene Elizabeth'. He paid the treasurer 6s. 8d. to the use of the company and received the oath of a freeman by ancient trade.

77. Edmond Burton, draper, 'a meere merchant and a trader into Spayne' was admitted into the freedom by redemption, paying £10 to the treasurer to the use of the company and taking the oath of a freeman by redemption.

78. Thomas Dalby, mercer, and Edward Davenant, merchant tailor,

whoe desyred the freedome by Redemption were not allowed at this court by reason they are supposed to be retaylors, and keapers of warehowses. And neither are they sonnes nor were they apprentizes of any marchants, and therefore thought not capable of the said freedome. Neverthelesse they are appoynted to attend the Committees hereafter named, whoe are entreated to advise and

consider fully of th'estate of their requests and to report their opynions att the
next generall courte.

79. [p. 23] It was ordered and agreed that two new members, Mr. Bates and
Mr. Castlyn, should be added to the committee of seven appointed at a
court of assistants on 23 August 1604, making nine in all. The seven
original members were the president, the treasurer, Mr. Bannyng, Mr. Ling,
Mr. Jaxon, Mr. Forman and Mr. Bostock. They or any five of them were

to meete togeather, and to cause all such persons to be warned before them that
either clayme their freedome by patrymony or service, or make suite to be
admitted by Redemption, and to examyne their claymes and understand the
nature of their suite and what trade or profession they have heretofore used and
what they nowe doe use, and whether by the trewe meaning of the Patent they
hold them capable and fitt to be receaved into this socyety, and from tyme to
tyme to make relation att the next generall court after such examination by them
or any fyve of them made as aforesaid.

80. The president exhibited a seal which he had had made, 'with the Scutch-
ion of the companyes armes, to be used for the sealing of such letters
as shalbe written in the name of the company, which seale was liked and
allowed and order gyven to Mr. Treasurer to make payement for the same'.

81. A petition to the lord high treasurer, drawn up on the advice of certain
committee members, was read out in court. It desired his lordship's resolution on the article in the peace-treaty concerning the sealing and registering
of English goods which bore any resemblance to those of Holland and
Zeeland. It also humbly requested his lordship's honourable letters to the
officers of the custom-house, 'that none may enter goods for Spayne or
Portyngale unlesse they should be certified by Mr. President or his deputy
or Mr. Treasurer to be free of this [p. 24] company'. The lord treasurer had
given the petition a very honourable and favourable answer, 'yett referring
the consideration of the first parte of the Petition to Sir Danyell Dun and
Sir Thomas Edmonds, whoe were ymployed in pennyng the said articles'.[1]
With regard to the latter part of the petition his lordship gave order to one
of his secretaries to draw up the letter.

Neverthelesse information is gyven att this court that some newe course is
entended whereupon Mr. President, Mr. Treasurer, Sir William Romeney, Mr.
Dorrington and Mr. Weech are entreated by this court to attend my Lord
Treasurer to understand what resolution is taken concerning the same wherein
they are entreated to advise and consider and to move his Lordshipp for the best
and easiest course that maye be for the good and safety of the company.

82. *A general court 'entended to be houlden' at Pewterers' Hall on Wednesday
19 September 1604.*

83. 'Unto which Court there onlie resorted Sir Thomas Pullison, Sir Robert Lee,
Mr. Chamberlen, Mr. Newman, Mr. Collymere, Mr. Hanger, Mr. Bannyng,

1. See above, p. xxxv and below, **723–6, 748.**

12

Mr. Jaxon, Mr. Dorrington, Mr. Savage, Mr. Toureson and Mr. Peele, and a smale nomber of the generallitie. Soe as for want of sufficyent apparance the said generall Court could not be held'.

84. *A general court held at Pewterers' Hall on Thursday 20 September 1604, in the presence of the president, the treasurer, and the following assistants:*

85. Sir Thomas Pullison, Sir William Romeny, Mr. Staper, Mr. Chamberlen, Mr. Cockayne, Mr. Collymere, Mr. Newman, Mr. Hanger, Mr. Bannyng, Mr. Lyng, Mr. Bowyer, Mr. Jaxon, Mr. Dorrington, Mr. Savage, Mr. Castelyne, Mr. Parslowe, Mr. Furner, and also divers of the generality.

86. [p. 25] After the reading and confirmation of the minutes of the last general court, the following business was transacted.

87. At this court the Companie falling into consideration how many courts have byn warned and nothing done for want of a competent number of Assistants to have byn presente at the same, and fynding that dyverse of the assistants latelie elected make default of apparance, some by reason of other ymployments, and some being beyond the Seas, and for other spetiall occasions, as namely Sir Thomas Cambell knight and Alderman, Mr. John Hawes, Mr. ffraunces Barnes, and Mr. William Jennyngs. Therefore for the better service of the Companie it is agreed that the said foure shalbe dischardged and noe longer be assistants, and foure others such as may attend the service to be elected in their places, ffor which purpose dyverse woorshipfull persons were named and put to election. But by moast voyces th'ellection did fall upon, Mr. Nicholas Style, Mr. John Castelyn, Mr. Gyles Parslowe, and Mr. Symion Furner.

The latter three being present were all sworn in as assistants, but as Mr. Style was absent he was to receive his oath at some other court.

88. The court also discussed whether Edward Davenant and Thomas Dalbie, who had lately sued for their freedom and paid £10 each to the treasurer, 'were by the true entent and meanyng of the Companies charter capable, and fitt to be received into the freedome'. It was agreed by majority vote that they were not capable and that their money should be returned, 'yett in the end the Companie thought fitt to take a further tyme to consider thereof'.

89. [p. 26] The following five persons were admitted into the freedom by service: John Stokeley by service with Thomas Owen, merchant tailor, John Stronginarme by service with Thomas Wilford, president, Clemens Fryer by service with Thomas Fryer, draper, Bryan Janson by service with Sir Thomas Pullison, and Roger Gomeldon by service with Mrs. Parnell Toureson. They all paid 6s. 8d. to the treasurer for the use of the company, taking their oaths as freemen by ancient trade.

90. George May, son of Richard May, merchant tailor, was admitted into the freedom by patrimony. He paid 6s. 8d. to the treasurer to the use of the company, and took the oath of a freeman by ancient trade.

13

91. The following four persons were admitted into the freedom by redemption: William Hungate, ironmonger, Phillip Jones, ironmonger, Thomas Church, draper, and Ralph Wight, grocer, 'being all mere merchants and free of noe other Companyes'. They each paid the treasurer £10 to the use of the company 'amounting in the whole to fortie powndes'.

92. [p. 27] *An assembly held at Pewterers' Hall on Wednesday afternoon, 30 January 1605 in the presence of the right worshipful Mr. Thomas Wilford, president, Mr. Roger Howe, treasurer, and the following assistants:*

93. John Newman, Nicholas Ling, Robert Bowyer, Arthur Jaxon, John Dorrington, John Bate, and Mr. Bostock one of the generality.

94. A letter was openly read out from the lords of the privy council.

95. It was addressed to the lord chief baron of the exchequer, Sir Daniel Dun master of the requests to his majesty, Sir Edward Coke the attorney general, and Sir Thomas Edmonds, secretary to his majesty for the French tongue, or to any three of them. Its contents were as follows.

96. After our very hartie commendations to your Lordship and the rest. Wheras upon his Majesty's Cominge to this Crowne and the ceasing of the trobles formerlie dependinge betwene this kingdome and the State of Spaine, the marchants of this Realme which use the trade of Spaine, and which have bine auncientlie made and Constituted a Corporation by the favor of former Princes, with the graunt of all priviledges therunto belonginge, did adresse themselves unto me the Lord Chancelor, and made suyte for [p. 28] the ratyfyinge of their Corporation by his Majestie, upon the knowledge which was taken that Aucthoritie was given by his majestie to me for the better ease of his Majestie, and for the expedition of the subiect, to renewe all Corporations of this Realme, according to their present forme. And accordinglie the said merchants obteyned the renewinge of their said Corporation, by aucthoritie whereof they pretend to have carefullie endevored the setlinge of their said trade, by establishinge such necessarie orders for goverment as are meete to be observed in the same, and to appoynte Consulls to reside for that purpose in the principall Portes of Spayne. But the said merchants doe complayne that they are ympeached and disturbed in their said proceedings by Certaine Retaylers and Shoppkeepers, which are prohibited by their charter to use the trade of merchandize and also by others not free of the said Company, which doe (as yt is informed) disable and discredit the power of the said Charter, pretending that the same is not sufficiently aucthorized and warranted by lawe, for that their Charter graunted by the late Queene became voyde by Non User, during the longe tyme of the Contynuance of the warr, which doth therfore dissolve the said Corporation, unles the same be restored againe by a new Creation. By reason of the which scruple (which is alleaged to be the opynion of some lawyers) the saide Company beinge doubtful how to proceede, and to governe themselves for the ordringe of their trade, have forborne to make any assemblies, and to putt their Charter in execution till our pleasures weare knowne, concerninge the validitie of the said Charter. And although wee holde the foresaide allegation of the non-user in this case to be a strict interpretation, Considering that ther was noe default in the merchant, but that the warres weare the occasion thereof: neverthelese we have thought good

14

both for our owne better satisfaction, and likewise at the humble suyte of the said merchants, to recommend to your Lordship and the rest, to Consider of the validitie of their present graunt, prayinge you not only to certifie us your opynions what you Conceave of the sufficiency therof in poynt of Lawe, but in case there be defect in the said graunt, and that it be needefull to obteyne a newe Charter from his Majestie, to advyse also how far forth yt is Convenient to yeelde to the enlargement of the said charter, in such farther matters as shalbe propounded unto you by the said merchants for the Comon good (as it is affirmed) of the said trade, and [p. 29] thereof lykewise to Certifie us your opynions as speedilie as you maie because it importeth that expedition be used therein. And so wee bid yow hartelie farewell from the Courte at Whitehall the 28 of January 1605.

97. Your lordships very loving friendes Thomas Ellesmere Cancellarius, Thomas Dorsett, Nottingham, Suffolke, Northumberland, E. Worcester, Devonshire, H. Northampton, Cranborne,[1] E. Zouche, Thomas Burghley, E. Wotton.

98. After the letters had been read out, 'and a good tyme spent in debating and considering of the same, with an expectation that a greater nomber of the Company wold have mett at this tyme and upon this occasion', it was finally agreed that 'all diligence should be used and care taken in prosecution of the honorable entent of the Lords'. For this purpose a committee was set up to confer together and to attend the lords' committee in order to ex-pedite the business. It was composed of the president, Sir William Romeney, Mr. How the treasurer, Mr. Jaxon, Mr. Dorrington, Mr. Bostock and the secretary, or any five of them. The company agreed to authorise the ex-penditure of any money that the committee should 'disburse or bestowe in gratuities touching or concerning the same'.

99. [p. 30] *An assembly held at Pewterers' Hall on the afternoon of Friday 8 February 1605 in the presence of the following assistants:*

100. Thomas Wilford, president, Roger How, treasurer, Sir William Rom-ney, John Newman, George Collymere, George Hanger, Robert Cobb, Nicholas Lyng, Arthur Jaxon, John Bate, Robert Savage, Lawrence Greene, John Castlyn, Gyles Parslowe, Simon Furner, and William Jennings one of the generality.

101. A copy of a letter was read out from the lord chief baron, Sir Daniel Dun, Sir Edward Coke and Sir Thomas Edmunds, to the lords of the privy council in answer to their letter entered up in the proceedings of the last assembly.

102. It was endorsed as sent to the lords of the privy council, and its con-tents were as follows.

103. Our humble duties to your lordships remembred. Wee have according to your honorable letters considered of the Chartre made to the merchaunts trading into Spaine, and the confirmation thereof by his Majesty, and Doe fynde two imperfections or defects in their charter, first in the forme of the incorporation

---

1. Cecil had been created Viscount Cranborne on 20 Aug. 1604, and earl of Salisbury on 4 May 1605.

being incorporated, per nomen Presidentis assistentium et societatis mercatorum Hispanie et Portugalie, where they should have byn named of England or some parte thereof, trading into Spaine and Portingall, secondly by the charter they ought to have elected yerely a President for one yere to endure, which they have neglected [blank in ms.] yeres. Also the confirmation is insuffitient for it is made, nunc Presidenti Assistenti et societati et cetera and there was no Presedent att the tyme of the [p. 31] Confirmation, wee thincke it fitt that a newe charter be made (with reformation of these errors and defects) for as without a charter good order (the only meanes to avoid confusion) cannot be observed, so is it necessary that the charter be so tempered and framed as nothing may be omitted necessary for the advauncement of trade and traffique, nor any thing inserted into it that may be repugnant to lawe, or preiudiciall to the comon wealth which being as much as was required of us, wee humbly take our leaves, and ever remayne, moast humbly att your Lordships Commandment.

104. Thomas ffleming, Daniele Dun, Edward Coke, Thomas Edmonds.

105. The above letter was read out in court in addition to the letter written by the lords and entered under the last assembly. It was then resolved that a new charter should be procured with all convenient speed, and a committee was appointed 'to conferr and consider of all things needefull to be incerted or added to the same charter for the good of the Company'. Its members were the president, the treasurer, Sir William Romney, Mr. Cockayne, Mr. Weech, Mr. Jaxon, and Mr. Dorrington.

106. It was also agreed that the sum of £100 in the hands of the treasurer, borrowed at interest some time earlier, should be disbursed by the treasurer in furtherance of the same business, at the direction of the members of the above committee or any four of them. If the original £100 had already been repaid then another £100 was to be borrowed. The members of the committee, or any four of them, should make out a warrant under their hands which would be 'a sufficient dischardg to the said Mr. Treasurer for payment thereof or any parte or parcell thereof'.

107. The copy of a letter from Viscount Cranborne, the principal secretary of his majesty, to the attorney-general.

108. Mr. Atturney. Whereas there was a graunt made att his Majesty's first commyng to the Crowne unto the company of merchaunts trading into Spaine upon my Lord Chancellour's [p. 32] generall graunt, which synce being viewed and perused by my Lord Chief Baron and others appointed Commissioners for that purpose, is found defective in some particulers, these are now to lett you knowe that it is his Majesty's pleasure you should draw a new graunt in due forme of lawe, whereunto hereafter no iust exceptions neede be taken for the satisfaction of the said merchaunts, towards whom his Majesty is graciously disposed to use all the favor that may be. And so I committ you to god. From the Court at Whitehall the [blank in ms.] day of ffebruary 1605.[1]

109. *An assembly held at Pewterers' Hall on 18 March 1605 in the presence of the following worshipful assistants:*

1. 8 Feb. 1605 (*Cal. S.P. Domestic 1603–10*, 193).

110. Thomas Wilford, president, Richard Staper, Nicholas Ling, Richard Weech, John Bate, Robert Chamberlen, George Collymore, Andrew Banning, John Castlyn.

111. A letter, recently received from Viscount Cranborne the king's principal secretary, was read out. It was endorsed as sent to Thomas Wilford and the rest of the merchants trading to Spain, and was as follows:

112. After my hartie Comendations, fforasmuch as his Majesty hath appointed Sir Charles Cornwalleis knight, to be his Ambassadour resident with the king of Spaine, and that it is Convenient both for the good of his majesty's service, and for the Advancement of your trade into those parts, that he be fully enstructed and informed of the present state of your trade, which he cannot be better then from your owne relation, I have thought good to require yow, that yow will depute some persons amongste yow of sufficiency and understandinge in those busines, to resorte to the said Sir Charles Cornewalleis, and to Conferr with him about the same, as also to informe him what ancient rights and priviledges you doe Claime in those parts, what taxes or Impositions are exacted upon yow, [p. 33] Contrary to former treaties, and all other incidencies of Complaints or grievances, which yow shall thinke fitt for his knowledge, and his interposition, wherein I hope yow wilbe the more carefull and diligent to waite on him, seing it Concerneth wholy your owne good and benifitt. And so I Comend yow to god, ffrom Grenwich this 18 of March 1605.

Your Loving frende

Cranborne.

113. It was therefore ordered that the president, the treasurer, Sir William Romeney, Mr. Cockayne, Mr. Robert Bowyer, Mr. Jaxon, Mr. Dorrington, Mr. Bate and Mr. Lawrence Greene should attend the ambassador, to inform him of the matters mentioned in the letter.

114. A draft for the new charter was also read out, 'which the Company praie may be procured and dispatched with all Convenient speede'.

115. *An assembly held at the house of Thomas Wilford the president, on Wednesday afternoon 20 March 1605 by the following worshipful persons:* Mr. Wilford, president, Mr. Cokayne, Mr. Jaxon, Mr. Dorrington.

116. Although the meeting was called to consider some information to be given to the ambassador, and the speedy effecting of the charter, several of those who had been notified failed to attend.

Yet nevertheles it is thought fitt and so agreed that Mr. Presedent Sir William Romeney and the Secretary (who have promised to undertake the Jorney) and Mr. Bowyer and Mr. Greene yf there leyzure will permitt, shall tomorrow morning procure a Coach and undertake a present Jorney to Mr. Attorney, to his house in the Country, for the speedy dispatch of the charter, before my Lord Admirall the great Ambassador, and Sir William Cornewalleis the lidgeor Ambassador goe over, which is expected shalbe within few daies. And the said fyve persons present have sent a noate under their hands to Mr. Treasurer to deliver £4 towards the Charges of the Jorney.

117. [p. 34] It was also thought fit that a collection of documents should be drawn up and sent to the ambassador, including the ancient privileges granted to the English merchants by the kings of Spain and Portugal. The documents were to be procured by Mr. Dorrington from Portugal, 'where he saieth the same may be obteyned'.

118. [p. 35] *A court of assistants held at Pewterers' Hall, 8 June 1605, in the presence of Thomas Wilford, president and the following assistants:*

119. Sir Robert Lee, Sir John Watts, Sir John Swynnerton, Sir William Romeney, Robert Chamberlen, William Cokeyne, Nicholas Ling, Arthur Jackson, John Dorrington, Robert Savage, Edward James, Symion Furner, John Newton, William Towreson, Nicholas Stile, Thomas Owen, Richard Wych, Robert Cobb, George Hanger, Thomas Forman, John Whitson of Bristol, Richard Langley, secretary, Roger Howe, late treasurer, Percival Brooke of York.

120. First, the president announced that the king had been graciously pleased to grant the company a new charter which had been sealed with the great seal of England on the preceding Saturday and bore the date 31 May 1605. The charter was then read out in its entirety by Richard Langley the secretary.

121. After the reading it was resolved

that letters should be presently written by Mr. President to the severall port townes to intimate and make knowne unto them his Majesty's gratious favour in that behaulf, to th'end they may ioyne and advise with the company for the laying Downe of good orders and constitutions for the government of the societie.

122. [p. 36] It was agreed in the meantime to set up a committee composed of the president, Sir John Swynnerton, Sir William Romeney, Mr. Cokayne, Mr. Wyche, Mr. Howe, Mr. Dorrington, Mr. Jaxon, Mr. Whitson of Bristol, Mr. Newton, Mr. Brooke of York, Mr. Owen, Mr. Towreson and Mr. James or any seven of them. They were entreated to meet at Merchant Tailors' Hall the following morning,

to consider of the oathes and ordinances for the government of the company, and to prepare the same in all readines against the next court of Assistaunts, to th'end Mr. President, Assistents and other officers and freemen may then be sworn, and so to proceed for the establishing of goverment in the company with speed, and to take order with the Customers that no entries be made of the goods of any but only of such as be free of the company.

123. *An assembly held at Merchant Tailors' Hall on Saturday 8 June 1605 by the following worshipful persons:*

124. The president, Sir John Swynnerton, Mr. Cokayne, Mr. Wyche, Mr. Dorrington, Mr. Jackson, Mr. Newton, Mr. Howe, Mr. Owen, Mr. James, Mr. Whitson of Bristol, Mr. Brooke of York, Mr. Chaple of Exeter.

18

125. In accordance with the order made at the last court of assistants the abovenamed persons

spent the forenoone in perusing the awncient oathes and divers of the old ordynaunces awnciently made for the goverment of this Company and according as tyme and occasion did require did alter some few thinges therein, and did defer the consideration of the residue of the said ordynaunces untill some other tyme.

126. [p. 37] *A general court held at Pewterers' Hall on the morning of Wednesday 12 June 1605 in the presence of Thomas Wilford, president and the following assistants:*

127. Sir Robert Lee, Sir William Romeney, Mr. Staper, Mr. Chamberlen, Mr. Cokayne, Mr. Newman, Mr. Ling, Mr. Jackson, Mr. Dorrington, Mr. Savage, Mr. James, Mr. Bowyer, Mr. Newton, Mr. Towreson, Mr. Cobb, Mr. Hanger, Mr. Sweene, Mr. Forman, Richard Langley, secretary.

128. Also present were Sir Thomas Pullison, Mr. Howe the former treasurer, Mr. Brooke of York and divers of the generality.

129. ffirst at this generall court the King's Majesties moast gracious charter under his highnes greate seale of England conteyning fyve skyns of vellam and bearing date the 31 day of May last being in the Third yeere of his Majesty's Raigne of his Realmes of England ffrance and Ireland, and of Scotland the eight and thirteth was openly redd in the presence of the Assistants and generallity here present.

130. After reading, Thomas Wilford the president named in the charter took his oath of office.

131. Richard Langley as the secretary named in the charter also took the oath appointed for his office.

132. [p. 38] The eighteen assistants who were present at the court, as before named, 'did also receive and take the oath for th'execution of the said places'.

133. Sir William Romeney, named in the charter, took the oath of a freeman by ancient trade, 'and paied the fine due upon such admission, viz. to the use of the said society 6s. 8d., and to the Secretary 12d. and to the Beadle 6d.'.

134. *A general court held at Pewterers' Hall on Thursday 13 June 1605 in the presence of Thomas Wilford, president, and the following assistants:*

135. Sir William Romeney, Robert Chamberlen, John Harby, Nicholas Ling, Robert Savage, Symion Furner, William Towreson, Thomas Owen,

Robert Cobb, George Hanger, Laurence Greene, Thomas Forman; the secretary of the company and divers of the generality.

136. It was agreed by general consent

that the names of Mr. Thomas ffarington, Thomas Bostock and William ffreeman (being meere marchaunts by auntient trade) are omitted out of the newe charter lately graunted by the king's Majestie, yett by the generall words they are made as capable of the freedome as any other that is named in the charter. Neverthelesse for the better manifestation of their right to posterity for the benefite of their servaunts and children it is thought fitt that some mention be thereof made in the [p. 39] books and records of this company, and some indorsement thereof to be made upon the back of the charter, and that all others that be in the like case shall receave the like favour and have the like entry and endorsement as aforesaid.

137. John Harby, Symion Furner, and Thomas Owen, three of the assistants who have been absent from the previous court, took their appointed oaths of office.

138. William Harrison, named in the charter,

was recommended to the Company by certen Lords of his Majesty's privie counsaill and for other causes the company moving, he had therefore administred unto him the oath of a freeman by auncient trade, and only paied the fine and sommes due upon such admissions viz. to the use of the Society 6s. 8d. and to the Secretary 12d. and the Beadle 6d.

139. James Flesher, who was named in the charter, had previously paid Mr. Howe the former treasurer £10 to the use of the society in return for his inclusion in it. Similarly Robert Brooke, Henry Peyton, Humphrey Slany, Francis Olyver, Thomas Eaton 'also Heaton', and Daniel Hills had each paid £10 to the president for the inclusion of their names, which were accordingly inserted into the charter on his instructions. 'Nowe at this court after some debate and discourse whether they should take the oath of freemen by auncient trade or by redemption in th'end it was concluded and resolved, and they had all administred unto them the oath of a Redemptioner'. Each paid 6d. to the secretary and 12d. to the beadle.[1]

140. [p. 40] *A court of assistants held at Pewterers' Hall on Friday morning 14 June 1605, the following being present:*

141. Mr. Thomas Wilford, president, Sir William Romeney, William Cokayne, John Newman, Nicholas Lyng, Arthur Jackson, John Dorrington, Edward James, Symion Furner, John Newton, William Towreson, Thomas Owen, Richard Wyche, Robert Cobb, George Hanger, Laurence Greene, Thomas Forman; the secretary of the fellowship.

---

1. Presumably a mistake for the usual sums of 12d. to the secretary and 6d. to the beadle.

142. First, the claims of several persons 'who pretended right and interest to the freedome of this society' were heard and examined, but 'it was resolved and held fitt to deferre their freedome untill a generall court which is appointed this afternoon for the same purpose'.

143. Nicholas Dickins, a ship's master,

praying his freedome by Redemption was Denyed the same, by reason that it was neither thought fitt nor allowable by the charter to admitt of any master of a Shipp or common Marryner because they are speciallie excepted out of the charter.

144. A letter from the lord chief baron was read out requesting the freedom of the company for certain merchants of Southampton.

But forasmuch as some of them are shopp keapers, and some officers of the custome house, and that his Lordship desireth to have them all to be admitted free without paying any money for the same, therefore Mr. President is entreated to take some of the Assistents with him and to attend my Lord chief Baron and to informe his Lordship howe Dangerous a president it were and how inconvenyent for the company to yeld to his lordship's request.[1]

145. [p. 41] It was agreed that a committee should be appointed to attend with all convenient speed upon the honourable lords who had furthered the granting of the charter, to convey the humble thanks of the whole company. Moreover the committee was 'to desire their honourable patronage and ayd in the using maynteyning and enioying of the liberties which the king's moast Excellent Majestie by the advice of their Lordships hath graunted unto the company'. The members designated were the president, Sir John Swynnerton, Sir William Romeney, alderman, Mr. John Jowles, Mr. Cokayne, Mr. Wyche, Mr. Dorrington, Mr. Jaxon and Mr. Towreson, or any four of them.

146. It was also ordered and agreed that Roger Howe the former treasurer should hand over to the president the sum of £50 to be used presently in the affairs of the company. The money was to be allowed him when he presented his account. Mr. Howe was also asked to bring in his account with all convenient speed, and a copy of this order would be delivered to him by the secretary for his discharge.

147. *A general court held at Pewterers' Hall on Friday afternoon 13 June 1605 in the presence of*

148. Mr. Thomas Wilford, president, Mr. Newman, Mr. Harby, Mr. Ling, Mr. Jaxon, Mr. Dorrington, Mr. Savage, Mr. James, Mr. Furner, Mr. Newton, Mr. Towreson, Mr. Owen, Mr. Hanger, Mr. Greene; the secretary and divers of the generality.

149. [p. 42] Eleven persons claimed their freedom by apprenticeship to

1. See above, p. xli.

merchants who were ancient traders. Their cases were examined and found valid, whereupon each of them paid 6s. 8d. to the use of the company and was admitted, taking the oath of a freeman by ancient trade. The claimants were Richard Stephens by service with Richard Hale, Thomas and Phillip Honnyman by service with William Dawks, William Walton by service with Sir John Spencer, Edmond Traves by service with Sir Thomas Blanck, John Wormell by service with Nicholas Bond, Edmond Peshall by service with William Villars, Robert Jenny by service with Robert Brooke, Thomas Hukeley by service with William Bond, John Strachey by service with Sir John Spencer and Henry Ball by service with Sir George Bond.

150. Three other persons claimed their freedom by apprenticeship to merchants who had been redemptioners. Their cases were examined and found valid, each paying a fee of £5 to the company, 'being asmuch as their severall Maisters paied at the tyme of their severall admittances', and taking the oath of a freeman by redemption. The claimants were Christopher Cardinall of Ipswich, named in the previous charter and formerly apprenticed to Robert Lymer of Ipswich, who was admitted by redemption within a year after the granting of the charter of 1577; Thomas Burge, formerly apprenticed to George Hanger who paid £5 to be admitted into the freedom on 14 August 1577; and lastly Francis Dent, salter, formerly apprenticed to John Dent who was similarly admitted for £5 by redemption on 14 August 1577.

151. [p. 43] Two further persons claimed the freedom by patrimony 'in the right of their fathers who were auntient freemen well knowne to the company'. They were William Wilford son of Thomas Wilford the president, and Hugh Bourman son of Simon Bourman.[1] Their claims were allowed, whereupon they took the oath of freemen by ancient trade and paid 6s. 8d. each to the use of the company.

152. Also William Palmer and Richard Waltham were admitted as redemptioners, taking their oaths accordingly, since each had formerly paid £10 to the president to have his name included in the charter, 'which Mr. President caused to be performed accordingly'.

153. It was agreed and enacted

that every person and persons, that is or shalbe free of this society which hath already ioyned with any partener or parteners not being free of the Company shall presently make relacion thereof in wryting to the Secretary of the Company, signifying with whom, and in what manner he hath so ioyned, upon payne that every one that shall not performe the same (besides the infringing of his oath) shall pay such fyne, as by a generall Court shalbe agreed. Moreover yt is enacted

1. Simon Bourman was one of the best-known English factors in Seville before 1585. He married a Spaniard and on his return to England the Inquisition made several attempts to prevent his wife and children from accompanying him. The half-Spanish Hugh Bourman was later elected consul for Seville and San Lucar, and the Simon Bourman who stood for Malaga may have been his brother (see below **351**; Cott. Vesp. C. vii f. 375; Madrid, Archivo Historico Nacional, 2946, 16 July 1577).

and agreed that every person and persons not free of this Company, which hath adventured any marchandizes into Spayne or Portugale, or any places Comprehended within our priviledges, and also all such as have ioyned with [p. 44] any freeman, shall have the favour and liberty of sixe moneths (viz) betwene this and the feast of Christmas next ensuing for retorning of their wares and merchandizes from the said places. Provided alwaies, that no such person or persons, not being free, nor any who have ioyned with freemen shall at any tyme or tymes from hensforth, adventure any wares or merchandize outward unto any the said places before mentioned. And moreover that after this day no person or persons free of this fellowshipp shall ioyne or deale as parteners in occupying with any person or persons not free of the Company, nor with any retailor artificer Inholder farmor Common Marryner or handycrafts man of or for any goods wares or merchandize, to be transported or brought to or from Spayne or Portugall or any place or places comprehended within our priviledg upon payne to forfeyt twenty in the hundred, to the use of the said fellowshipp. Provided alwaies, that this acte, shall not extend to any person, that doth occupy with any other being beyond the sea, that may at his retorne enioy the freedome.

154. *A general court held at Pewterers' Hall on Friday 28 June 1605, there being present Thomas Wilford, president, and the following:*

155. Sir Robert Lee, Sir John Watts, Sir John Swynnerton, Mr. Staper, Mr. Chamberleyn, Mr. Newman, Mr. Lyng, Mr. Jackson, Mr. Dorrington, Mr. Savage, Mr. Bowyer, Mr. Furner, Mr. Newton, Mr. Towerson, Mr. Owen, Mr. Wyche, Mr. Cobb, Mr. Hanger, Mr. Greene; the secretary, and also divers of the generality.

156. [p. 45] After the confirmation of the business concluded at the last general court, a letter was read out which had been procured from the lord high treasurer to send to the customers, ordering them not to take entries for any cargoes to be sent to Spain or Portugal unless their owners were free of the company. The letter was as follows.

157. After my harty comendations. Although yt hath pleased his majesty by his letters patents under his greate seale of England, to graunt a large Charter unto his highnes subiects, the mere marchaunts of England trading into Spaine and Portugal, and thereby inhibiting all others to use any trade, to those two Realmes or either of them, other then such as may lawfully Clayme by vertue of the said Charter, or be admitted by the true meaning thereof, and by the same letters patents hath graunted that they and such only as shalbe of the said Incorporation shall have the whole entier and sole trade to and from thence, straightly prohibiting all others from trading to those parts, and also thereby requiring all Customers Comptrollers and other officers, that neither they their Clarcks or substitutes shall take any entry of any merchaundizes to be transported into Spaine or Portugall, or make any agreement for Custome, but only with such as are or shalbe free of that Company, and thereby excluding all retaylours Artificers Inholders ffarmors, Comon Marryners, and handycrafts men, out of the said society, as by the said charter may fully and at lardg appeare. Yet neverthelesse I am informed that diverse persons not being free of the said society, doe presume and adventure to trade thether, contrary to the tenour and effect of the said charter, and to the manifest Contempt thereof. Wherefore these are to will and

23

requier you to have due and speciall care for the true observance of his Majesty's gratious pleasure in that behalf. And for the better performance hereof, I require you [p. 46] not to take entry for any merchaundizes to be transported as aforesaid nor make any agreement for custome with any person other then of and with such as shall produce, and have sufficient testymony under the hand of the President or his deputy that they are of that fellowshipp, and are neither Retailours or Artificers, and by their orders allowed to use trade thether as meere merchaunts, inhibiting and refrayning all others that shall attempt any thing to the contrary. And thereof fayle yow not; ffrom Dorset howse this 27 of June 1605.

Your loving freind

T. Dorset.

158. Since the form of the letter was well liked, it was agreed that twenty copies of it should be procured and sent out to the following places: London, Bristol, Bridgwater, Chichester, Ipswich, Chester, Gloucester, Sandwich, Lynn, Yarmouth, Poole, Boston, Hull, Plymouth, Exeter, Newcastle, Southampton, Barnstaple, Cardiff, Milford Haven.

159. The company then proceeded to the election of deputies for the following port towns,

and putting two in election for every severall place the election (being made by lifting up of hands according to usuall manner) did fall upon these worshippfull parsons following, who were elected to supply the said place or office of Deputie to the president of this Company for the severall places whereof they are severally and respectively chosen as hereafter followeth and also for all those places which in former tymes were allotted to be under their severall Jurisdictions.

160. John Barker for Bristol 'cum membris ut supra'; Richard Dochester for Exeter etc.; Nicholas Downe for Barnstaple etc.; John Hassard the elder for Lyme etc.;[1] James Bagg for Plymouth etc.; Fulk Aldersey for Chester etc.; [p. 47] Alexander Jones for Bridgwater etc.;[2] John Clynch for Ipswich etc.; William Harebrowne for Yarmouth etc.;[3] John Lister for Kingston upon Hull etc.; William Nevey for Southampton etc.; Thomas Higgins for Rye etc.; Thomas Sendall for Lynn etc.[4]

161. The election of deputies for Sandwich and Newcastle was deferred for the time being 'for want of names and understanding who are fytt men for such a service'.

162. It was not thought proper to appoint deputies for Totnes, Taunton and Chard, 'because they are members, and under the devision of the Cytties and townes before mencioned'.

163. It was agreed that the president and the secretary, assisted by Mr. Howe, Mr. Wyche, Mr. Dorrington, Mr. Jackson and Mr. Towrson, or any

1. Margin note, 'under Excetor'.
2. Margin note, 'under Bristoll'.
3. Margin note, 'Aunciently under Lynn'. In the right hand margin is written 'Leonard Holmes', presumably inserted after the latter had succeeded William Harebrowne as assistant for Yarmouth (see below, **231**).
4. The name 'Henry Ball' has been crossed out.

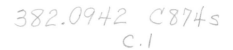

four of them, 'shall presently consider of fytt and convenient letters to be written to the severall deputies before mentioned and to cause the letters to be procured from my Lord Treasurer to be sent and conveyed awaie with all speed'.

164. Another letter was read out from the king's principal secretary the earl of Salisbury, urging the appointment of one Bertrand Crosmer as consul in Valencia.

165. It was endorsed as sent to the president, assistants and other members of the company trading to Spain, and its contents were as follows:

166. [p. 48] After my harty comendations. This bearer Bertrand Crosmer, being well knowne, as I am informed, to diverse of you, hath entreated my recomendation, in a suite of his, which he makes unto you, for the Consullshipp of the Province of Valencia. How fitt he may be for it, and of what use he may prove to our nation in that place, being a stranger, I leave to your owne considerations, onely my intent being to afforde him this favorable recomendation that he is reported unto me to be both an honest man and of good discretion and experience in those places. And so I leave you to god's protection, from the Courte at Greenwich this 11 of June 1605.

Your loving freind
Salisbury.

167. After the letter had been read out, the company resolved

to take further tyme to advise and consider what is fitt to be doen concerning the same. And yf any sufficient Englishman may be fownd out, to undertake the service, they rather hold it fitt to preferre one of our owne nation then any stranger whatever.

168. The assembly was then notified of 'the greate chardge disbursed and to be paied about the procuring of the Companies charter'. A committee consisting of the president, Mr. How, Mr. Newman, Mr. Wych, Mr. Lyng, Mr. Dorrington, Mr. Jackson or any five of them was formed, 'to consider of the charge alreddy disbursed and what payments or gratifications are fyt to be made or bestowed upon all such as have taken paines in and about the same'. The company agreed to approve whatever decisions the committee should reach.

169. [p. 49] John Newman, Nicholas Ling and Lawrence Greene all stood as candidates for the post of treasurer in the coming year,

and by full election by hands Mr. Lawrence Greene was chosen Treasurer, who being here present in open Court did receave and take the Oath for the due execution of the said Office and hath promised against the next Court to nomynate his suertie according to the auncient order.

170. It was ordered that Roger How the former treasurer should prepare his accounts for the next court, so that auditors for them might be appointed. In the meantime Mr. How hath promised to satisfie the said newe Treasorer the some of Forty pownds to be ymployed in the Companies affaires, uppon the Companies promise that he shalbe allowed the said some in his Accompt and that the Companie will have hym harmlesse concerning the same.

171. Four persons claimed their freedom by patrimony in the right of their fathers who were all ancient freemen: John Newton, mercer, son of John Newton, William Hill, grocer and Edmond Hill, draper, sons of Edmond Hill, grocer, and George Whitmore son of William Whitmore. They were all admitted, taking the oath of a freeman by ancient trade, and each paid 6s. 8d. to the use of the society.

172. [p. 50] Eight other persons also claimed their freedom by apprentice-ship to merchants who were ancient traders: Edward Collyns, clothworker, by service with Jon Symcotts,[1] John Cage, grocer, by service with Augustine Fulke, John Barnaby, draper, by service with John Combes, Richard Howse, mercer, by service with Robert Wincoll, Thomas Stokeley, merchant tailor, by service with John Stokeley, Thomas Hanson, ironmonger, by service with Sir Thomas Cambell, Bartholomew Holland, clothworker, by service with Richard Stapers, and Edward Cox, mercer, by service with Leonard Harward. The claims were examined and found valid, whereupon each claimant paid his fine of 6s. 8d. to the use of the fellowship and was admitted, taking the oath of a freeman by ancient trade.

173. After the above oaths were administered and received,

and the contents thereof being fully weyed, and considered and to th'end every one of this society may be the more carefull to performe and fulfill the same, it is agreed and ordered that the Secretary of this Company shall deliver to every freeman of this society the true copy of the oath mynistred unto every such free-man, at his admission into this society, for which copy it shalbe lawfull for the Secretary to demaund and take the some of six pence of every such freeman of this society.

174. [p. 51] *An assembly held at Pewterers' Hall on Monday 1 July 1605 in the presence of the president, Mr. Newman, Mr. Harby, Mr. Lyng, Mr. Dorrington, Mr. Savage, Mr. Bowyer, Mr. Newton, Mr. Owen, Mr. Cobb; the secretary.*

175. The president urged those present to consider that, by the words of the charter, the company was enjoined to receive 'meere marchaunts to be so quallified as by the charter appeareth'. He therefore asked them to decide 'what person (in their opynions) should be accompted a meere merchant'. After due consideration and debate,

they delivered their opynions that they accoumpt him a meere marchaunt that hath only delt and traded as a marchant, without any retayling or shopp keeping, the full space and terme of Eight yeres, (in which tyme an apprentize by his service may attayne to the freedome) shalbe accoumpted a meere marchant, and (if he be otherwise qualified) may be receaved into the freedome by Redemption.

1. 'John' has been crossed out and 'Jon' written above.

176. The draft of a letter to be sent to John Barker of Bristol, recently elected deputy for that port and the other places within the division, was read out to the assembly. It was approved 'and appointed to be sent away with all speed'.

177. *An assembly held at Pewterers' Hall on Saturday 6 July 1605 in the presence of the following:*

178. The president, the treasurer, Mr. Staper, Mr. Chamberlen, Mr. Newman, Mr. Ling, Mr. Dorrington, Mr. Bowyer, Mr. Furner, Mr. Newton, Mr. Towreson, Mr. Cobb, Mr. Hanger, the secretary.

179. [p. 52] First, the form of the letters to be sent out to the recently-elected deputies was agreed and orders were given that they should be despatched with all speed.

180. It was agreed that the president should not

deliver any warrants under his hand to the Customers for transportation of merchaundizes into Spayne or Portugall but only for such as shalbe certified by the Secretary under his hand to Mr. President that they were either sworne upon the first or last charter wherein the Secretary shall sett downe certenly upon what day every such person was sworne.

181. It was also ordered that former precedents for impositions should be sought out, 'to th'entent that ymposicions may be rated and levied in such manner as by a generall court or court of assistaunts shalbe thought fitt and aunswerable to the tyme'.

182. It was also agreed that 'the like allowance shalbe made for the use of the Pewterers hall as in former tymes hath ben accustomed, the same to be paied by Mr. Treasurer and to be allowed him in his accoumpt'.

183. It was further agreed 'that Mr. President shall make provision of a Carpett and a dozen of Cushions for the use of the company, and Mr. Treasurer to disburse the money for the same'.

184. Lastly, two letters sent to the company from Spain were read out, one from the resident ambassador Sir Charles Cornewalleys and the other from Nicholas Oseley a brother of the company. 'But it was thought fitt to referre the consideration thereof unto a generall court'.

185. [p. 53] '*A generall court warned and entended to have been kept upon Wednesday the 10 of July Anno Domini 1605 at Pewterors hall. But for want of apparance of a competent nomber of assistants which cannott be held without 13 Assistaunts at least, therefore it amounted only to an assembly of these viz.*'

186. the president, Sir Robert Lee, Mr. Chamberlen, Mr. Jackson, Mr.

Bowyer, Mr. Newton, Mr. Towreson, Mr. Owen, Mr. Wyche, Mr. Cobb, Mr. Greene; the secretary, and divers of the generality.

187. Albeit it hath not ben thought fitt to admitt any into the freedome but at a generall court yett forasmuch as a generall court was appointed to have kept this day and summaunce gyven accordingly, and because 11 of the Assistaunts are here present and only 2 assistants wanting to make a full court and forasmuch as diverse grave and woorshipfull persons of the generallity are nowe present and certen persons make clayme to the freedome against whom there can be no opposition or obiection, therefore it is held fitt that they be admitted and sworne at this assembly whereupon Robert Lewes also Anwell a meere merchaunt bound apprentize to a merchaunt and free of no other Company of marchaunts was for the fine of ten pownds, admitted into the freedome of this society by redemption, and tooke the oath of a freeman by redemption accordingly.

188. [p. 54] Four other persons made claim to their freedom by ancient trade. Their claims were examined and allowed, whereupon each of them paid 6s. 8d. to the use of the society and was admitted, taking the oath of a freeman by ancient trade. The claimants were Richard Wych the younger son of Richard Wych, skinner, by patrimony; Nathaniel Cobb son of Robert Cobb, girdler, also by patrimony; John Couchman by service with Paul Banning, and John Caplyn by service with George Collymere, all the latter being ancient traders.

189. At the last general court Henry Ball was elected deputy for Lynn, but

forasmuch as the company are enformed that one Mr. Thomas Sendall is a more auntient sufficient and fitter man for the said place, it is therefore ordered that the name of the said Thomas Sendall shalbe entred in the place of the said Henry Ball, and that the said Thomas Sendall shalbe Deputy for Lynne and the membres thereof for this yere ensuing.

190. *A general court held at Pewterers' Hall on Friday 12 July 1605 in the presence of Thomas Wilford, president, and the following assistants:*

191. Sir John Swynnerton, alderman, Sir William Romeney, alderman, Mr. Staper, Mr. Chamberlen, Mr. Cokayne, Mr. Newman, Mr. Andrew Banning, Mr. Ling, Mr. Dorrington, Mr. Bate, Mr. Savage, Mr. James, Mr. Bowyer, Mr. Towreson, Mr. Owen, Mr. Wych, Mr. Cobb, Mr. Hanger; the secretary and also divers of the generality.

192. [p. 55] The acts and agreements of the last assembly were 'liked allowed and confirmed'.

193. Andrew Banning and Richard Wych, two of the assistants, then took their oaths for the due execution of their office.

194. The two letters previously read out, from Sir Charles Cornewalleys the ambassador in Spain and from Mr. Oseley, were read again, together with a letter from Alderman Sir Stephen Soame of London 'but the court held it fitt to take further tyme to consider of all the said letters'.

195. William Anys son of Dunstan Anys who had been made free by ancient trade on 26 July 1577, claimed his own freedom by patrimony. The claim was examined and allowed, 'but by reason he departed before th'end of the court he was referred to take his oath at some other tyme'.

196. Hewyt Stapers also claimed his freedom by patrimony in the right of his father Richard Staper one of the assistants. His claim was allowed, whereupon he paid 6s. 8d. to the use of the society and took the oath of a freeman by ancient trade.

197. At a court of assistants on 8 June 1605, 'divers committees were appointed to consider the Auntient oathes and ordinaunces for the government of this society'. They were asked to revise them as they should think fit and [p. 56] bring them up to date, before finally presenting them to a general court for its confirmation.

Whereupon diverse of the said committees having mett at three severall tymes in performance of the trust in them reposed, finding moast of the ordinances fitt to be contynued without alteration, and having altered some and leaving some others with blancks, referring all their proceedings to be altered and reformed by a generall court, doe nowe at this court offer and present the same to the whole assembly here present; who caused as many of them to be redd and debated upon as tyme would permitt, and in some points did alter reforme make perfect, and fully conclude and agree of so many of the oathes and ordinances as are entered in the booke of ordinances beginning page 1 and ending page 29. And being prevented by tyme were dryven to breake of and to referre the consideration of the residue of the said ordinances untill the next generall court.

198. The court granted Richard Langley the secretary an annuity of £20 over and above the ancient yearly standing fee of £20 and the other fees and profits due to him for the execution of his office. The annuity was granted to him only for the duration of his service [p. 57] as secretary, and the total sum of £40 was to be paid quarterly by the treasurer and allowed him in his account.

199. The court also granted Richard Colman the beadle an annuity of £6 13s. 4d. in addition to his ancient yearly standing fee of 20 marks and the usual profits of his office. He was to receive these fees only during the pleasure of the company, the total sum of £20 being paid quarterly by the treasurer and allowed him in his account.

200. *A general court held at Pewterers' Hall on Wednesday afternoon 24 July 1605, in the presence of Thomas Wilford, president, and the following assistants:*

201. Nicholas Ling, John Dorrington, John Bate, Robert Savage, Edward James, Robert Bowyer, John Newton, Thomas Owen, Richard Wych,

George Collymere, George Hanger, Laurence Greene; the secretary and divers of the generality.

202. [p. 58] The business of the last general court was read out and confirmed, then the company proceeded as follows.

203. First, three persons claimed their freedom by ancient trade. Their claims were allowed, whereupon they were sworn in as freemen by ancient trade, paying the fine of 6s. 8d. to the use of the society. The claimants were John Howard by service with Mrs. Margaret Bond the widow of Alderman William Bond, Gregory Bland by service with Peter Collett, merchant tailor, and Edward Lynch by service with John Ramridge, mercer, all these merchants being freemen by ancient trade.

204. William Castle and Richard Syms, both mere merchants and free of no other company, sued to be admitted as freemen by redemption. They were accepted 'with free and generall consent', and paid their fines of £10 each to the treasurer before taking their oathes as freemen by redemption.

205. Whereas the names of a great nomber of parsons are inserted into his majesty's Chartre lately graunted to this society whereof divers are of the auncient freedom or discended from the same, and some others paid and disbursed money to Mr. President to have their names put in the charter, and yet nevethelesse did voluntarily consent to accept of their freedom by way of Redemption; and some others procured their names inserted by the Recommendation of honorable parsons or men in aucthority, and some by one meanes, and some by another. And whereas greate debate and dispute hath byn had in what manner the severall parsons named in the said Chartre are to be admytted, whether as freemen by auncient [p. 59] trade or else by way of Redemption, for the deciding of which doubt and for the more orderly proceeding therein; yt is at this Court agreed that Mr. Cokayne, Mr. Wych, Mr. Howe, Mr. Dorrington, Mr. Hanger, Mr. Newton and Mr. James, or any fyve of them, shall peruse over the names of all such as are inserted into the said Chartre, and inquire and learne out, by what right or how and in what manner and by whose procurement they obtayned their names to be soe inserted and to consider and lay downe aswell howe many and which are to be admytted by auncient trade as also how many and which are to be admitted by redemption, and thereof to make relation at a generall Court for further therein to be done as shalbe then thought fytt and convenient.

206. Complaints had been made to the members of the privy council that persons capable of the freedom of the company 'know not when or whether to resort to challeng the same'. It was therefore ordered

that there shalbe a generall Court held heere every Wensday morning begyning at seaven of the Clock in the sommer, and at eight of the Clock in the winter, and to end at eleven of the Clock upon every of the same daies, and so to contynue untill order shalbe taken to the contrary.

207. [p. 60] It was also ordered that 'for the more certen observing of the said Court daies, the ease of Mr. President and the better goverment of the Company, a fytt and discreete person should be elected and chosen deputy'. Three candidates, John Newton, Roger Howe, and Arthur Jackson stood for election, 'but by lyfting up of hands th'election did fall uppon the said Mr. John Newton, who was thereupon admitted and sworne for the due execution of the said office'.

208. It was also ordered that Alderman Sir Stephen Soame,

by reason that he is free of the Company of the marchaunts of the Staple and also of the East marchaunts cannot by the true meaning of the charter be admitted into the freedom of this society, unlesse he procure the like freedom for one of this Company or pay according to the words and trew meaning of the charter.

209. By the last charter granted to the society they are required to receive into the freedom any of his majesty's subjects

which then were or shalbe meere marchaunts, and which by the lawes and statutes of this Realme may lawfully use the trade of Marchaundize from or into the Realme of England (excepting Retaylers and such other persons as in and [p. 61] by the said charter are mentioned).

The question has arisen

whether a man that hath byn a shopp keeper, and for the space of divers yeres hath given over his trade who was not brought up in the trade of marchandize seaven yeres at the least as an apprentize may be refused to be admitted into the freedome of this society by the words of the said charter.

The company, 'being desirous to carry an even and indifferent hand', observed that by the laws of the realm no man might use any trade or occupation, 'being farre inferior to the profession of a merchant', without serving at least seven years as an apprentice. After due consideration it was therefore agreed

that every parson and parsons, which during the full space and terme of seaven yeres together, hath only used, or hereafter shall use, the trade of marchandize, without keeping any shopp, or using any other trade withall, but only lyved as a meere marchaunt, (Except all such as now be or hereafter shalbe free of any spetiall incorporation or Company of merchants trading by force of any Act of parliament, charter or letters patents, into any the partes beyond the seas) shall and may from and after such tyme, as hee or they have or hath or hereafter shall have only used the trade of a mere marchaunt, during such full terme of seaven yeres in form abovesaid, be admytted and receaved into the freedome of this society by Redemption, for such fyne and fynes, (according to the tyme they shall require the said freedome) as in and by the said charter is lymitted.

210. [p. 62] It was also agreed that an act passed at the last general court, entitled 'In what tyme the freedome of this company shalbe claymed', should be reviewed and considered more carefully at 'a more full and ample generall Court'.

211. *A general court held at Pewterers' Hall on Wednesday 31 July 1605 in the presence of Thomas Wilford, president, John Newton, deputy, and the following assistants:*

31

212. Laurence Greene, treasurer, Robert Chamberlen, Nicholas Ling, Arthur Jaxon, John Dorrington, John Bate, Edward James, Robert Bowyer, Symion Furner, William Towreson, Nicholas Style, Thomas Owen, Richard Wych, George Hanger, Richard Langley, secretary, and divers of the generality.

213. The business of the last general court was read and confirmed.

214. First, an election was held to fill the vacancy left among the assistants by the election of John Newton to the post of deputy. Two candidates were nominated, Roger Howe and William Harrison, 'and the triall being made by lyfting up of hands the Election did fall upon the said Mr. Roger Howe'.

215. [p. 63] Roger Howe and two other assistants, John Bate and Nicholas Stile, then took the oath appointed for the execution of their office.

216. John Jolles, named in the charter and subsequently elected an alderman of London, 'being generally knowne to have ben an auncient trader into Spayne and Portugall' was admitted as a freeman by ancient trade. He took the appointed oath and paid the treasurer 6s. 8d. to the use of the society.

217. It was agreed that Thomas Boothby should be given a certificate by the president for the officers of the customs, 'testifying only that he is free of this society, And upon his humble suit he is only tollerated to keape open his shopp untill Michaelmas next and no longer, upon the paynes conteyned in the companies orders, or as they shall thinck fitt to ympose upon him'.

218. Humphrey Wyms, named in the charter, was refused admittance to the company unless he paid the sum of £10 and took the oath of a redemptioner, 'which he denyed to performe, and therefore departed the court for this tyme'.

219. James Boyle, mercer, claimed his freedom by service with Michael Boile, a freeman by ancient trade. His claim was allowed and he was admitted, paying his fine of 6s. 8d.

220. [p. 64] Rowland Backhouse son of the late alderman Nicholas Backhouse of London, claimed his freedom by patrimony. His claim was allowed and he was admitted, paying a fine of £10, 'being the lyke some that his father paied at his admission'. Since he was also free of the Merchant Adventurers, Backhouse 'tooke that oath which is appointed for freemen by redemption being also already free of some other company of marchaunts'.

221. Furthermore six other persons claimed their freedom by redemption, 'being all brought up as meere marchaunts or ells for the space of Seaven yeres last past and above only used the trade of a marchaunt without any manner of retailing whatsoever and being free of no other society of marchaunts'. They were John Buffeild, armourer, William Greene, cutler, Ralph

Belfeild, skinner, John Davies, haberdasher, John Greenewood, draper, and Edward Skeggs, haberdasher. They each paid the treasurer £10 to the use of the society and took the oath appointed for freemen received by redemption who were not free of any other company of merchants.

222. Laurence Horton requested his freedom by redemption, but 'forasmuch as he may challenge by patrymony the freedome of the society of the marchaunt Adventurors and did refuse to renownce the same or to take the oath auntiently administred to freemen by redemption', he was thought unfit to be admitted under the terms of the charter.

223. [p. 65] The court designated a group of new committee members: the president or the deputy, Mr. Jolles, alderman, Mr. Staper, Mr. Allabaster, Mr. Dorrington, Mr. Jaxon, Mr. Ling, Mr. Bate, Mr. Towreson, Mr. Harrison and Mr. Boothby. They or any four of them were asked to join with the seven members designated at the last general court, or any five of them,

to consider of aunsweres to be presently written to Sir Charles Cornewalleys now Lord Ambassador resident in Spayne, and to Mr. Nicholas Oseley, and to advise and Consider whether it were that any of the company and which of them should resort unto the right honorable John Baptista de Taxus the Spanish Ambassador nowe resident here and shortly to returne into Spayne (as is reported) to desire his favour for the confirmation and enlardging of our Auntient liberties in Spayne.

They were also asked to think of suitable persons to be consuls in Spain and Portugal, 'and of any other matter that shall concerne the good estate of the company, and to make relation of their proceedings at the next generall court'.

224. [p. 66] *A general court held at Pewterers' Hall on Wednesday 7 August 1605 in the presence of John Newton, deputy, and the following assistants:*

225. Sir William Romney, Lawrence Greene, treasurer, Richard Staper, Robert Chamberlen, William Cockayne, John Newman, Nicholas Lyng, John Dorrington, John Bate, Robert Savage, Edward James, Robert Bowyer, Symion Furner, William Towerson, Richard Wych, George Hanger, Roger How, assistants of London; William Harebrowne of Yarmouth, William Nevey of Southampton, Richard Langley, secretary, and divers of the generality.

226. Robert Towerson, skinner, son of Mr. William Towerson claimed his freedom by patrimony 'in the right of his father who was an ancient freeman'. His claim was allowed, whereupon he took the oath of a freeman by ancient trade and paid 6s. 8d. to the use of the society.

227. [p. 67] The following seven persons claimed their freedom by ancient trade: Robert Bromley by service with Sir Thomas Pullison, Leonard Holmes of Yarmouth by service with the above-named William Harebrowne of Yarmouth, William Nevey of Southampton, named in the charter, by service with Paul Stavely of Southampton, John Feild by service with

William Towerson, Richard Dalby of Southampton by service with William Nevey, William Payne by service with Alderman Thomas Starky, and John Colmer by service with Henry Colthurst. Their cases were examined, and as all their masters were ancient traders they were all admitted, each paying 6s. 8d. to the use of the society and taking the oath of a freeman by ancient trade.

228. Eight other persons claimed their freedom. They had all been brought up as mere merchants, or else had traded exclusively as a merchant for the last seven years without any retailing, and were free of no other society. The claimants were Henry Kynnersley, merchant tailor, Emanuell Francklyn, clothworker, Thomas Wakeman of Yarmouth, Bartholomew Wormell of Lynn, Francis Rumbald, fishmonger, William Thurston, salter, Thomas Ball, haberdasher, and Nicholas Lockwood, leatherseller. The claimants were admitted into the freedom by redemption, paying £10 each to the treasurer and taking the oath appointed for freemen by redemption who are not free of any other company of merchants.

229. [p. 68] In addition Simon Smyth claimed his freedom by patrimony. He was the son of Simon Smyth who was admitted into the freedom by redemption on 27 February 1577 for the sum of £5. His claim was allowed, whereupon he paid the fine of £5 to the use of the fellowship as his father had done before him, and took the oath appointed for a freeman by redemption who is also free of another company.

230. Thomas Waltham, named in the charter, was refused the freedom of the society 'unlesse he shall satisfie the some of £10, and also receive and take the oath appointed for a Redemptioner which he Denyed to performe, and therefore departed the court for this tyme'.

231. At this courte Mr. William Hareborne lately elected Deputy for yarmouth, did deliver some speciall reasons declaring that he cannot conveniently execute the said office, and therefore according to the purport of the companies letter, he hath caused to come up the aforenamed Leonard Holmes being sometymes his servaunt and the only man in those parts that can clayme his freedome by aunrient trade, as a man fitt to supply the said office of Deputy, upon whose recommendation so made by the said Mr. Hareborne, and his loving promise to be ayding counselling, and assisting of him, the said Leonard Holmes was elected and chosen Deputy for the said towne of yarmouth and the lymitts thereof.

232. [p. 69] After the above election William Hareborne and William Nevey of Southampton, both assistants named in the charter, then took their oaths of office.

233. Mr. Nevey, earlier elected deputy for Southampton, and Leonard Holmes who had been elected deputy for Yarmouth at this court, both took their oaths as deputies for their respective divisions.

234. The following persons were delegated to form a committee: Mr.

Cockayne, Mr. How, Mr. Wych, Mr. Hanger, Mr. Dorrington, Mr. Bate, Mr. Towerson and Mr. Harrison. They, or any four of them, were asked

to consider and lay downe what power and aucthority is fitt to be given to the Deputies for government in their several divisions and that the Secretary shall deliver them such copies of oathes ordinances and other things as they or any 4 of them shall thinck fitt.

235. A petition was read out from Richard Candler 'humbly desiring the freedome of this company for his owne person gratis', but consideration of it was deferred to the next court.

236. Also Hugh Hamersley named in the charter, clayming the freedome by patrymony, for as much as his father died before the graunting of the charter of Decimo Nono of Queene Elizabeth, the company have taken further tyme to consider of his clayme.

237. [p. 70] *A general court held at Pewterers' Hall on Tuesday 13 August 1605 in the presence of Thomas Wilford, president, John Newton, deputy, and the following assistants:*

238. Richard Staper, John Harby, Andrew Bannyng, Nicholas Lyng, Arthur Jackson, John Dorrington, Robert Savage, Nicholas Style, George Hanger, Roger How, Martyn Bond, Thomas Bostock, assistants of London; John Clynch of Ipswich; Richard Langley secretary and divers of the generality.

239. After due examination the court allowed William Fisher son of John Fisher of Ipswich to receive the freedom of the society by patrimony in the right of his father, who had received his freedom by ancient trade on 21 August 1577. As the claimant was absent from the court,

Mr. President or his deputy and fowre of the assistaunts (according to aucthority graunted by the charter) may administer unto the said William ffisher the oath of a freeman by auncient trade, he first paying to Mr. Treasurer to the use of this society the some of 6s. 8d.

240. [p. 71] Two other persons claimed their freedom by patrimony in the right of their fathers who were ancient freemen. They were Samuel Garrett, mercer, son of Anthony Garrett, and Richard Barne son of Alderman Sir George Barne, haberdasher. Their claims were allowed, whereupon they took the oaths of freemen by ancient trade and each paid 6s. 8d. to the use of the society.

241. At former courts the question had been debated

in what manner Edward Davenant, merchauntailor, should be admitted into the freedome of this society, whether by auncient trade, or as a Redemptioner by reason that the said Edward Davenant not knowing of his right by patrymony delivered Mr. Roger Howe the last Treasurer the some of Tenn poundes, making then suit to be admitted by Redemption, which the cort at that tyme refused to graunt, by reason it was supposed he was not then capable of the freedome. And sithence his name being inserted into the charter he challenged thereby the free-dome as amply as any Auncient trader, which the company did not allowe. After all which upon serch made in the old books it appeareth that John Davenant, merchauntailor, deceased late father of the said Edward Davenant was an auncient free brother of this society, admitted by auncient trade and sworne the 26 of June Anno Domino 1578 whereby the said Edward Davenant claymed by his patrymony, to be admitted by auncient trade. Whose case being examyned he was found enhabled, and thereupon paid for his admittance 6s. 8d. and tooke the oath of a freeman by auncient trade, and was admitted into the freedome accordingly.

242. Four other persons claimed their freedom by ancient trade: Joseph Jackson by service with Alderman Sir John Spencer, clothworker, Thomas Witherall by service with Thomas Boothby, [p. 72] merchant tailor, Humphrey Wotton by service with William Shawcrost, girdler, and John Clynch of Ipswich by service with John Barker the elder of Ipswich. Each claimant's case was on examination found valid, for all the masters were ancient traders. Each paid 6s. 8d. to the use of the society and took the oath of a freeman by ancient trade.

243. Moreover Edward Grent, mercer, and John Dade, merchant tailor, 'being both brought up as mere merchaunts, or ells by the space of seaven yeres last past and above only used the trade of a merchaunt without any manner of retayling whatsoever, and being free of no other society of merchaunts' were admitted into the freedom by redemption. Each paid £10 to the treasurer and took the oath appointed for freemen by redemption who were unfree of any other company.

244. Peter Muffett, skinner, claimed his freedom by service with Lawrence Carlill, who became free by redemption on 20 November 1582 for the sum of £10. His case was examined and found valid, whereupon he paid £10 being the same fine paid by his master and took the oath of a freeman by redemption who was also free of another company.

245. [p. 73] According to a note made by Richard May the former secretary of the company, Richard Reynolds the apprentice of Simon Lawrence an ancient freeman claimed his own freedom on 1 February 1589 'when the keeping of Corts was discontynued'. Since he may rightfully claim the freedom,

forasmuch as he is not in estate to come abroad, therefore upon humble request made in his behalf, it is ordered that he shalbe admitted by vertue of his said service, and that Mr. President or his Deputy and fowre of the assistants (according to the aucthority graunted by charter) may administer unto him the oath of a freeman by auncient trade, he first paying to the use of the society 6s. 8d.

246. John Clynch, named in the charter as one of the assistants for Ipswich and recently elected deputy for that port and its division, 'did in open corte receave and take the two severall othes for the due execution of the said two severall offices'.

247. Whereas it is found by experience, that (when corts of Assistaunts are called) much tyme is spent, and no business can be performed, for want of a competent nomber of Assistaunts to make up a full courte, and forasmuch as Mr. Thomas Cordell and Mr. John Castlyn, two of the Assistaunts named in the charter, by reason of other occasions cannot attend the service, nor appeare at courts, (as Assistaunts ought to doe) and therefore desier to be dischardged thereof, and some others elected in their places; therefore at this corte the company dischardged the said Mr. Thomas Cordell, and Mr. John Castlyn, and proceeded to election of two other Assistaunts in their roomes ffor which purpose these woorshipfull persons following were put in election (viz) Mr. Martyn Bond, Mr. William Harrison, Mr. Thomas [p. 74] Bostock, Mr. Thomas Boothby, Mr. John Ramridge and Mr. Gyles Snoade whoe being all entreated to walk forth, the company (according to their usuall manner) proceeded to election, by lyfftyng up of handes, and by the greatest nomber of hands the election did fall upon the said Mr. Martyn Bond, and Mr. Thomas Bostock, whoe were thereunto admitted, and in open courte did receave the oath for the due execution of the said office.

248. A letter was read out from Thomas Sandyll, recently elected deputy for Lynn,

whereby he desireth to be dischardged of the said office of Deputy. But forasmuch as he is knowne to be a fitt and worthy man, the company resolve not to alter their election, and therefore doe agree that a letter shalbe written unto him for the same purpose.

249. Two other letters were read out, one from John Bagg, recently elected deputy for Plymouth, the other from John Lister, deputy for Hull.

After the reading of which letters and consideration thereunto had, and forasmuch also as diverse other Deputies have not retorned any answeres to the companies letters, yt is ordered and thought fitt, that for the swearing of the severall Deputies, and to setle government, and give direction in every of the said places, that Mr. Deputy Newton and Mr. Arthur Jackson shall with all convenient speede ryde to all the severall places, where the said deputies are elected, and that a Commission shalbe drawne and sealed with the seale of this society, to give them sufficient aucthority for the performance of the said service, and that Mr. Treasurer shall deliver them money to defray their chardges in the said Jorney. And upon the earnest motion and entreaty of the company Mr. Deputy hath gyven his absolute consent, and Mr. Jaxon hath promised (his owne private affaires being setled which will hold him almost a moneth) to prepare himself ready to undertake the service.

250. [p. 75] The court also appointed a committee of auditors for the accounts of George Hanger and Roger How, the last two treasurers of the company. The auditors were Mr. Lyng, Mr. Dorrington and Mr. Harby from among the assistants, and Mr. Harrison, Mr. Boothby, Mr. Stone, Mr. Snoade and Mr. Stokeley, five of the generality, together with either the president or the deputy.

251. The drafts of two letters were then read out, one to Sir Charles Cornewallis the ambassador in Spain 'in answere of a letter written by his Lordshipp to this company in favour of Mr. Nicholas Osely', and the other to Nicholas Osely himself. The latter was in answer to his letter touching the procuring of a newe graunt and confirmation of the Companies charter and liberties, wherein the company doe signifie they have agreed to give his wief here in England ffyfty pounds, and to make over unto him ffowre hundred Ducketts and when the charter and priviledges are confirmed (in respect of the chardg he shalbe at) to gratifie him with Eight hundred Duckatts more.

Both drafts were approved; orders were given to provide the money and send off the letters with all convenient speed.

252. fforasmuch as many of the Assistaunts made default of apparance at this courte, therefore the names of all the Assistaunts were openly redd, and the Beadle examyned (by vertue of his oath taken to this societie) what particuler summons, and warning, he gave to every of them, and as many as were in the Country, at the tyme of the summons, or otherwise specially ymployed, were excused, but these six following viz. Mr. Robert Chamberlen, Mr. John Newman, Mr. John Bate, Mr. Edward James, Mr. Symion Furner and Mr. Robert Cobb, being duly sommoned, and making default of apparance, are to pay such fynes, as in such case, by the orders of this society, are lymitted and appointed.

253. [p. 76] Certain committee members were authorised at the last general court, to fix the powers and authority to be given to the outport deputies in their divisions. The secretary was also to deliver to the deputies such copies of oaths and ordinances as the committee, or any four of its members, should think fit.

According to which aucthority Mr. William Cokayne, Mr. Richard Wych, Mr. Georg Hanger and Mr. John Dorrington, four of the said committees, (being accompanied with Mr. Newton the Deputy) did assemble and meete togeather the 7 day of August 1605, and did cause their opynions and conceipts to be laid downe in wryting to be presented to the next generall corte to be confirmed or disallowed as the court should thinck fitt. The tenor whereof followeth in these words viz.
254. Imprimis every Deputy to have an abstract of the charter, or a copy at lardg, if they will pay for it.
255. Also coppies of the oath of a freeman by auncient trade.
The Oath of the Deputy
The Oath of the Assistaunts
The Oath of the Treasorer
The Oath of the Clark in the Country
256. The copy of the Act for Apprentizes that the words Marchaunt of Spayne and Portugall should be inserted in their Indentures.
257. Also the Copy of the order of Dispensation, notwithstanding the omission of the words, Spayne and Portugall, sithence 1585 which order was taken at a generall court holden ultimo Augusti 1604.
258. The copy of the Act against Marchaunts using retayling.
259. And it is agreed that the Deputies severally and respectively in their severall Divisions may admitt and sweare into the freedome, the sonnes and servaunts of such as may clayme the freedome by auncient trade, and being discended from such fathers or masters as have byn sworne to this company, and none other whatsoever, unlesse they have byn sworne, notwithstanding they be named in the Charters or either of them, and that this power and aucthority shall only have contynuance untill the feast of All Sainctes next ensuing, and no longer, and then all to come up hether.

260. [p. 77] It was also agreed that the deputy should summon to him four or five freemen, 'if so many may be had, or ells as many as the place will aford' to give their consent to the acceptance of those admitted as freemen by patrimony or service.

261. Furthermore, they should with all convenient speed certify the names of all those admitted, 'and under whome, and by what right they made their clayme'.

262. Notwithstanding this authority for admitting sons and servants claiming their freedom by patrimony or ancient trade, it was also agreed that if any of the claimants by patrimony or ancient trade could not make clear proof of their rights, or if any doubts should arise in any way, 'that then every such person shalbe remitted and sent up to London, to receave their freedome here'.

263. It was also absolutely agreed that any claimants by redemption should be sent up to London, with a certificate from the deputy and six assistants

or speciall Marchaunts of the Company (yf so many may be had) or ells so many as the place will afford, testefying that they are meere Marchaunts fitt to be admitted, and have only traded in marchaundizing, seaven yeres at the least, and not free of any other company of marchaunts, and that they are neither retailours, Artificers, Inholders, farmors, comon Marryners or handycrafts men, but esteemed and knowne to be sole Marchaunts, trading beyond the Seas.

It was also agreed that all sons and servants of redemptioners should be sent up to London with similar certificates from the deputy and such merchants or assistants 'testefying whose sonnes they are, and their Masters report for their service, and no Redemptioner, nor the sonne or servaunt of any Redemptioner to be admitted without such certificate as aforesaid'.

264. [p. 78] The deputy was also to keep a full account of all the fees he received 'for admissions or for fynes, brokes or any other thing for the company, and to Accoumpt to the Treasorer when he shalbe required, and if he be not required, yet once a yere at the least'.

265. The deputy was to inform the company if any merchant also retailed goods, so that a penalty could be fixed.

266. He must also advise the company 'from tyme to tyme upon all occurrences, what is fitt for governement in those severall places to th'end it may be considered of heere, and order taken accordingly'.

267. Lastly he must give 'certificates to the Customers for freemen that have taken their Oathes, that they may Shipp, and none other, and to have a care to restraine all others'.

268. 'And concerning ymposicions the company will presently consider, and advertize the severall Deputies.'

269. This report from the committee was read out in court, receiving general approval. It was agreed that it should be entered as an act of the court and that all the deputies should have a copy of it and of everything mentioned in it, 'and this order to be a sufficient warrant to the Secretary in that behalf'.

270. [p. 79] *A general court held at Pewterers' Hall on Wednesday 21 August 1605 in the presence of Thomas Wilford, president, John Newton, deputy, and the following assistants:*

271. Richard Staper, Robert Chamberlen, John Newman, Nicholas Ling, Arthur Jaxon, John Bate, Robert Savage, Edward James, Robert Bowyer, Symion Furner, Thomas Owen, Robert Cobb, George Collymore, George Hanger, Roger Howe, Martyn Bond, Thomas Bostock, being assistants of London; John Clynch of Ipswich, Richard Langley, secretary, and divers of the generality.

272. First, the business of the last general court was read out and confirmed.

273. Then three persons claimed their freedom by patrimony in the right of their fathers who were all freemen by ancient trade: Roger Collymore, draper, son of George Collymore, Richard Hollworthy of London, mercer, son of John Hollworthy of Bridgwater and also formerly apprenticed to James Boyle a freeman by ancient trade, and Salaman Shorter, merchant tailor, son of William Shorter. They were all admitted, paying 6s. 8d. each to the use of the society and taking the oath of freemen by ancient trade.

274. [p. 80] The following four claimants were made free by virtue of their service with freemen by ancient trade: James Bagg of Plymouth by service with Nicholas Ball of Plymouth, Thomas Style, skinner, by service with William Cokayne, William Boornford by service with William Coles, grocer, and John Hale by service with Richard Hale, grocer. They paid 6s. 8d. to the use of the society and took the oath of freemen by ancient trade.

275. Richard Candler, mercer, the clerk for policies of assurance, petitioned the company

shewing that he was bound apprentize to a merchaunt whose master was Sir Thomas Gresham being a freeman of this company. Also that he having a dwelling house in the Royall exchange will have a roome necessary for the Assistaunts to meete together at any convenyent tymes upon any sudden buisness for the company which shalbe at their commaund, and that he is not free of any forren Company. And therefore he humbly prayed the Company to graunt him the freedome gratis.[1]

The company after considering his petition granted him his freedom without charge, for his person only, 'but not to make either sonne or servaunt free'. He was admitted and took the oath of a freeman by ancient trade.

1. See above, p. xli.

276. The seven persons following, all mere merchants and free of no other company, were admitted into the freedom by redemption: William Yonge, Benjamyn Cooper and Augustine Yonge of Yarmouth, 'upon the Certificate of Mr. William Harburne and of the Deputy of Yarmouth, and Isack Cooper of Yarmouth upon the report of Mr. Staper and others, [p. 81] and Thomas Carrowe of Lynn upon sufficient report and certificat'. In addition there were Humphrey Phipps of London, joiner, and Richard Newman, fishmonger, mere merchants for fourteen and twenty years respectively. All seven claimants paid £10 each to the use of the society and took the oath ordained for freemen by redemption who are not free of any other company.

277. Thomas Girling of Lynn son of William Girling was admitted into the freedom by patrimony, paying £10 to the use of the society as his father had paid on his admission by redemption on 18 August 1584. Thomas Girling took the oath of those freemen by redemption who were also free of some other company.

278. John Langham, leatherseller, who had traded as a mere merchant for sixteen years, 'saving only he maried a Dutchwoman who keapeth a shopp in ffanchurchstreete selling Lawnes and cambricke' requested his freedom by redemption for £10. He was denied it 'during so long tyme as his wief doth contynue the keaping of her shopp or retailing as aforesaid. And it is agreed that when shee shall gyve over the same he shalbe accepted and allowed according to his desire'.

279. Richard Hobby also claimed his freedom by service with William Sherrington 'whom he alledgeth to have ben free'. Richard Washer, John Amherst and Silvanus Payne also requested their freedom by redemption for £10 each.

fforasmuch as question is made whether by the trewe entent and meaning of the charter and the orders of the Company they be capable and fitt to be admytted, it is therefore ordered that certen Committees shalbe appointed to consider of the claymes and requests of them, and of such others as shalbe doubtfull and questionable.

280. [p. 82] There was 'eftsoones commended to the consideration of the Company the request of Sir Stephen Soame knight and Alderman of London to be admitted into the freedome of this society'. Sir Stephen Soame was already free of the Merchant Staplers and the Eastland Company;

he therefore doth desire that some one of this company (not being free of the marchaunt adventurors) may be nomynated by this court and made knowne unto him, whom he will procure to be admitted either into the freedome of the Staple or ells into the freedome of the Eastland company.

When the company was considering the matter, Thomas Boothby one of the freemen of the society but not free of the Merchant Adventurers

did offer to gyve unto this Company the some of Twenty Pownds to procure him the freedome of the Marchaunts of the Staple. Whereupon it is ordered and agreed that yf the said Sir Stephen Soame will procure the said Thomas Boothby to be made free of the company of merchaunts of the Staple, that then the said Sir Stephen Soame shalbe admitted and receaved into the freedome of this society of marchaunts of England trading into Spayne and Portugall without any other fine to be paied for the same.

281. Among those present at this court were Richard Dochester, recently elected deputy for Exeter and an ancient freeman, 'and as appeareth by a faire Register booke of Excetor sworne at Excetor 16 Januarii 1578', together with James Bagg, deputy for Plymouth, who was made free at this same court, and Nicholas Downe of Barnstaple, 'an auntient freeman admitted and sworne 21 Junii 1583 as by the records here remayning may appeare'. [p. 83] All three,

making their apparaunce hether according to letters unto them in that behaulf directed, did in open court receave and take the oath for the due execution of the office of Deputy for the severall places whereof they are elected and the Auntient lymitts within their severall Jurisdictions.

282. The above deputies

did present and deliver in open Court certen Demaunds in writing. But forasmuch as the tyme being spent they could not resolve or Determyne of them at this cort, and because the said Deputies desire expedition having speciall occasion to hasten homeward, it is therefore ordered that Mr. President and Mr. Deputy and the Committees named at a court of Assistents holden here the 7 of this instant August, viz Mr. Cokayne, Mr. How, Mr. Wych, Mr. Hanger, Mr. Dorrington, Mr. Bate, Mr. Towreson and Mr. Harrison, or any fowre of them shall meete and conferre together with the said Deputies upon and touching their said Demaunds, or any other thing for the good of the company. And what they shall determyne or conclude upon this Court doth and will approve and allowe. And it is ordered that the Secretary shall deliver unto the severall Deputies such copies as the said persons and Committees before named or any fowre of them shall appoint, and this order shalbe his sufficient warrant and dischardge in that behalf.

283. 'Lett the demaundes and resolutions entred page 87 come in here.'[1]

284. Memorandum: that on 27 August 1605 in the presence of John Newton, deputy, John Bate, Robert Bowyer and Thomas Owen, three of the assistants, and Richard Langley, secretary, according to an order taken at a general court on 13 August 1605, Richard Reynoldes took the oath of a freeman by ancient trade, paying 6s. 8d. to the use of the society.

285. [p. 84] *A general court held at Pewterers' Hall on Wednesday 28 August 1605 in the presence of Thomas Wilford, president, John Newton, deputy, and the following assistants:*

286. William Cokayne, John Newman, Andrew Bannyng, Nicholas Lyng, Arthur Jackson, Robert Savage, Edward James, George Hanger, Roger

---

1. This paragraph has been inserted into the text. See below, **297–305**.

How, Martyn Bond, Thomas Bostock, being assistants of London; John Whitson of Bristol, James Bagg of Plymouth and divers of the generality.

287. The business of the last court was read out and confirmed.

288. Two persons claimed their freedom by patrimony in the right of their fathers, 'auncient freemen, well knowne to the company': John Pytt of Weymouth son of Mr. Richard Pytt of Weymouth and Robert Peacock, grocer, son of Mr. Robert Peacock. They were admitted, taking the oath of freemen by ancient trade and paying 6s. 8d. to the use of the society.

289. [p. 85] Five other persons claimed their freedom by apprenticeship to ancient traders: William Waltham of Weymouth by service with John Peter of Exeter, John Stradling of Bridgwater by service with Robert Bucking of Bridgwater, Henry Jennyngs, draper, by service with Robert Cox, William Morse, skinner, by service with William Cokayne the elder, and Charles Colfox, haberdasher, by service with Edmund Eyton. Their claims were examined and found valid, whereupon the claimants paid 6s. 8d. each to the use of the company and were admitted, taking the oath of freemen by ancient trade.

290. John Erick of London, a mere merchant and free of no other company, 'making suite to be admitted by Redemption, was with free and generall consent accepted'. He paid his fine of £10 and took the oath of a freeman by redemption.

291. Thomas Stoner of Southampton came to this court to claim his freedom by patrimony through his father Peter Stoner of Southampton an ancient merchant named in the charter of 1577. 'But his clayme was referred to be further considered of, and determyned, by Mr. Deputy Newton, att his commyng downe into those parts.'

292. At a general court on 28 June 1605, the company elected Alexander Jones as deputy of Bridgwater, 'and by letter written unto him did require him to make his repaire hether, to take his oath for the due execution of the said place'. At this court a letter was read out from Alexander Jones [p. 86]

wherein he alleadgeth that by reason of dishabillity of body, he is not hable to undertake the travell and chardg of the said place, and therefore having procured a counsell or meeting of the said society within the said towne, they made choice of Mr. John Stradling a freeman by auncient trade, to supply the said place of Deputy, whom they sent up of purpose to receave the said oath. But forasmuch as sithence the wryting of the said letter, the company doe fynde that the towne of Bridgwater hath byn heretofore a member, and under the Jurisdiction of the citty of Bristoll, therefore they have forborne the swearing of any Deputy there, unlesse the Deputy and merchaunts of Bristoll give their consents thereunto. And therefore it is agreed that the said Mr. John Stradling shalbe allowed to beare his charges in commyng up hether the some of Three poundes, the same to be paid by Mr. Treasuror, and to be allowed him in his accompt.

43

293. A letter to the company from Sir Charles Cornwallys the lord ambassador in Spain was openly read out.

294. It was endorsed as sent to the right worshipful the Spanish company of merchants in London, and its contents were as follows.

295. After my harty commendations, et cetera, understanding that the office of Consulshipp for Portugall was by the king's majesty of Spaine long before my hether commyng, given to one Rowland Maylard, Englishman and Inhabitant of the said citty, conceiving him thereby to be of good sufficiency every way for the executing and dischardg of that place, I thought good at his very ernest suite, so far as in me lay to confirm and Ratifie unto him the said graunt of the King yet with condition on his parte, under his hand wryting to be performed, that if hereafter it [p. 87] shall appeare to me, that any iust complaint of his bad and evill dealing in the said place, be by the company made against him, he will at my direction forthwith resigne the same to whome the election of an other shall be found to appertayne. And so hoping that you will rest well contented with what herein I have done, I bid you hartely farewell from Vallodolid of July the 26.

Your loving freind
Charles Cornwalys

296. After reading the letter the company decided that

by vertue of the charter graunted by our soveraigne lord the king's majesty, the election of Consulls doth belong to this company. Therefore they held it not fitt to give any allowance or assent to the election made either by the king of Spaine, or by the said Lord Ambassadour, but to appoint and elect a fitt man of their owne knowledg and nomynation.

A letter to that effect was to be sent to the ambassador.

297. Lett these Demandes of the Westerne Deputies, and the resolutions thereupon be entred in th' end of page 83.[1]
298. Demaunds by the Deputies of the westerne Devisions 21 Augusti 1605.
299. Item that our courts may contynue of so many assistaunts as in tyme past, that is 16 of Exceter, 12 of Plymouth, and that Barnestable which before had ben 6 Assistaunts may (for better government) be allowed 8.
300. Item that wee may have the Charter Exemplefied under the seale, to be in Exeter, as in tyme past.
301. [p. 88] Item that our courts may have power, to make and establish lawes, and ordynances for the beter government of the company, and ordering of their goods and marchaundizes.
302. Item that our Deputies, and other officers, may take their oath for the executing of their offices at our generall corts holden for that purpose, and not to be compelled to come to London, being so greate a Jorney, and needlesse chardg.
303. Item, that sonnes, Apprentices, and Redemptioners, may be made free there, and not compelled to come to London for the causes aforesaid.
304. Item that the moyety of our fynes, Impositions, Amerciaments and all other penalties, and brokes, may remayne and be amongst us, towardes the Defraying of any needfull chardg, and relief of decayed bretheren.
305. Item that whereas the President, and Assistaunts, have power to make lawes,

---

1. See above, **283.**

that wee may no further be bound by oath to the observations of them then as they may stand with the good of our Countrey, and the consent of our severall courts there.

306. *A committee held at Pewterers' Hall on Wednesday afternoon, 21 August 1605, in the presence of*

307. Mr. Wilford, president, Mr. Newton, deputy, Mr. Ling, Mr. Howe, Mr. Hanger, Mr. Harrison; deputies Mr. Dochester of Exeter, Mr. Bagg of Plymouth, Mr. Downe of Barnstaple, Mr. Clynch of Ipswich.

308. The committee assembled according to the order taken at the general court held on the morning of 21 August 1605, 'to advise and consider of the Demaundes before mentyoned, being delivered in open corte by the severall Deputies, before named'. Their answers to the demands were as follows:

309. [p. 89] The first Demaund is assented unto, and allowed by the said Committees.
310. To the second wee thinck that a copy of the Charter wilbe sufficient, which our Secretary (for reasonable consideration) shall deliver. And it shalbe allowed them againe out of their ympositions, whereupon the said Deputies were well satisfied and content with the same.
311. To the third wee thinck that by our letters patents all Acts and ordynaunces for the good goverment of the whole society, are to be made, and agreed upon here, at a generall corte. Otherwise greate confusion might growe in making of Acts and therefore it is requisite the Deputies, and Assistaunts, should conforme themselves, and be bound to governe by such Acts and ordynaunces, as shalbe made and agreed here by the generall courte. Nevertheless for there owne better goverment wee thinck it lawfull and fitt, that the Deputies, Assistaunts and generallity in their severall Divisions from tyme to tyme may devise, and lay downe acts and ordinaunces amongst themselves, which acts and ordynaunces before the putting of the contents thereof in execution, they shall send unto us in wryting, and being allowed, and ratified by our generall courte, they shall stand in force, or ells not.
312. Item, to the 4th that the like order and course be observed, as in auncient tyme was accustomed, aswell for electing as for swearing of Deputies, Assistaunts and officers.
313. Item to the ffyft, that the Indenture of every apprentice bound in the Countrey, shalbe sent up hether to be enrowled with our Secretary here, within the ffirst yere after his bynding, and that the Secretary shalbe allowed for every such enrowlment 12d., and that every such Apprentice whose Indenture shalbe so enrowled within the first yere and shalbe bound to a freeman by auncient trade, shall at the expiration of his terme (yf he shall faithfully serve his Master according to such Indenture) be sworne before the Deputy, Assistaunts and generallity [p. 90] in the Countrey. But every such Apprentice, whoe shall not be enrowled within the first yere, shalbe sent up hether to receave his freedome here. And all Redemptioners whatsoever, and the sonnes and servaunts of all Redemptioners shalbe sent up hether to receave their freedome with such certificate from the Deputy and Assistants there, as by an order taken at a former Committee entred at Corte holden the 13 of August 1605 is mentioned.

314. Item to the 6th the severall Deputies and their Treasurers to rendour accoumpt of all receipts, as in former tymes hath byn accustomed.

315. Item to the 7th they are to be bound (as wee and all brothers in the company are) according as in the oathes and ordynaunces is mentioned, and according to the true entent and meaning of the same.

316. And for the present the said Committees doe thinck fitt, that the severall Deputies shall have such copies delivered them and be only aucthorised to proceede so farr, as was formerly thought fitt by the Committees, to whome the same was referred, according as it is agreed and entred at a generall courte holden the said 13 day of August 1605, and hereafter to have such further addition or detraction, as circumstaunces and tyme may Minister iust occasion. Vide page 83.[1]

317. [p. 91] *A general court held at Pewterers' Hall on Friday 30 August 1605 in the presence of Thomas Wilford, president, John Newton, deputy, and the following:*

318. Lawrence Greene, treasurer, William Cokayne, John Newman, Andrew Bannyng, Arthur Jackson, Edward James, Robert Bowyer, Thomas Owen, Robert Cobb, George Hanger, Roger Howe, Martyn Bond, assistants of London; John Whitson of Bristol, James Bagg of Plymouth, Richard Langley, secretary, and divers of the generality.

319. The business of the last general court was read out and confirmed.

320. And this corte being specially appointed only to conclude of the Acts and ordynaunces for the goverment of this society, and of a commission or aucthority to be graunted to Mr. John Newton (the Deputy generall) and Arthur Jackson (one of the Assistaunts) whoe at a former courte were entreated and appointed to ryde to Bristoll, and the other severall porte townes, to keepe Courte and performe services, and ymployments for the good of the company. They caused a draught of a comission prepared for the same purpose to be openly redd, the tenour whereof followeth in these words, viz.

321. [p. 92] To all true Christian people to whom this present wryting shall come, the President, Assistaunts and fellowshipp of Marchaunts of England trading into Spaine and Portugall send greeting. Whereas our moast gratious soveraigne Lord the King's moast excellent Majesty that now is, by his highnes letters patents under the greate seale of England, bearing date at Westminster the 31 day of May last, did incorporate us into a society or fellowshipp, with aucthority to keepe courts, Elect officers, and to admitt freemen into our society, and to make and ordayne lawes and statutes for the goverment of our Society, and with diverse other privileges and ymmunities as in and by the said letters patents at large appeareth. Now knowe yee that aswell for the present ease of all the Deputies, and other freemen (whoe ought to come up to London to receave their oathes) and for the setling of goverment in every severall place where Deputie [sic] are or heretofore have byn appointed, and for keeping of courts, electing and swearing of officers, and Ministers in the said severall places (which have not byn lately sworne here at London) admitting and swearing of freemen, aswell as by Patrymony and service, as also by Redemption and doing and performing all other things which wee the President Assistaunts and fellowship can or may doe, by vertue of the said charter, wee have nomynated constituted and appointed, And

---

1. See above, **282.**

46

by these presents Doe nomynate, constitute and appoint our trusty and wel-beloved, John Newton (the Deputy generall of our said society) and Arthur Jackson (one of the Assistaunts of the same) whome wee have aucthorised and entred to performe, execute and undertake this greate trust and ymployment before mentyoned, of whose approved wisdomes and [p. 93] fidelity wee have sufficient experience. And forasmuch as they have byn present with us at moast of our courts and thereby are fully acquainted with our orders and manner of government here, wee are confidently perswaded they will keepe their courts, and so dispose of busines by vertue of this commission, with that integrity and indifferency as they have observed, and knowne us to governe here, wherein we desier one and the self same order to be observed without respecting of persons, or any favour or parcially to be shewed to any whatsoever. Especially requiring them that if (upon examynation) they shall fynd the name of any person to be inserted into the said charter, whoe cannot lawfully clayme the freedome thereof, as sonne or servaunt to some freeman heretofore admitted and allowed by auncient trade, that then (according to the Ordynaunce and our proceedings here) they shall not admitt or swere him or them into the freedome of this society, unlesse he or they first satisfie the use of the society the some of Tenn pounds apeece, and take the oath appointed for a Redemptioner, and that if any of them shall refuse soe to doe, that then they admonish and warne him and them to desist and forbeare trading under the paines contayned in the companies ordynaunces. And for the better directions of the said John Newton and Arthur Jackson in their proceedings wee have delivered unto them a perfect and true copy of our Charter and of certen Ordynaunces and statutes already made, devised, and allowed, for the goverment of the Company. And whatsoever they shall doe in the premisses wee doe by these presents, promisse to [p. 94] ratifie and allowe. In witnes where-of wee have hereunto caused our comon seale to be putt, the fowrth day of September Anno domino 1605.

322. After the commission had been modified in some points and finally embodied in the form given above, it was ordered

that the same shalbe ingrossed against the next generall courte to be then sealed with the auncient Common seale of this society, being in open courte produced and shewed furth by Mr. President, in whose custody the same hath remayned sithence the dissolving of our auncient Courts.

It was also ordered that the treasurer should deliver £20 to Mr. Newton and Mr. Jackson towards the costs of their journey, and the sum be allowed him in his account. 'And what chardges they shall disburse in their said Jorney upon an Accompt by them made and delivered up, shalbe allowed and paid by this company.'

323. The company then went on to the reading of various acts and ordinances for the government of the society,

whereof parte of them were taken out of the auncient ordynaunces of this Company, with some alterations and aditions, as to certen Committees, appointed to consider of them, were thought fitt and convenient. And so many as were thought unnecessary, and which tyme had worne out of use, were frustrated, made void, and omitted, and the residue which were held fitt, and proffitable for the goverment of the company, were ratified and allowed, and all such as are appointed now to stand in force, are entred in a faire register booke, (called the booke of ordynaunces) made and appointed for that purpose.

324. [p. 95] *A general court held at Pewterers' Hall on Wednesday 4 September 1605 in the presence of Thomas Wilford, president, John Newton, deputy, and the following assistants:*

325. Lawrence Greene, treasurer, John Newman, John Harby, Andrew Banning, Nicholas Lyng, John Dorrington, Robert Savage, Edward James, Robert Bowyer, Symion Furner, Thomas Owen, Richard Wyche, George Hanger, Roger How, Martyn Bond, Thomas Bostock, assistants of London; Richard Langley, secretary, and divers of the generality.

326. The business of the last general court was allowed and confirmed.

327. The commission to John Newton the deputy general and Arthur Jackson one of the assistants, agreed on at the previous general court, 'and now ingrosed in parchment, was sealed with the common seale of this society'.

328. Three persons claimed their freedom by patrimony in the right of their fathers who were all freemen by ancient trade: Henry Newton mercer, son of John Newman the deputy, Nathaniel Isam, mercer, son of Henry Isam, and Leonard Shawe, clothworker, son of Francis Shawe. They were all [p. 96] admitted, paying 6s. 8d. each to the use of the society and taking the oath of a freeman by ancient trade.

329. Also the following five persons were made free by service with merchants who were free by ancient trade: Richard Cox, grocer, by service with Robert Peacock, John Skybow, grocer, by service with Richard Reynolds, John Morris, haberdasher, by service with Robert Dawborne, Robert Criste 'now of London' with William Godbeare of Taunton, and Robert Greene, grocer, by service with Robert Brooke the younger. Each paid 6s. 8d. to the use of the society and took the oath of a freeman by ancient trade.

330. The following four persons 'being all mere merchaunts, and free of no other society of merchaunts, and having used merchaundising above the space of seaven yeres' were admitted into the freedom by redemption: William Whitwey of Dorchester,[1] John Roye of Weymouth, Richard Archdale of London, draper, and Richard Washer of London, fishmonger. Each paid £10 to the use of the society and took the oath appointed for redemptioners free of no other company.

331. John Hawes, salter, claimed the freedom by service with John Cage. He was admitted, paying a fine of £5 'being the like some that his Master paid', and took the oath of a freeman by redemption.

332. [p. 97] At the motion and request of the right worshipfull Mr. John Doderidge Esquiour, the king's Majesty's Solicitour generall, it is concluded and agreed that William Gamyng of [blank] in the County of Devon, shalbe admytted and

1. Presumably Dorchester, Dorset, rather than Dorchester near Oxford.

receaved into the freedome of this society for his owne person gratis. And it is agreed that Mr. Deputy Newton and Mr. Jaxon when they come into the Country may mynister unto him the oath of a freeman, according to his admyttaunce.

333. Also Richard Hobby, haberdasher, apprenticed formerly to William Sherrington, requested his freedom by ancient trade 'by vertue of his office'. However, no record could be found that William Sherrington had ever been made free,

so as the said Richard Hobby cannot directly prove himself capeable thereof. Nevertheless it hath pleased the Company, to bestowe upon him the freedome of this society for his Owne parson gratis and thereupon in open courte he was admytted and sworne accordingly.

334. Upon the humble petition of Josias Brand, a poore brother of this Company, it is agreed, that Mr. Treasurer shall deliver him the some of fyve pownds, upon his Bond to the Company in £10, to repay the same at our Lady Day next.

335. It was also agreed that the sum of £10, which Edward Davenatt deposited with Mr. Howe the former treasurer, should be repaid to him 'because it appeareth that he had right to the freedome by Patrymony, whereupon he was lately admytted'.

336. [p. 98] It was agreed that the president

shalbe allowed, (for and in respecte of the Execution of his said office, and his care and dilligence in the affaires of the Company) a yerely some of one hundreth pownds, whereof £50 to be accoumpted for his standing fee, and £50 by way of gratuity. And the same allowaunce to comence and begyn at our Lady Day was Twelve moneth, which was Anno Domino 1604.

He would thus receive £150 next Michaelmas to cover one and a half years' service. Thereafter the fee was to be paid quarterly by successive treasurers and allowed them in their accounts.

337. It was also agreed that Mr. Newton the deputy 'for and in respect of his greate care and dilligence in the service of the Company' should receive an annuity of £50, of which £30 was his standing fee and £20 a gratuity. It was to be paid quarterly by the treasurer, beginning at Michaelmas next.

338. [p. 99] *A general court held at Pewterers' Hall on Friday 6 September 1605 in the presence of Thomas Wilford, president, and the following assistants:*

339. Sir Robert Lee, alderman, Sir William Romeney, alderman, Lawrence Greene, treasurer, Richard Staper, Robert Chamberlen, Andrew Bannyng, John Newman, John Harby, Nicholas Lyng, John Dorrington, Robert Savage, Edward James, Robert Bowyer, Richard Wych, George Hanger, Roger How, Martyn Bond, Thomas Bostock, Richard Langley, secretary.

340. 'There was also then and there present not being of the Assistaunts the right worshipfull Sir John Spencer and Sir Thomas Pullison knights and divers of the generallity.'

341. Nicholas Leate, ironmonger, claimed his freedom by service with Sir Thomas Cambell an ancient freeman. He was admitted after paying a fine of 6s. 8d. and taking the oath of a freeman by ancient trade.

342. [p. 100] Robert Sandy, grocer, a mere merchant for twenty years 'and free of no other society of marchaunts (saving onely of East India)', requested his freedom by redemption. He paid a fine of £10, took the oath of a redemptioner, and was admitted accordingly.

343. And notwithstanding the company have heretofore held the freedome of East India not to be any barr or ympedyment to restraine any from being admytted into the freedome of this society, yet upon the motion of some of the Company it was held fytt, that some order might be laid downe and Recorded concerning the resolution of the Company in that case, whereupon being put to question to the howse, it was resolved and fully agreed, that the said Company of East India is dissolved, and not to be any longer accoumpted for a Company, and that any such freedom of itself, is not thought sufficient to barr or hinder any marchaunt (being otherwise lawfully quallified, according to the charter and the Companies ordynaunces) to be admytted and received into this society.[1]

344. The company then proceeded to the election of consuls

to rule and governe in Spayne and Portugall, according to the true intents and meaning [p. 101] of the charter (ffor which purpose this Courte was specially called). And first they entred into consideration how many, and for what places Consulls were to be elected. And in the end they agreed to make election of severall Consulls, for these severall places following (viz)

345. '(1) Biskey (2) Baion in Galitia[2] (3) Lisboine (4) St. Lucar and Sivill (5) Malaga (6) Valentia (7) Canaries (8) Matheres[3] (9) St. Michael's, and the 7 other Islands'.[4]

346. They then proceeded to elect consuls for the above places, with nominations as follows:

347. 'Bisky: James Wych, Thomas Chace and William Palmer. An then by lifting up of hands the Election did fall upon the said James Wych'.

348. The following elections then took place. Bayona in Galicia: Francis Lambert, Hugh Lea and John Audley, of whom Francis Lambert was elected.

349. [p. 102] Lisbon: Hugh Lea, John Audley and Phillip Gregory, of whom Hugh Lea was elected.

350. San Lucar and Seville: Hugh Bourman, John Audley and John Ramridge, of whom Hugh Bourman was elected.

1. See above, p. xl.
2. Bayona in Galicia.
3. Possibly Madeira.
4. São Miguel and the Azores.

351. Malaga: Simon Bourman, Humphrey Wootton and Jeffrey Davies, of whom Humphrey Wootton was elected.

352. 'But for Valentia and other the places before named, they take longer and further tyme to make inquiry, and to informe themselves of fytt and worthy men to be Consulls in the said severall places.'

353. After the above elections were concluded, a committee was set up with the following members: the president, Sir William Romeney, Mr. Staper, Mr. Andrew Banning, Mr. Harby, Mr. Wych, Mr. How, Mr. Hangar, Mr. Dorrington, Mr. Lyng, Mr. Bond, Mr. Bostock, Mr. James, all of them assistants; Mr. Parslow, Mr. Harrison, Mr. Davies, of the generality.

354. [p. 103] They or any seven of them were asked to meet on Monday next, 9 September 1605,

and to send for so many of the said Elected Consulls as are nowe remayning about London, and to conferr with them touching their allowaunce and entertaynement for th'execution of the said places, and to consider and lay downe what allowaunce is fytt to be given to the other elected Consulls that are absent.

355. The committee was also asked to consider the levying of impositions and, if any were to be levied, at what rates.

356. Furthermore they were

to consider of an act drawne by Mr. President prohibiting that no stranger shall lade with or amongst the freemen of this society, and to make relation of all their proceedings at the next generall Courte, for further therein to be donne, as shalbe then thought fytt and Convenient.

357. *An assembly held at Pewterers' Hall on Wednesday 11 September 1605 in the presence of the following assistants:*

358. Mr. Wilford, president, Andrew Banning, Nicholas Ling, John Dorrington, Robert Savage, Roger Howe, Martyn Bond, Thomas Bostock, Richard Langley, secretary, and certain of the generality.

359. [p. 104] A general court was to be held this day, but

for want of a Competent nomber of assistaunts they could not proceede, nor determyne the businesse, for which the Court was specially summoned. And therefore it was earnestly desired that such as were absent should pay the penalties, due by the ordynaunces to be inflicted upon such as make default of apparaunce at such Courts.

360. The draft of a letter to the deputy of Southampton was read out and passed. It concerned

an information that was given, that one Mr. Janveryne not being free, was in hand to lade a French Barck for Spayne, requiring the Deputy (if it were trew) to make stay thereof. And Mr. Davies one of this society being in Courte hath undertaken for 10s. to send a foote post with the letter and to retorne an aunswer, which some is agreed shalbe delivered and payd.

361. *A general court held at Pewterers' Hall on Friday 13 September 1605 in the presence of Thomas Wilford, president, and the following assistants:*

362. Sir Robert Lee, Lawrence Greene, treasurer, Richard Staper, Robert Chamberlen, Andrew Banning, William Cokayne, John Newman, Nicholas Ling, John Dorrington, Robert Savage, Nicholas Stile, Roger Howe, Martyn Bond, Thomas Bostock, Richard Langley, secretary.

363. [p. 105] Also present was Alderman John Jowles, 'not being of the Assistaunts' and divers of the generality.

364. The business of the previous general court was read out and confirmed.

365. First, John Garrett, merchant tailor, claimed his freedom by service with Peter Collett an ancient freeman. He was admitted after paying a fine of 6s. 8d. and taking the oath of a freeman by ancient trade.

366. Richard Aldworth, grocer, and John Cooper, fishmonger, both mere merchants for many years and members of no other society, were admitted into the freedom by redemption. They paid £10 each 'and tooke the auntient Oath for Redemptioners in that case ordayned and provided'.

367. Then the report of the committee authorised at the last general court was read out. The committee was to consider the question of allowances for the consuls in their different posts, the levying of impositions, and the president's draft of an act forbidding strangers to load with or amongst those free of the society. Their report was as follows:

368. According to the aucthority graunted at the last generall Court, we Andrewe Banning, Roger Howe, Richard Wych, George Hanger, John Dorrington, Nicholas Lynge, Martyn Bond, Thomas Bostock, and Edward James, being [p. 106] of the Assistaunts and Gyles Parslowe, William Harrison and John Davies of the generallity (being accompanied with Mr. Wilford President) did assemble and meete together at Pewterers hall upon Munday and Tuesday being the 9th and 10th daies of this instant moneth of September 1605 and did cause our opinions and conceipts to be laid downe in writing to be presented to the next generall Courte to be confirmed or disallowed as the Court shall thincke fytt, the tenour whereof followeth in these words viz.:
369. We the said Commyttees upon long conference amongst ourselves, and regarding the severall expences and charge that will growe upon the severall Consulls, within their severall divisions and cercuits, in executing the office of Consulshipp, are of opinion, that yf they faithfully parforme the office and charge incident to such a place, that they may deserve those stipends and allowaunces heereafter following:
370. Inprimis the Consull for St. Lucar and Civill the yerely allowaunce of two hundreth pounds of lawfull English money.

371. And to the Consull resident in Lisborne the yeerely allowaunce of one hundreth and fifty pownds of like money.

372. And the severall Consulls resident in Baion in Galitia, Biskey, and Maliga, the severall yerely allowaunces of forty pownds apeece, of like lawefull English money.

373. And we are further of opynion that it were fytt that every Shipp whatsoever fraighted into, or from Spayne or Portugall, of the burden of one hundreth Tonnes or under shall pay one ducket, and every shipp above one hundreth tonnes shall pay two ducketts, the same to be paid by the master or owner of every such shipp or shipps at such places where any such shipp or shipps shall first discharge or unloade any goods or Marchaundizes, and the same to be [p. 107] Levied and receaved by the severall Consulls (in the parts of Spayne and Portugall) within their severall devisions, to the use of this society, for which they shall make iust and true accoumpts and be aunswerable to the Company for all they shall receave.[1]

374. And concerning the levying of Impositions upon all and every the goods or Marchaundizes transported or retorned into or from the parts of Spayne and Portugall, the said Commyttees the first day did thinck fytt that the some of 2s. 6d. outward, and 2s. 6d. homeward, shalbe levied uppon the value of every hundreth pounde so to be transported or returned as aforesaid. But at the second daies meeting, uppon further consideration they thought fytt to increase the same 2s. 6d., unto the some of 3s. 4d. owtward, and asmuch homeward. And that the same Impositions should generally be receaved and entred in a faire booke heere in England by such parson as heereafter upon further consideration (by the Company at a generall Courte) shalbe aucthorized and allowed, to receave the same.[2]

375. And towching the order drawne by Mr. President they referr the same to a generall Courte.

376. After the report of the committee had been read out,

greate dispute and reasoning grewe concerning the same, some holding the allowaunce greater then th'estate of the Company as yett fytt or hable to defray. Others wishing their allowaunce as greate in substaunce, but utterly disliking that the same should be made by such certen yerely fee from the body of the Company.

In the end, 'after along tyme spent in debating and discoursing thereof' it was noted that there was a sum given to the cape-merchant or his factor,

to be distributed for [p. 108] Romaging, wynding, hasar, Primage, Pilatage, petit lodagie money,[3] and in rewarding of the master and others of the Company as they shewe themselves dilligent about the Marchaunt's goods. And in some parts of Spayne and Portugall they pay after one rate, and in some after an other, but in noe place above two royalls and a half plate money of Spayne[4] upon a tonn.

It was therefore suggested that in addition to this allowance, half a royal per ton might be paid to the consuls together with the fine of a ducat on

---

1. Margin note, 'This Point is allowed at the next general court'.
2. Margin note, 'Concerning Impositions 3s. 4d. upon the hundreth allowed at the next generall court'.
3. Rummaging, the arranging of casks in the hold; winding, the hauling or hoisting of a sail, or the vessel itself, by means of a winch; hawser, to pull on a hawser or cable, usually in mooring; primage, the customary allowance made to the master and crew for the loading and care of the cargo; pilotage, the cost of hiring a pilot wherever necessary or compulsory; petit lodagie money, probably relating either to the loading of the vessel or to the hiring of a 'lodesman' or pilot.
4. 'Royalls' or 'ryalls', the English corruption of the Spanish *real*.

each ship, which would be 'as greate and a more fytt and proper allowaunce to be made unto them, then the said certen yerely fees before mentioned'. Although the suggestion was 'well allowed and apprehended by some, yet by others for speciall causes was not approved, and therefore referred to be considered better of, at the next generall Courte'.

377. [p. 109] *A general court held at Pewterers' Hall on Wednesday 18 September 1605 in the presence of Thomas Wilford, president, and the following:*

378. Lawrence Greene, treasurer, Andrew Banning, John Newman, John Harby, Symion Furner, Thomas Owen, Richard Wyche, Robert Cobb, George Collymore, George Hanger, Roger How, Martyn Bond, Thomas Bostock, Richard Langley, secretary, and divers of the generality.

379. Three persons claimed their freedom by ancient trade: Hugh Hamersley, haberdasher, 'being named in the last charter and the sonne of Hugh Hamersley decessed who was well knowne to have ben an auntient trader before Anno 1568'; William Anys, grocer, son of Dunstan Anys who was made free in 1577; and Robert Barker of London, mercer, [p. 110] son of William Barker of Ipswich, 'who is named in the charter of 19 Elizabeth, knowne to diverse of the company present to have ben an auntient trader and to have ben present at many courts, albeit it cannott be fownd when he was sworne'. They were all made free by ancient trade, paying 6s. 8d. each and taking the oath provided for that case.

380. Ninus Lane, merchant tailor,

being made free of that company by patrimony, but bound by Indenture (orderly made with the words Spayne and Portugale in the same) unto John Challenger, haberdasher, and having faithfully served his whole terme as Mr. Challenger being present in Court doth make report, is by vertue of his service admitted into the freedome of this society.

He paid £5, 'being the like somme that Mr. Challener paid at his admission', and took the oath appointed for such a redemptioner.

381. The three persons following, all mere merchants free of no other company, were granted the freedom by redemption. They were Robert Cox, grocer, George Dunscombe, merchant tailor, and Abraham Beavoir of Guernsey ('Garnsey'). Each paid £10 and took the oath appointed for them, being admitted accordingly.

382. [p. 111] The report of the committee on consuls, entered up under the last general court, was read out and considered. It was resolved that every ship of the burden of 100 tons or less, freighted to or from Spain and Portugal, should pay one ducat, and every ship above 100 tons should pay two ducats. The sum was to be paid by the master or owner at the first port at which any goods were unloaded. The money would be collected by each consul in his division, 'to the use of the society ffor which they shall make Just and trewe accoumpts, and be aunswerable to the Company for all they shall or may receave'.

383. As regards the impositions to be levied on any goods transported to or from Spain and Portugal, 'it was demaunded what sommes were fitt to be levied upon the value of every hundreth pownd, both outward and inward'. The sums of 2s. 6d., 3s. 4d. and 5s. were each suggested in turn, 'and first by triall by lyfting up of hands to every of the said sommes the greatest nomber of hands were for the two first somes viz. 2s. 6d. and 3s. 4d., and the fewest nomber for 5s.'.
The two smaller sums were voted on once more, 'and then by moast hands and voices it was agreed that 3s. 4d. outward and 3s. 4d. inward shalbe levied for ymposition upon all merchaundize of the value of £100, and so after the same rate for merchandizes of greater or lesser value'.

384. [p. 112] The goods would be valued according to the custom-house rate, but for wines, which are not rated there, it was agreed 'that for all sorts of wynes whatsoever a butt or pipe shalbe rated and valued at £5. But it is not as yett concluded when the said ymposition shalbe collected'.[1]

385. With regard to the additional half royal per ton mentioned previously, 'the same is disalowed and by the greatest number disliked and not thought fitt to be graunted'.

386. And forasmuch as greate varyety of opinyons was shewed when the allowaunces to Consulls should begin and much tyme spent and little concluded upon concerning the same, it was in th'end thought that a Court of Assistaunts might better resolve and determyne of such and the like business.

The general court therefore thought fit to refer the whole matter to a court of assistants, asking them not only to settle it but also to consider 'what directions and aucthority is fitt to be gyven to the Consulls, and what letters are to be procured either from his Majestie or the lords of the Counsaill (for their better Creditt) to be carried over with them'. The general court will confirm whatever sums the assistants think fit to grant the consuls 'for their better furnishing before they goe over', and also ratify the orders and directions they decide on for them.

387. As for the consuls' yearly standing fees, the general court approved the sums as set out in the report of the committee.

388. [p. 113] A letter was read out in court from the earls of Dorset and of Salisbury, 'in favour of William Masham to be admitted into the freedome of this society'.

389. A letter was also read out from Bristol, sent by the deputy Mr. Newton and Arthur Jaxon, 'shewing that the merchaunts of Bristoll pretende to

---

1. Crossed out underneath are the words, 'And the same ymposition to be collected from michaelmas next ensuing'.

stand and governe of themselves, and refuse to submitt themselves to the orders and government of this society'.

390. Lastly a letter was read from Hugh Lee the newly-elected consul for Lisbon. However, it was decided to take further time to consider all these letters before drafting any replies.

391. *A general court held at Pewterers' Hall on Wednesday 25 September 1605 in the presence of Thomas Wilford, president, and the following assistants:*

392. Mr. Greene, treasurer, Mr. Banning, Mr. Newman, Mr. Ling, Mr. Dorrington, Mr. James, Mr. Bowyer, Mr. Furner, Mr. Cobb, Mr. Collymere, Mr. Hanger, Mr. Bond, Mr. Boston; the secretary and also divers of the generality.

393. [p. 114] The business of the last general court was read and confirmed.

394. Thomas Higgins 'the late elect deputy for Rye, was admytted into the freedome of this Company for his owne parson gratis'. He took two oaths, that of a freeman and that of a deputy, and the president and treasurer were authorised 'to satisfy him such allowaunce for his charge in coming up as in their wisdomes shalbe thought fytt'.

395. The letter from the earls of Dorset and Salisbury to the company on behalf of William Masham was read out as follows.

396. To our loving frends the President Assistaunts and fellowship of Marchaunts of England trading Spayne and Portugall, be these et cetera.
397. After our harty commendations. Whereas before the sealing of your Patent, William Masham of London made suite unto us to be the meanes for his admytaunce into your society, who uppon his earnest suite and greate reasons alleadged of his discontynuance of his other trade to Stoade, and long frequenting and using his whole trade, into the Countries of the King of Spain the greatest parte of his estate being there [p. 115] ymployed, and his servaunts there resident, obtayned our favourable promise therein, which was by us omytted and forgotten to be spoken at the sealing of your graunt. Wherefore although (having of late byn sued by many) we have ben, and are very loathe to presse you with any inconvenience, yet have wee thought good in regard of our former promise to pray and entreate you, onely to entertayne into your Company the said William Masham assuring you that by yelding to this our request, you shall drawe us from henceforth not to importune you in the behalf of any other. And so we bidd you hartely farewell, from Dorsett Howse the ffyfth of September 1605.
Your very loving friends
Thomas Dorset   Salisbury

398. After considering the letter

the Company were very desiorous to graunt asmuch as by their charter they lawfully might, yet finding that the said William Masham is free of an other Company of Marchaunts, they have admitted and sworne him into the freedom of this Companie for his owne person gratis, whereunto he rested well satisfied.

399. Two persons claimed their freedom by apprenticeship: Thomas Symonds, skinner, by service with Percivall Hassall and Nicholas Heath, mercer, by service with Richard [p. 116] Culverwell, both masters being ancient traders. They were both admitted and Nicholas Heath who was present in court paid his fine of 6s. 8d., taking the oath of a freeman by ancient trade. Thomas Symonds who was absent was to pay his fine and take his oath at some other time.

400. Also, two persons requested their freedom by redemption, both of them mere merchants for above seven years and free of no other company: John Greene of Wells in Norfolk and Thomas Fayrefaix of Walsingham in the same county. They were admitted 'with free and generall consent', paying £10 each and taking the oath of a freeman by redemption. 'And it is agreed that they shalbe assistaunts to the deputy of Lynn, who by letters is to be advertized thereof accordingly'.

401. Robert Myldmay, grocer, requested the freedom by redemption for £10 but was denied admittance since various members of the company 'did [p. 117] affyrme, that he is noe meere marchaunt, but keepeth an open warehowse, and servaunts contynually attending the same'.

402. *A court of assistants held at Pewterers' Hall on Friday 27 September 1605 in the presence of Thomas Wilford, president, and the following:*

403. Andrew Banning, Mr. Dorrington, Mr. James, Mr. Bowyer, Mr. Stile, Mr. Owen, Mr. Wych, Mr. Cobb, Mr. Cullimore, Mr. Hanger, Mr. Bond, Mr. Bostock; the secretary.

404. The business of the last court of assistants was read out and confirmed.

405. 'First, that the Duplicate of the Chartre, under the greate Seale of England, and florished with Armes, shalbe sent over into Spaine to the Ambassadour or Mr. Ousley, to procure the Confirmation.'[1]

406. [p. 118] It was resolved that

letters of two natures shalbe sent to Nicholas Oseley, the one verbatim, as the former, to be delivered unto him yf it shall appeare to Mr. Bowreman that he hath effected the busines to any purpose, and yf he have not, then other letters signifying the Companies dislike. And then letters to be delivered to the lord Ambassadour to entreate his honorable favour to procure the same effected. And the gratuity promised to Nicholas Oseley to be conferred where his Lordship shall appoint.[2]

1. This paragraph has a single line through it. Margin note, 'Upon the hearing hereof at the next court thought fitter to send a Copy'.
2. Margin note, 'This Course is altered at the next court'.

407. It was agreed that the president, the treasurer, the secretary and Mr. Boureman should 'take a iourney to the Court one sunday next to procure letters from his Majestie to the king of Spayne and the Ambassadour to be carried over by Mr. Bowreman'.

408. For the expenses of his journey with the letters Mr. Bowreman was to receive 200 ducats 'which Mr. Treasurer will deliver at Bilbo or St. Sebastians, at 5s. 8d. the Duckett'.

409. The sum of £50 to be delivered to Mr. Bowrman at his going over to Spain was 'to be accepted as parcell of his fee of £200 a yere, which fee is to take comencement from the tyme that he shall returne from the king of Spain's Court to St. Lucar'.

410. It was also agreed that he should have a letter of credit for a further 200 ducats, in case he had need of the money in Spain.

411. [p. 119] *A general court held at Pewterers' Hall on Friday 11 October 1605 in the presence of Thomas Wilford, president, and the following:*

412. Sir Robert Lee, alderman, Mr. Greene, treasurer, Mr. Bannyng, Mr. Newman, Mr. Lyng, Mr. Bate, Mr. Furner, Mr. Owen, Mr. Wych, Mr. Cobb, Mr. Howe, Mr. Bond, assistants of London; Thomas Symms, 'being one of the Assistaunts for Charde', and divers of the generality.

413. The business of the last general court was read and confirmed.

414. Three persons claimed their freedom by ancient trade: Christopher Goodlack by service with Mrs. Parnell Towerson widow of William Towerson, skinner of London, John Humffrey by service with Andrew Bannyng, grocer, and John Moxey now of Plymouth by service with John Newton the elder, mercer and deputy of this company. They were all admitted, paying 6s. 8d. and taking their oaths.

415. Also at this court Allen Thompson, merchant tailor, named in the last charter, requested admission to the freedom by ancient trade. 'But for asmuch as he was neither the sonne or apprentice of any freeman by ancient trade, therefore it was [p. 120] resolved that he was to be admitted and sworne and to pay as a freeman received by Redemption'. He therefore paid £10 to the treasurer and took the oath appointed for a redemptioner.

416. The company was informed that the king's letters to the ambassador in Spain on their behalf had already been procured. They required him 'to move the king of Spaine for allowance of our auncient priviledges and liberties, and enlardgment thereof as neede shall requier, for the better establishing of our Consulls in Spaine'. It was nevertheless agreed that the members of the committee set up previously should become humble sutors to procure his Majesty's letters to the Duke of Medina for allowance and confirmation of such liberties as his Auncestors graunted the Company in St. Lucar de Barameda, the same letter to be Carried over by our Consull, for his better Creditt. And that such money as the Comittees shall thinck fitt to be Disbursed for procuring the same shalbe paid by Mr. Treasurer and allowed him in his Accompt.

417. Various letters were read out and referred to a court of assistants for further consideration.

418. And because many of the Assistaunts make default of Apparance, so as for want of a Competent nomber the Courts are often deferred, it is ordered that the fynes agreed upon by the ordynaunces shalbe levied of all such as shall absent themselves, having no iust cause of excuse, without remission or pardon.

419. [p. 121] *A court of assistants held at Pewterers' Hall on Wednesday 16 October 1605 in the presence of Thomas Wilford, president, John Newton, deputy, and the following:*

420. Mr. Greene, treasurer, Mr. Chamberlen, Mr. Lyng, Mr. Jaxon, Mr. Bate, Mr. Savage, Mr. Wyche, Mr. Cobb, Mr. Collymere, Mr. Hanger, Mr. Bond, Mr. Bostock; the secretary.

421. At the last court it had been agreed that 'the faire Duplicat of the charter being Lymmed and bewtified with Armes' was to be sent to Spain, but now it was thought that a copy would be sufficient. This together with copies of all the privileges 'which in auncient tyme were graunted to the company in Spaine and Portugall, and are remayning with Mr. President' was to be delivered to Mr. Boureman before his departure for Spain.

422. The copy of a petition sent to the earl of Salisbury the principal secretary and a letter from the king to the ambassador in Spain on behalf of the company, were both read out. They were as follows.

423. [p. 122] The humble petition of the English marchaunts trading Spaine and Portugall.
424. Whereas in Anno 1517 certen landes, and diverse privileges and liberties were graunted to the English marchaunts in the Towne of St. Lucar de Barameda by Don Alonso Peres de Gusman Duke of Medina:
425. And Anno 1530 the same liberties allowed and proclaymed there, and sithence the same ratefied and confirmed by the succeeding Dukes:
426. And whereas King Henry VIII by his letters patents Dated primo Septembris 22 of his raigne (being Anno Domini 1530) Did aucthorise the English marchaunts to elect a Consull or Consulls in Spaine, and 12 Assistaunts to governe there, and to gather ymposisions, and aucthority to make lawes for the publique goverment of the generallity.
427. And afterwards Charles the Emperour by his charter dated 2 Septembris 1538 (reciting the former letters patents of Henry VIII) did confirme and approve the said letters patents of Henry VIII, and thereby gave lycence and faculty to the English nation to use the same amongst themselves, and comaunded his Justices

to suffer them soe to doe: and to pleasure the English nation not being prejudiciall to his owne subiects.

428. A charter graunted by Queene Elizabeth dated 8 Junii 19 Elizabeth whereby her Majestie doth graunt to the said Marchaunts liberty to appointe one or more to be their President in Spayne and Portugall who with six other discreete Marchaunts associat with him, shall have full power to governe there all the English marchaunts.

429. King James by his letters patents dated 30 Martii 2 Jacobi doth ratefy the foresaid charters of King Henry and Queene Elizabeth.

430. [p. 123] Also king James by his other letters patents, dated 31 Maii 3 Jacobi, hath graunted them power to Elect Consulls, who with six or more discreete marchaunts may governe there.

431. Item that the graunts and privileges given by the Princes to marchaunts of either of the kingdoms, coming to their said kingdoms, and which privileges through the warrs have ceased, shall from hensforth wholy be revived, and have their full force and strength.[1]

432. And whereas the English marchaunts have lately elected these fyve Consulls for these fyve severall places viz

433.

St Lucar and Sivill	Hugh Bourman
Lisborne	Hugh Lea
Biskey	James Wich
Bayon in Galitia	Frauncis Lambert
Malaga	Humfrey Wotton.

434. They most humbly pray his Majesty's gratious letters to the king of Spaine, to th'entent that all such Consulls, as the company have or shall elect, may enjoy all the said privileges and aucthorities graunted as aforesaid, and that the King of Spaine would write to the Duke of Medina in that behalf.

435. [p. 124] And also that yf they shall neede (for the better goverment of the English nation) any enlargement of the same, that the king of Spaine and the Duke of Medina would be pleased to graunt and allowe such reasonable suits and requests as the English nation shall make in that behalf.

436. And also they humbly pray your Lordshipps letters to the lord Ambassadour resident in Spaine, to be ayding and Assisting to the Consulls for the quiet establishing of them in their places, and also to Assist the English marchaunts in all their iust suits and requests, and if any grevaunces shalbe offered them or uniust ymposicions or taxes laid upon them to endeavour and help to ease, and free them of the same.

437. The king's letter to Sir Charles Cornwallis the English ambassador resident with the king of Spain.

438. Trusty and welbeloved, wee greete you well. Wee have perceaved by sondry your letters directed to our Cousin the Earle of Salisbury our principall Secretary, your care and iudgment in the handling of such our affaires as since your being in that ymployment, have byn directed unto you. And though that neither all those directions have come to you under our owne hand, nor any signification of our acceptance of your service, yet by this occasion wee thought good to lett you knowe, that both the directions given you, have byn with our privity, and your answeres Communicated to us, with good information of your diligence in the managing of them, wherewith wee doe rest well satisfied, ffor the present that which we have to say unto you is grounded upon a petition [p. 125] made unto us by our marchaunts trading in Spaine and Portugale, whoe having heretofore

---

1. Margin note, '24 Article in the last treaty of peace hath these words'.

enioyed diverse priviledges graunted unto them some by the Dukes of Medina within whose iurisdictions they have traffique, and some by the Princes of Spaine, some also by our Progenitours of this Realme confirmed by the kings of Spaine. All which were interrupted during the late breach of Amity in the Queene our Sisters daies, but are by the last Treaty betweene that King and us revived by generallity of woords. The Marchaunts entending now the setling thereof, and having made choice of servaunts and officers to reside in severall parts of Spaine for preservation of their liberties according to the auncient usage have humblie besought us to direct our letters both to the king and the Duke of Medina in furthering of their purposes. But because wee knowe that one letter written to either of them cannot worke so much to their good, as a continuall solicitation of you our Ambassador, aucthorized both by your place, and by this speciall commaundment to be a Solicitor for them upon all accidents that may happen to them, wherein to have neede of our mediation and Countenance wee have iudged it best for them to give direction to you to take information from them, of all such things concerning the setling of their trade as they desire to be obtayned of that king, or of the duke being grounded upon any former Treaty, accord of Princes or usage of our subiects in those parts whereof some particulars are contayned in this note enclosed by them exhibited to us, and more at lardg wilbe enformed to you by their Deputies and Agents appointed to followe this busines. In all which and in all other things concerning their good, and within your discretion, you shall thinck meete to be moved there, wee are pleased that in our name you shall from tyme to tyme, Deale either with the king or his Councell, or any private persons whome it may concerne, to obtayne what may be had for the benefitt of them in their traffiques, and for redresse of any wrongs that may chance to be offred unto them. And when wee shall perceive by advertysment from you, that any extraordynary letters shalbe requisite above your solicitation wee shall doe as upon advertisement from you in our iudgment, wee shall fynde to be needefull. Given under our Signett at our Palace of Westminster the 8 day of October in the Third yere of our raigne of great Britayne, ffraunce and Ireland 1605.

439. [p. 126] Since the king in his letters had required the ambassador to petition the king of Spain and the duke of Medina Sidonia for the reestablishment of the ancient privileges and their enlargement if necessary, the company thought it 'needeles, and unnessessary to use Nicholas Oseley any longer about the same'. They decided instead 'to depend and relye upon the lord Ambassador's Assistance therein, and of such as his Lordshipp shall ymploy in the said service'.

440. It was therefore ordered that the president, the deputy, the treasurer, Mr. Wych, Mr. Jaxon, Mr. Hanger and the secretary should meet to prepare suitable letters to be sent to the ambassador, Nicholas Oseley and others, 'as also such Commissions and instructions as shalbe thought fitt for Mr. Boureman to carry over with him'. Their decisions, or those of any five of them, would be confirmed by the company as a whole.

441. At the request of Sir Thomas Flemyng, lord chief baron of the court of the exchequer, it was agreed that John Long of Southampton should be received into the freedom. It was ordered that a letter should be sent to William Nevey, deputy of Southampton, enclosing a copy of the oath of a freeman admitted by redemption, willing and requiring him to admitt the said John Long into the freedome of our society, and to administer unto him the said oath, and to receive of him his fyne of £10 for his admission, and after the receipt thereof, to restore and deliver the same back, as the free gift of the Company.[1]

442. [p. 127] It was also agreed

that the Companies last charter shalbe enrowled in his majesty's high Cort of Exchequer, whereby the Barons of the Exchequer may be sufficiently aucthorized to send out writts to the Customers, to stay the entries of all such as are not free of the Company. And that the money disbursed for the same, shalbe paid by Mr. Treasurer and allowed him in his Accompt.

443. *A general court held at Pewterers' Hall on Wednesday 23 October 1605 in the presence of Thomas Wilford, president, John Newton, deputy, and the following:*

444. Mr. Greene, treasurer, Mr. Chamberlen, Mr. Newman, Mr. Lyng, Mr. Jackson, Mr. James, Mr. Owen, Mr. Cullymere, Mr. Hanger, Mr. How, Mr. Bond, assistants of London; Thomas Syms one of the assistants for Chard; the secretary and divers of the generality.

445. The business of the last general court was read out and confirmed, whereupon the company proceeded as follows.

446. Baldwyn Durham, mercer, son of Baldwyn Durham 'an auntient freeman well knowne to the Company' claimed his freedom by patrimony. He was admitted, taking the oath of a freeman by ancient trade and paying 6s. 8d. to the use of the society.

447. Four other persons claimed their freedom by apprenticeship to ancient traders: John Tedcastle, merchant tailor, by service with [p. 128] Jerrard Gore the elder, Richard Buckfould, draper, by service with George Collymere, Roger Rogell, haberdasher, by service with Sir Thomas Bramley, and Thomas Watson by service with Arthur Needham. They were all admitted, paying 6s. 8d. each to the use of the company and taking the oath of freemen by ancient trade.

448. John Mockett of Waymouth and Melcom regis producing severall Certyfycates under the hand of the Maior and under the Comon seale of the said towne, testyfying that he was an auntient trader before 1568, and upon the reporte of diverse of the Assistaunts here present affirming that the said Certyfycates were trew, and that the said John Mockett was for many yeeres beyond seas, so as hee could not come to make his Clayme, when the company kept their Corts, was at this Corte found Capable of the freedome by auncient trade.

He took his oath and paid his fine of 6s. 8d.

449. Phillip Dawkyns, grocer, and William Groce of [blank] mere mer-

1. See above, p. xli and **144.**

chants for many years and free of no other company, were admitted into the freedom by redemption. They paid £10 each 'and tooke the auntient oath for Redemptioners in that case ordayned and provided'.

450. [p. 129] Two other persons, William Atkyn of Lynn and George Garrard, grocer, affirmed that they had been mere merchants for more than seven years and were free of no other company. They requested admission into the freedom by redemption, each paying £10 to the treasurer and taking the oath of a freeman by redemption. They were admitted upon this condition

that yf within six monethes next ensewing they shall not severally and respectively produce to this Courte a sufficient certificate to the full satisfaction of the Company testyfying and proving their said affirmation, that then hee or they that shall make default shall not only be disfranchised and loose his freedome, but also forfeyt the money so paid as aforesaid.

451. Lastly, 'the petition of Nicholas Diggins now a marchaunt, but lately a marryner desiring the freedome of this society by Redemption for his fyne of £10 was openly redd'. Nothing was concluded on the matter which was referred to the next general court for further consideration.

452. *A general court held at Pewterers' Hall on Wednesday 6 November 1605 in the presence of Thomas Wilford, president, John Newton, deputy, and the following:*

453. Mr. Chamberlen, Mr. Newman, Mr. Dorrington, Mr. Savage, Mr. Furner, Mr. Towerson, Mr. Style, Mr. Owen, Mr. Wyche, Mr. Cobb, Mr. Collymere, Mr. Hanger, Mr. How, Mr. Bond; the secretary and divers of the generality.

454. [p. 130] The business of the last general court was read and confirmed, then the company proceeded as follows.

455. Henry Waade of Topsham in Devon, came 'making clayme to the freedome by auncient trade, by vertue of a clause included in the charter of Decimo nono Elizabeth because his father was a trader into Spaine before 1568'. On further examination it appeared that his father had died before the charter itself was granted,

whereupon the company perused over an order taken at a generall courte holden the 8 day of November 1577, at which tyme question was moved and intreated upon, for the admitting of such auncient merchaunts Children and servaunts whose fathers or masters were usuall traders into Spaine or Portugall before anno 1568 and nevertheless dead before the graunt of the said letters patents. And then it was agreed Concluded and adiudged by the whole courte that it was not necessary, that any such should be received or admitted, for that they be without the Compasse of the expresse words of the said graunt, as by the said order may appeare which order is also lately confirmed the 30th day of August last. Neverthelesse forasmuch as it is affirmed, that the company cannott make and order to

63

barr any man of his right graunted by charter, it is agreed that the opynion of Mr. Dodderidg his majesty's Solicitor generall shalbe used upon that point of the charter, and that Mr. Dorrington, Mr. Harrison and the Secretary togeather with the said Henry Waade, shall all resort unto him to understand his resolution therein, and the fee to be paid indifferently by the company and Mr. Waade. And upon relation made of his opinion the company will doe that which to right and equity shall appertayne.

456. [p. 131] The petition of Nicholas Diggins which was read out at the last court was again considered but it was generally resolved 'that he is neither capable nor fitt to be received into the freedome of this society'.

457. Four persons claimed their freedom by service with ancient traders: Humphrey Hamford, grocer, by service with Henry Colthurst, Humphrey Walweyne, grocer, by service with Nicholas Style, Gregory Guybon, mercer, by service with Nicholas Heath, and Zachery Parke by service with William Parkyn of King's Lynn. They were all found capable by ancient trade, paid their fines of 6s. 8d. and were admitted and sworn accordingly.

458. William Fisher son of John Fisher of Ipswich, whose claim to the freedom by patrimony was allowed at a general court on 13 August 1605, paid his fine of 6s. 8d. at this court, took the oath of a freeman by ancient trade and was admitted accordingly.

459. Whereas information was given to this courte that diverse exactions and greate somes of money are required of the freemen of this company, for Composition for wynes, Spices, and diverse other purveyance which would tend to the greate losse of the Company, if the same be not carefully looked unto; and forasmuch as it appeareth that [p. 132] by 2 severall charters graunted to the Citty of London the one of 1 Edward 3 and the other of 7 Richard 2 that the citizens of London are freed, and discharged from all such purveyance, exactions and chardges. Therefore at this court the company have earnestly entreated Mr. President, and Mr. Deputy or one of them, Mr. Treasurer, Mr. Wych, Mr. Howe, Mr. Dorrington, Mr. Bate, and Mr. Harrison, or any 4 of them, from tyme to tyme to take speciall care to prevent all such compositions, and exactions, and if neede be to take advise how the Company may be freed and dischardged of the same, and all chardges to be borne by the company concerning the same.[1]

460. Various letters written by factors and agents in Spain were read out. It was ordered that the president should answer them 'and therein to give them thancks for their advertisements, and to lett them knowe of the companies care here to their good'.

461. The court considered a letter recently received from Totnes 'showing how farr distant and inconvenient Totnes, and the other Townes following lye from Excetour'. It was therefore ordered that Totnes and these towns should be 'clerely exempted from the government of Excetour, and that a deputy shalbe elected for Totnes, and the same severall townes to be under the Jurisdiction of Totnes viz., Dartmouth, Tynemouth, Newton boshell,

1. See above, p. xxvi, and below, **484**.

Kingsware, Kingsbridg, Salcome, Asperton, Staffarton, Broadhenson, and Toore, and no allowance to be made either to Deputy or Assistauntz'.[1]

462. [p. 133] William Greenewell a mere merchant free of the Eastland Company came and requested the freedom of the society and, in accordance with the charter, offered to procure the freedom of the Eastland Company for any one member of this society. He was told

that he should have shortly delivered unto him, by Mr. President and 4 of the Assistaunts the name of one of this company, and upon procuring of the freedome of the Eastland Company for such person so to be named, the said William Greenewell should be received and admitted into the freedome of this society accordingly.

463. Two letters were read out, one from William Nevey, deputy of Southampton, and the other from Richard Dorchester, deputy of Exeter. The letter from Richard Dorchester was referred to a court of assistants but the former was dealt with here. It merely concerned a request on behalf of Henry Plomer of Southampton for the repayment of £10

which he paid for his freedome at Southampton, when Mr. Deputy Newton and Mr. Jackson were lately there, and which they promised to repay, if the consent of the Assistaunts here, might be obtayned in regard the said Henry Plomer is sonne in law to Mr. Apsten the Customer.

However when this request was voted on in court, 'the greater number would not give their consents to repay the same, nor thought it fitt to make any such president because all other Customers would expect the like favour'.

464. [p. 134] *A general court held at Pewterers' Hall on Friday 8 November 1605 in the presence of Thomas Wilford, president, John Newton, deputy, and the following:*

465. Mr. Greene, treasurer, Mr. Newman, Mr. Lyng, Mr. Jackson, Mr. Dorrington, Mr. Bate, Mr. Savage, Mr. Furner, Mr. Wyche, Mr. Collymere, Mr. Hanger, Mr. How, Mr. Bond and divers of the generality.

466. The business of the last general court was read and confirmed.

467. The draft of a grant or commission was read out, 'whereby Mr. Hugh Bourman is elected Consull of St. Lucar and Sivill, and the whole territories of Andaluzia extending by the sea coast and begynning at Aymonty in the Candado[2] and ending at Gibraltar, within the straights mouth'. The points of the commission were agreed, and it was ordered to be engrossed and sealed with the common seal of the company at the next general court.

1. Teignmouth; Newton Bushel, now a suburb of Newton Abbot; Kingswear; Kingsbridge; Salcombe; possibly Ashprington, three miles south-east of Totnes; Staverton; Broadhempston; and the Tor Bay area.
2. Ayamonte in the Condado, the area south-west of Seville.

468. The commission itself was as follows:

To all true Christian people to whome this present wryting shall come, the President Assistaunts and fellowshipp of marchaunts of England, trading into Spaine and Portugall, send greeting in our lord [p. 135] god everlasting. Whereas our late soveraigne Lord of moast famous memory king Henry the Eight by his letters patents under the greate seale of England bearing date at Westminster the first day of September in the 22nd yere of his raigne, for the better governement of the marchaunts trading into Spaine, did aucthorize the English marchaunts to elect Consulls and Assistaunts to governe there, and to gather ymposition and to make lawes for the publique government of the generallity. And whereas the most excellent Prynce, and Emperour Charles the ffyft, king of the Romans, and of Spaine et cetera by his charter Dated the second day of September 1538 (recyting the former letters patents of King Henry the eight) Did confirme and approve the said letters patents, as by the same charter more at large may appeare; and whereas the moast excellent Prince, Don Alonso Perez de gusman, Duke of Medyna Cydonia, Marques of Cacaca in Africa, Erle of Niebla, Lord of the noble Citty of Gebraltor, in the yere of our Lord god 1517, Did graunt certen Lands and diverse priveledges and liberties to the English marchaunts in the towne of St. Lucar de Barameda, which said liberties were allowed and proclaymed there in the moneth of October in the yere 1530, and sithence ratified, and confirmed by the succeeding Dukes; and whereas in the late Articles of peace, entercourse, and Commerce, concluded upon in the names of the moast high and mighty Kings and Princes our most soveraigne Lord James by the grace of god King of greate Brytaine ffraunce and Ireland defendor of the faith et cetera, And Phillipp the third King of Spaine et cetera, and Albertus and Isabella Clara Eugenia, Archdukes of Austria, Dukes of Burgundie et cetera: it is concluded and agreed, that the graunts and priviledges, given by [p. 136] the Princes to merchaunts of either of the kingdomes commying to their said kingdomes and which priviledges through the warrs have ceased shall from thensforth wholy be revived, and have their full force and strength. Whereas also our moast gratious soveraigne lord James the kings most excellent Majesty that now is, by his highnes letters patents under his greate seale of England bearing Date at Westminster the 31st day of May last past, being in the Third yere of his highnes raigne of England, ffraunce and Ireland and of Scotland the 38th Did of his especiall grace certen knowledg and meere motion, will and for him his heires and successors graunt to us the said President Assistaunts and fellowshipp of Marchaunts of England trading into Spaine and Portugall and to our successors, that the said President and his successors or his Deputy or Deputies with the assent and consent of the said Assistaunts, or the greatest parte of them then present, for the tyme being, may and shall have power to name choose and appoint, at their will and pleasure from tyme to tyme one or more of the said fellowshipp to be our Consull or Consulls or governor or governors, in the parts of Spaine and Portugall and the Islands thereto belonging, and that the Consull or Consulls, governour or Governours so named and chosen, and every of them, togeather with six others or more of the discreetest Marchaunts of the said fellowshipp for the tyme being, to be elected by the said Consull or Consulls, governour or governours for his or their Assistaunts in that place where the said Consull or Consulls governor or governours in the said parts of Spaine and Portugall shall then be [p. 137] resident, shall have full power, and aucthority to governe in the said Domynions within the Lymitts to them by us the said President, and Assistaunts of the said fellowshipp resident in England prescribed and assigned or the greater parte of them then present, all and singuler merchaunts his Majesty's subiects and of his highnes heires and successors, as well of the said fellowshipp, as others which be not of the said fellowshipp, and their factors, Agents and servants trading merchaundize in Spaine, and Portugall, and to administer unto them and every of them, full speedy and expeditt Justice in all and every their causes plaints and contentions amongest them begun or to be begun in the said Domynions of Spaine or Portugall, and to pacifie decide and determyne, all and almanner of questions discords and striffes amongest them in any of the said Realmes of Spaine and Portugall, moved or to be moved for the better goverment of the said merchaunts in Spaine or Portugall for the tyme being, and to doe and execute all things which by the President or his Deputy and Assistaunts of the said fellowshipp for the tyme being or by the more parte of them then present, shalbe to the said Consull for the tyme being prescribed and commaunded, according to the statutes, acts and ordynaunces of the said fellowshipp, so as any of the orders ordynaunces directions or constitutions so to be prescribed be not to the hindraunce of the trade and traffique of any of the said fellowshipp, behaving him or themselves duly and orderly as becommeth good marchaunts of the said fellowshipp, without any fraudulent or disorderly attempt or practize, as by the said letters patents more fully and at lardg appeareth.

469. fforasmuch as wee the said President, Assistaunts and fellowshipp have byn sufficiently informed by diverse men of good reputation, Judgment and accoumpt [p. 138] in our Company of the aptness, experience, integrity and sufficiencie of Hugh Bourman one of our society, for the dischardg and supply of the roome office and place of a Consull, Knowe ye therefore that wee the President with the assent, not only of the greatest parte of the Assistaunts but also of the generallity of our said society being assembled and mett for that purpose at an ample and generall courte, Have named, chosen and appointed, and by these presents doe name choose and appoint the said Hughe Bourman to be our Consull or governour for St. Lucar and Sivill, and the whole territories of Andaluzia extending by the seacost and begynnyng at Aymonty in the Condado and ending at Gibraltar within the straights mouth, to have and to hold the said office during the pleasure of us the said President, Assistaunts and fellowshipp, giving and by these presents graunting unto the said Hugh Bourman full power, and aucthority to elect such discreete merchaunts of our said fellowshipp for his Assistaunts in that place, where he shalbe resident, or in any other place or places within the lymitts to him prescribed and to governe within the said lymitts, according to the purport true intent and meaning of the said graunts charters and priviledges before mentyoned, willing and requiring all the merchaunts there resident to be ayding, assisting, and obedient unto the said Hugh Bourman, in the due execution of the said office and aucthority so graunted as aforesaid, assuring ourselves that he will rule and governe with that diligence integrity and indifferency, that wee shall have no iust complaint against him, for any thing that he shall doe by vertue of the power and trust which wee comitted unto him. In witnes whereof wee the said President, Assistaunts and fellowshipp, have hereunto caused our common seale to be putt the Thirteenth day of November Anno Domini 1605, and in the yeres of the raigne of our soveraigne Lord James by the grace of god King of England, Scotland ffraunce and Ireland Defender of the faith et cetera, that is to say of England ffraunce and Ireland the Third, and of Scotland the Nyne and Thirtieth.

470. [p. 139] It was also agreed that similar commissions should be drawn up for the other four elected consuls, omitting the privileges granted by the dukes of Medina Sidonia, which related only to San Lucar and Seville, and laying down the limits allotted to them as follows:

471. Hugh Lee, consul for Lisbon, 'and the whole territories of Portugall, extending by the sea coast, and begynnyng at Caminha, and ending at Castromarin'.[1]

472. James Wych, consul for the coast of Biscay, 'begynnyng at Fuenterabia, and ending at the hethermost parte of Galitia'.

473. Francis Lambert, consul for Bayona in Galicia, 'begynnyng on the Esterne parte of Galitia and ending at the hether parte of the Kingdome of Portugall'.

474. Humphrey Wootton, consul for Malaga 'extending by the sea coast and begynnyng at Stepona and ending at Barsolona'.[2]

475. All the commissions were to be engrossed, sealed with the common seal of the company, and sent to the consuls in Spain with all possible speed.

476. Thomas Forman one of the assistants

hath ben long visited with sicknes so as he cannott Conveniently attend the service, therefore (at his request) the company have freed and dischardged him of the said place, and in his roome have elected Mr. John Castlyn one of the Assistaunts named in the charter who was by a former corte dischardged, by reason that he was for the moast parte remaynying in the Countrey, but being now abiding in the Citty, is restored to the said place and admitted accordingly.

477. [p. 140] On the first day of parliament, some objections were made in the lower chamber to the charter recently granted to the company. A committee was appointed to consider it, and to draw up a bill to be presented to the house against the charter. The company took note of this, and the president, the deputy and the secretary

resorted to the midle temple hall where the Committee satt, desiring to understand of them, in what points they did except against our charter, whereupon they delivered two propositions to this or the like effect, viz., ffirst whether the merchaunts incorporated to trade Spaine and Portugall, will permitt, and suffer that all manner of persons, that shall adventure to the sea to take fysh, may carry their fysh freely for those Countries, and there sell it at their will and pleasure and returne from thence all sorts of merchandizes att their will and pleasure.
478. The second, whether the company will permitt and suffer all gentlemen, yeomen, ffarmers and all others of what quality soever to carry corne into Spaine and Portugall, and to make their retorne in marchandize from thence at their will and pleasure.

479. The committee required the president to confer with the company, and reply before Wednesday next,

which was the chief and speciall matter that moved him to call this courte, upon full and deliberate consideration, whereunto had it is resolved and agreed that the company shall depend and stand upon the vallidity of their charter, and not to give any consent or agreement to the propositions required.

1. Castro Marim.
2. Estepona.

480. [p. 141] *A general court held at Pewterers' Hall on Wednesday 13 November 1605, in the presence of Thomas Wilford, president, John Newton, deputy, and the following:*

481. Mr. Greene, treasurer, Mr. Chamberlen, Mr. Cokayne, Mr. Newman, Mr. Jackson, Mr. Dorrington, Mr. Bate, Mr. Savage, Mr. Bowyer, Mr. Owen, Mr. Wyche, Mr. Cobb, Mr. Hanger, Mr. Bond, Mr. Bostock, Mr. Castlyn; the secretary and divers of the generality.

482. A letter was read out from Lord Knowles and Lord Wotton, the comptroller and treasurer respectively of the king's household, concerning the composition for wines and spices.

483. It was endorsed as sent 'to our loving freinds' the governor and assistants of the Spanish Company, with the rest of the merchants trading to Spain, and was as follows:

484. Whereas by the complaint of Mr. Jacobb Compounder for sweete wynes, for the expence of his Majesty's howse, as also by the answere of the said Complaint delivered in, by you the marchaunts of the Spanish Company that you not only contrary to your former course in the late queenes tyme, but also contrary to that which you have willingly paid and yeelded unto since the begynning of his Majesty's moast happy raigne, untill this present tyme, doe refuse both to pay the composition of sweete wynes, and also deny to obay his Majesty's Comision, except the full valewe [p. 142] and present payment be made for such goods as shalbe taken from you, alleadging both the stricte words of the lawe, and also the words of the charter of the Citty of London, for your defence therein, which may not (without the preiudice of his Majesty's Honor, and Royall prerogative) be suffered. These are therefore in his Majesty's name to chardg and Commaund every of you, fforthwith upon the receipt hereof, either to deliver unto the said Mr. Jacobb such wynes as he or his Deputy hath or shall marke for his Majesty's provision, according to the effect of the Commission, or to pay him such composition, as you have formerly done, and for any greviance that you shall fynde by reason of this service, hereafter upon your iust Complaint you shall fynd us ready to doe you such Justice, as in these cases with the maynetaunce of his Majesty's Prerogative is fitt and requisitt. So nothing doubting but that in your wisdomes you will forthwith satisfie this our demaund, which if you shall deny you will enforce us to a course which in our owne dispositions, and for your good wee desier to avoide considering that you in your duties ought not to deny that unto the king's majesty, which you have performed to the late Queene, wee bid you ffarwell, ffrom the courte the 12 of November 1605.
485. We requier the like at your hands for the king's Grocer in all such provisions as he hath to deale in for his Majesty's service.
W. Knowllys   E. Wootton

486. After full consideration of the matter it was agreed that the president, the deputy and the treasurer should 'take advise of some learned Counsell in the lawe, how the company may be freed from the said Composition for Wynes, Spices and diverse other purveyance'.[1] The fees would be disbursed by the treasurer and allowed him in his account.

1. See above, pp. xxvi, xlvi and **459**.

487. Edward Man of Poole in Dorset son of John Man claimed the freedom by virtue of a clause in the charter of 1577, 'because his father was an auncient trader into Spaine before Anno 1568 and was lyving when the said charter was graunted, the same being testified in open court'. Also [p. 143] Thomas Baker of Lynn son of George Baker claimed the freedom by patrimony since his father had been made free by ancient trade in 1579. They were both admitted, paying 6s. 8d. each and taking their oaths as freemen by ancient trade.

488. The two persons following were admitted by service with ancient freemen: William Cockayne, skinner, with Henry Sherratt deceased, and George Berrisford with William Cockayne the elder. They each paid 6s. 8d. to the use of the society and took the oath of a freeman by ancient trade.

489. Robert Hardy of 'Culleton' in Devon, an ancient trader into Spain before 1577 'as is well knowne to diverse present att this courte', cannot however request his freedom either by patrimony or service.[1]

Nevertheless because he hath ben so auncient a trader, it hath pleased the Company upon his humble suite to bestowe upon him the freedome of this society for his owne person gratis, and thereupon in open courte he was admitted and sworne accordingly.

490. John Andrewes, haberdasher, requested the freedom by service with William Sherrington, an ancient trader to Spain well known to divers of those present in court. However, 'there can be no record fownd to prove that the said William Sherrington was ever admitted, sworne, or made free of this society, so as the said John Androwes cannott directly proove himself capable thereof'. The company therefore agreed to bestow his freedom on him gratis for his own person, and he was admitted and sworn accordingly.

491. [p. 144] Thomas Tessemond of Norwich, a mere merchant free of no other company came to the court bringing a certificate from Leonard Holmes the deputy of Yarmouth. It testified

that the said Mr. Deputy Holmes had received of the said Thomas Tessemond to the use of this society to be sent up to Mr. Treasurer here the some of £10, for the admission of the said Thomas Tessemond into the freedome of this society by Redemption, and thereby testyfying that the said Thomas Tessemond was a meere merchaunt Capable by the true meaning of the charter.

He was therefore admitted and sworn in as a redemptioner, 'and order given to Mr. Treasurer to call for the said £10, from the said Mr. Deputy Holmes'.

492. *A general court held at Pewterers' Hall on Friday 22 November 1605 in the presence of Thomas Wilford, president, John Newton, deputy, and the following:*

1. ?Collaton near Kingsbridge, ?Collaton near Paignton, or ?Colyton near Seaton, Devon.

70

493. Mr. Greene, treasurer, Mr. Newman, Mr. Harby, Mr. Lyng, Mr. Jackson, Mr. Dorrington, Mr. Bate, Mr. Savage, Mr. James, Mr. Furner, Mr. Owen, Mr. Wyche, Mr. Hanger, Mr. How, Mr. Bond, Mr. Bostock; Mr. Harborne 'one of the Assistaunts of Yarmouth'; the secretary and divers of the generality.

494. [p. 145] The business of the last general court was read and confirmed.

495. The two persons following were admitted to the freedom by service with ancient traders: Henry Johnson, clothworker, by service with William Hancock, and John Spence [blank] by service with [blank]. Each paid 6s. 8d. to the use of the society and took the oath of a freeman by ancient trade.

496. On the humble petition of John Sozar, 'who hath byn for many yeres resident in Spaine, and thereby growne very perfect in the Spanish tongue, and upon his promise to be ready to doe the company service, either in translating of their Spanish letters or otherwise', the court decided to grant him his freedom gratis for his own person. He was admitted, taking the oath of a freeman by ancient trade.

497. Henry Waade of Topsham in Devon again resorted to this court, claiming his freedom in the manner noted at the court of 6 November 1605. He

did produce the opynions of diverse lawyers, upon that point in the charter which is mentyoned in the said order. But foreasmuchas he did not intreate the Committees aucthorized for that purpose, to be present at the conference with the said lawyers, therefore the company take further tyme to advise and consider thereof.

498. [p. 146] A petition from the merchants of Weymouth and Melcombe Regis was offered to the consideration of the court, 'to be freed and exempted from the government of Southampton, and to have a Deputy, and to governe of themselves'. The company deferred it for further consideration until the general election day, 'when the severall Deputies out of the Contry come up, that their opynions may be used therein'.

499. *A court of assistants held at Pewterers' Hall on Friday 5 December 1605 in the presence of Thomas Wilford, president, John Newton, deputy, and the following:*

500. Mr. Greene, treasurer, Mr. Newman, Mr. Harby, Mr. Jackson, Mr. Dorrington, Mr. Furner, Mr. Towerson, Mr. Style, Mr. Hanger, Mr. How, Mr. Bond, Mr. Bostock, Mr. Castlyn; the secretary.

501. A letter was read out from Sir Charles Cornewallis the ambassador in Spain to Mr. Wilford,[1]

[1] See below, **727–32.**

intymating that he expected better allowance to be made to Mr. Nicholas Oseley, alleadging he detayned him only for the companies service, and also taxing the Company with negligence and unkyndnes in not making him sooner accquainted that the King's Majesty had confirmed our Company, and that he hath not byn saluted by any of our Company sithence his going over.

502. [p. 147] The draft of the company's reply to the ambassador was read out, together with a draft of reminders and directions for Mr. Boureman to take with him to Spain, and also the draft of a letter to James Wyche the consul for Biscay. It was ordered that all these, as well as the draft of a letter to the other consuls and one to Nicholas Oseley, should be prepared and sent away with all convenient speed.

503. It was agreed that the consuls should collect, in their respective divisions,

these ympositions following, viz of the goodes and marchaundize, of all and every person and persons being free of this society, and which have taken their Corporall oath to this Company, and of all such as are beyond the seas, and may lawfully Clayme the freedome, at their retorne, a quarter of the hundreth Inward, and a like quarter of a hundreth outward, and of the goodes and merchaundizes of all and every other person and persons, one in the hundreth inwards, and one in the hundreth outwards.

504. *A court of assistants held at Pewterers' Hall on Thursday 2 January 1606 in the presence of Mr. Thomas Wilford, president, Mr. John Newton, deputy, and the following:*

505. Mr. Greene, treasurer, Mr. Newman, Mr. Lyng, Mr. Dorrington, Mr. Bowyer, Mr. Towerson, Mr. Wyche, Mr. Cobb, Mr. Hanger, Mr. How, Mr. Bond, Mr. Castlyn; the secretary.

506. [p. 148] At the request of Hugh Lea, recently elected consul for Lisbon, it was agreed that the treasurer should deliver £50 to him 'the same to be accompted as parte of his yerely fee of £100, paid unto him before hand, the better to furnish himself, for his present dispatch, and going over into Spaine to undertake the execution of the said office'.

507. It was also agreed that the treasurer should

make provision of a peece of plate of the value of £30 or thereabouts, to be presented and bestowed for a new yeeres guift, upon such person as the company have in private accquainted Mr. President, Mr. Treasurer and the Secretary, they meane to conferr and bestow the same upon.[1]

508. As the treasurer informed the company that he had disbursed in the company's affairs more than he had received, it was agreed that he should

take upp at interest the some of £200 to be used and ymployed aswell for the payment of the said £50 to Mr. Lea, and providing the said peece of plate of £30,

1. See above, p. xlvi.

as also to pay officers fees, and otherwise to be expended in the affaires of the company.

509. A petition, delivered by the company to the privy council, was read out

concerning diverse wrongs and iniuries offered us in Spaine, the same petition being also by order from the Lords of his Majesty's Most honorable privie Counsell, translated into Spanish, which their Lordshipps intend shalbe delivered to the Spanish Ambassador, the same being carefully translated by Mr. Thomas Honnyman, at the request of the Company.[1]

1. See below, **733–51.**

BOOK OF OATHS, ACTS AND ORDINANCES

(Bodleian Library, MS. Rawlinson C. 178)

510. [p. 1] The oath of a freeman by ancient trade.

You sweare to be true and faithfull to our soveraigne Lord the king, and to his heires and successors. You shalbe obedient unto the President, his deputy or deputies, and Assistaunts of the Marchaunts of England trading into Spayne and Portugall, as well on this side the Seas as beyond, in all matters touching or appertayning to the said society or fellowshipp. And you shall come to all Courts and assemblies, uppon due warning, having no reasonable excuse to the contrary, or els pay such fyne as shalbe appointed for your default when it shalbe demaunded. You shall not willingly doe consent or knowe to be done, any thing that may tend to the breach, violation, or ympeachment of any of the Privileges or graunts geven, or to be geven to this Company, on this side the Seas or beyond, without the comon consent of the same. And yf you shall knowe of any thing to be attempted, or done to the contrary; you shall with all convenient speede discover and shewe the same to the said President, or his deputy, for the tyme being. The goodes or Marchaundizes of any straunger borne, you shall not in any wise avowe, cooller or conceale, whereby the kings Majestie, his heires or successors may be defrauded of his or their Customes or duties, nor shall avow, culler, or conceale the goods or Marchaundizes of any other parson, not being free of this society. And yf you shall knowe any parson that so doth, you shall with all convenient speede, thereof informe the said President or his deputy for the tyme being. All Acts Ordinaunces and constitutions made, and hereafter to be made, and standing in force, concerning the good governement and order of this fellowshipp, or their goods wares or Marchaundices, you shall on your parte maynetayne, supporte and fullfill to your power and knowledge. Or els shall pay such fynes, paynes, penalties and mulkts, being accused condempned and orderly demaunded, As for the offendors and violaters of the same, shalbe ordayned provided and established to be paide. So help you God et cetera.

511. [p. 2] 'The Oath of a freeman receaved by Redemption (being free of some other company of Marchants). The same Oath also to be mynistred to such as are named in the patent, that neither are nor were discended of, or from the auntient freedome, and therefore nowe to be admytted and receaved as Redemptioners'.

512. You sweare to be true and faithfull to our soveraigne Lord the king his heires and successors; you shalbe obedient unto the President, his Deputy or Deputies and Assistaunts of the Marchaunts of England trading into Spayne or Portugall, (whereunto you are nowe admytted by Redemption), aswell on this side the Seas, as beyond, in all matters touching or appertayning to the said society or fellowshipp. [Thereafter as **510.**]

74

513. [p. 3] The oath of a freeman received by redemption, not being free of any other company of merchants and not being named in the patent.

514. You sweare to be true and faithfull to our soveraigne Lord the king his heires and successors, you shalbe obedient unto the President his deputie or deputies, and Assistaunts of the Marchaunts of England trading into Spayne and Portugall, (whereunto you are now admitted by Redemption) as well on this side the Seas, as beyond, in all matters touching or appertayning to the said societie or fellow-shipp: you likewise sweare that you neither are free, nor will clayme by Patry-mony or service the freedome of any other society of marchaunts, which was incorporated at the tyme and date of his Maiesties letters patents of Incorporation to this Company graunted, nor that you are any Retayler, Artificer, Inholder, Farmor, common Marriner, or handicrafts-man. You shall come to all Courts and Assemblies. [Thereafter as **510**.]

515. [p. 4] The oath of the president.

You sweare to be true and faithfull to our soveraigne lord the king his Heires and successors, you shall support and maynetayne to your power all the Marchaunts of England trading into Spayne and Portugall, so long as you shall remayne in the Office of President. Right and iustice you shall doe to all parsons, in all matters and questions that shall depend before you as President, without favour or affeccion malice or displeasure. All acts ordynaunces and constitutions by you, or your deputy and the Assistaunts and fellowshipp made, or to be made, you shall truly and indifferently observe mayntayne and execute, so long as they shall stand in force, having no singular respect unto yourself in derogation of the Comon wealth of the Company. And also to your power shall assist and help all the Officers of this Corporation and Company in all their lawfull and iust doings touching or concerning the mayntenaunce of the privileges graunts and ordyn-aunces, made or to be made, by force of the said letters patents or otherwise. So help you god et cetera.

516. [p. 5] The oath to be administered to the deputy for London and also to the deputies for the country.

You sweare to be true and faithfull to our soveraigne Lord the king, his heires and successors; you shall supporte and mayntayne to your power, all the Mar-chaunts of England trading into Spayne and Portugall, so long as you shall remayne in the office of Deputy. Right and Justice you shall doe to all parsons, in all matters and questions that shall depend before you as Deputy, without favour or affection, malice or displeasure. All Acts, Ordynaunces and constitutions by the President and Assistaunts, or by the President Assistaunts and fellowshipp made, or to be made, you shall truly and indifferently observe maynetayne and execute, (within your charge), so long as they shall stand in force.[1] [Thereafter as **515**.]

517. [p. 6] The oath of the sixty-one assistants.

You sweare to be true and faithfull to our soveraigne Lord the king his heires and successors, you shall in all your power, knowledg and best advise assist the President his Deputy or deputies, and fellowshipp of Marchaunts of England

---

1. Opposite the words 'within your charge' is a note in the margin, 'Omytt these wordes out of the Oath for London'.

trading into Spayne and Portugall, in making good and quiett order and governement, aswell of the Marchaunts of this society, as of their goods and Marchaundizes without any singuler regarde to your self, and also in the iust and indifferent execution of all such Acts, and ordynaunces, as by comon consent according to the letters patents are or shalbe made, so long as they shall stand in force, without shewing any favour, or doing any oppression to any parson. The privileges and graunts contayned in the letters patents of Corporation lately graunted, or hereafter to be graunted, to this society, either on this side the Seas, or beyond the Seas, you shall to your uttermost power maynetayne supporte and observe, without consenting to the violation or breach of them, or any of them, without the common consent of the said Company. Right and iustice you shall doe to your power to all parsons in all matters and questions depending afore you, without favour affection malice or displeasure. So help you God et cetera.

518. The oath for the assistants in the country [is identical to **517**, 'saving they are onely to be Assistaunt to the Deputy and the Marchaunts within their lymits and Jurisdiction'].

519. [p. 7] The oath of the treasurer general.

You sweare to be true and faithfull to our soveraigne lord the king his heires and successors, and the whole society of the Marchaunts of England trading into Spayne and Portugall. And for the tyme you shalbe Treasorer, you shall duly and truly receave and pay, all manner of duties, fforfects, Arrerages,[1] or other charges to the said Societie growing, or in any wise belonging, so as it may lawfully come to your possession and knowledge; and also shall truly Accompt for your tyme to the President Assistaunts and Society, for the tyme being, or to such parsons as shalbe by them assigned. So help you God et cetera.

520. The oath of the treasurer in the country [is as **519** except for the insertion of the words 'within your Jurisdiction' after 'Arrerages or other charges', and the addition of 'or appointed' after the final word 'assigned'].

521. [p. 8] The oath of the secretary.

You sweare to be true and faithfull to our soveraigne Lord the king his Heires and successors; you shalbe dilligent and attendaunt in the affaires of the President Assistaunts and fellowshipp of Marchaunts of England trading into Spaine and Portugall, at all tymes lawfull and requisite, (not infringing or violating your Oath or duty to other services formerly made). You shall make due reporte to the President or his Deputy, and to the said Assistaunts and fellowshipp (when you shalbe required) of all manner of things apperteyning to your office and charge (to your knowledge). You shall Justly and truly Register and write, or cause to be registred and written, All Ordinaunces, Decrees and Statutes made, or to be made, by the said President or his Deputy, and the Assistaunts for the tyme being, or by them, and the generalitie, during the tyme that you shall execute the office of Secretariship, in reasonable and convenient tyme after they or any of them shalbe concluded and made, and come to your knowledge and understanding. The Secrets of the Company you shall keepe, and nothing thereof disclose to others to th'entent to hurt the Company, or any Brother of the same. Copies of Acts and ordynaunces passed at any Court of Assistaunts or generallitie, you shall not deliver, without the consent of the President, or his Deputie, and of the Assist-

1. Arrears.

aunts, or the more parte of them present at some Courte. And you shall honestly
and faithfully execute the said Office of Secretariship during such tyme as you shall
use and enioy the same, in all points, as a faithfull Assistaunt and Secretary of the
said Fellowshipp ought to doe. Soe help you God et cetera.

522. [p. 9] The oath of the beadle.

You sweare to be true and faithfull to our soveraigne Lord the king his heires and
successors. You shalbe attendant and dilligent to the President, or his Deputy or
Deputies, concerning the Common wealth or behoof of this society of Marchaunts
of England, trading into Spayne and Portugal during the tyme you shall contynue
in the Office of Beadle or Officer. And you shall honestly and curteously behave
yourself to the said President or his Deputy or Deputies, and to all and every
other of the same society: you shall duly truly and faithfully make reporte of all
manner of thinges appertayning to your Office and charge. And you shall truly
from tyme to tyme Accoumpt and discharge yourself, aswell to the said President,
or his Deputy, as to the Treasorer, for the tyme being of all such somes of Money
as may in any manner of way come to your hands, for and to the use of the said
society. So help you God et cetera.

523. The oath of the servant sent into Spain and Portugal.

You sweare to be true and faithfull to our soveraigne Lord the king his heires and
successors, you shall not cullour convey nor take in charge, any the Goods wares
or Marchaundizes of any parson or parsons, borne within the kings maiesties
Dominions not free of this fellowshipp, to be transported or brought to or from
any the parts of Spayne and Portugall, or either of them, or to, or from any the
Islands comprehended within our priviledge, contrary to the Ordynaunces of this
Society. So help you God et cetera.

524. [p. 10] The oath of the clerk in the country.

You sweare to be true and faithfull to our soveraigne lord the king, his heires and
successors. You shalbe dilligent and attendant to the Deputy for the tyme being
of that place, and for that Jurisdiction whereof you are elected Clarck, and to
the society of marchaunts of England trading into Spain and Portugal, at all
tymes requisite. You shall duly and truly observe and obey all such commaunde-
ments as you shalbe commaunded to doe by the said Deputy for the tyme being,
touching the Companies affaires and busines. And you shall honestly and curteously behave your self, to the said Deputy and all other of the said society. You
shall also make due reporte to the said Deputy, of all manner of thinges appertayning to your office and charge. You shall iustly and truly register and write, or
cause to be registred and written, All Ordynaunces, Decrees and Statutes made,
or to be made, by the said Deputy, and the Assistaunts for the tyme being, or by
them and the society, during the tyme that you shall execute the office of Clarcke,
Incontynently after they or any of them shalbe concluded and made. The Secrets
of the Company you shall keepe, and nothing thereof disclose to others, to the
hurt of the Company, or any brother of the same. Coppies of any Acts, privileges,
ordynaunces or other things passed at any Courte of Assistauntz or generallity,
you shall not deliver, without the consent of the Deputy and Assistaunts. So help
you God et cetera.

525. The oath of the beadle in the country [is similar to **522**, substituting the
words 'to the deputy for the tyme being of that place, and for that Jurisdiction

whereof you are elected Beadle', for 'to the President, or his Deputy or Deputies', and 'deputy' for 'president' in the following sentences].

526. [p. 11] Acts and ordinances. An act for choosing the president.

There shalbe then Three or more worshipfull and discreete parsons named, free of the Company, which shalbe thought fitt by the greater nomber assembled, to supply the roome and office of the President, whereof the old President shalbe named to be one. Which nomynation being made and agreed, the Deputy (or in his absence two of the auntientest of the Assistaunts then present) shall sitt in the place of the President, and by question mynistred to the whole company, they shall proceede to the Election by holding up of hands, and he of the three which shalbe chosen by the greater nomber of the hands, shalbe and remayne President for one whole year, and from thence untill an other shalbe chosen and sworne, according to the tenor of the letters patents, and shall take the Oath appointed for the President.

527. [p. 12] An act for choosing the deputy. Three or more freemen of the company, including the previous deputy, shall be nominated, 'being named by question mynistred to the whole Company'. The person then elected

shalbe and remayne deputy during the pleasure of the President, Assistaunts and fellowship, and to be removed, when they or a greater nomber of them present at any generall Courte shall thincke fitt, according to the tenor of the letters patents; and shall take the Oath appointed for the deputy, like as the President, mutatis mutandis.

528. An act for choosing the assistants in London.

After the choosing of the President and his Deputy, the Assistaunts that were the yere before, shalbe discharged of their office and roome of Assistaunts, and then the generalitie shall nomynate such and so many others, as they shall thinck meete to supply the roome and office of Assistaunts for the Cittie of London, out of which parsons, there shalbe chosen by Election of the greatest nomber of hands Thirtie parsons: which thirty parsons so elected shall remaine for Assistaunts one whole yere following, and untill a new election be made of the Assistaunts of the same fellowshipp, and shall take the Oath appointed for the Assistaunts [p. 13] Provided allwaies, that yf any of the Assistauntz so chosen, fortune to dye, or will wilfully absent himself from the Courte when he shalbe lawfullie warned thereunto, or be in the parts beyond the Seas: in the roome of such there shalbe others chosen in a generall Courte, from tyme to tyme, to supply the roome of hym or them so dying, or absenting himself, to contynue the residue of the yere and untill a new election as aforesaid, and shall take the like Oath appointed for the Assistaunts. Provided also that he or they that hath served as an Assistaunt one whole yere, shalbe one whole yere after, free from election, to be an Assistaunt againe.

529. An act for choosing the thirty assistants in the country, according to the charter.

There shalbe Thirtie parsons named to be Assistaunts, out of such Citties, townes, and places out of the Cittie of London, as shall seeme good to the Company, from tyme to tyme. Of which Assistaunts, every Deputy in every Division of the Country shalbe one, which said Thirty Assistaunts together with the other Thirty Assistaunts to be chosen for London as aforesaid, and the Secretary of the Company for the tyme being, make up the full nomber of 61 Assistaunts, according to the trewe intent and meaning of the Chartre lately graunted to this Societie.

530. [p. 14] An act for choosing the treasurer. Three or more nominations shall be made for the office of treasurer, by questions asked of the whole company. The elected treasurer shall hold office for one full year, taking the oath appointed. 'And having once executed the Office of Treasorer, shall never after be charged againe with that Office.'

531. The office of the treasurer.

Every parson chosen Treasorer, and refusing it without lawfull cause shewed to the contrary shall forfeit Tenn pounds. The Treasorer shall yerely at the tyme of his Election or the next Court after, become bounden by one obligation to the said Society by such name or names as they are by Chartre incorporated in the some of ffyve hundreth pounds with condition to make a just and trew Accompt[1] of all such somes of money as he shall receave to the use of the Company, and truly to pay the remaynder due uppon the foote of the Accompt within ten daies after the publishing thereof.
532. [p. 15] He shall during his Office use all dilligence, to levy and receave all manner of Debts, fforfeits and brocks belonging to the Company, and attend at every Courte generall or of Assistaunts, without speciall lycence to the contrary, uppon payne of ffive shillings forfeiture, of and for every his default.
533. Yf any parson being indebted to the Company for any cause, doe refuse to pay to the Treasorer the some due, he requiring the same; he shall informe the President or his Deputy thereof, who by the advise of the Assistaunts, shall take order for the levying of it.
534. Yf any presentment be made to the Treasorer of any offence commytted against ordynaunce, he shall cause the same to be registred in a Booke, therefore to be appointed. But he shall not bewray the name of the Presentor to any parson, but to the President or his Deputy. But if the parson presented requier to knowe his accuser, he shall iustifie his presentment in Courte.
535. He shall likewise receave of the Beadle the absence money, and charge his Accompt with it.
536. He shall at the next generall Court after he shalbe dismissed from the office of Treasorer, exhibite his Accompt of all the money that he hath receaved and paid during his office to the Companies use.
537. He shall deliver to his Successor all such Bonds money and other things, as shalbe found to remayne in his hands, by the Auditors assigned for the taking of his Accompt, within Tenn daies after the Auditing and determynation thereof.

538. [p. 16] For auditing the treasurer's account.

The Munday yerely before the Assention day or at the next generall Court, Eight expert parsons of the Companyes affaires, whereof three at the least to be of the Assistaunts shalbe appointed Auditors for the Treasorer's Accompte.
539. The Auditors warned at any tyme for the taking of that Accompt, shall appeere at the hower and place appointed by the President or his Deputy, upon payne of Three shillinges fowre-pence of every of them that maketh Default.

1. The original version which has been crossed out reads 'put in two sufficient suerties in a reasonable some to be allowed by the Assistaunts to make a iust and true Accompt'. A note in the margin records that the alteration was made at the general court of 12 July 1605.

540. They shall examyne the ould Ballaunce and make a newe, subscribed with their hands, or ffyve of them at the least.

541. They shall not passe the Accompt, without the hands of ffyve of them at the least.

542. They shall allowe no some of Money without Act of Courte, nor any fee or Annuity without a Quittaunce.

543. They shall at the next Court of Assistaunts after the Accompt is fully audited, bring in the iust rest of the Treasorer's Accompt in writing.

544. [p. 17] An act for choosing the secretary after the death or resignation of Richard Langley, the present secretary, who holds the office granted to him by the charter for his lifetime.

545. There shalbe two or more discreete and meete parsons named, to supply the roome and Office of the Secretary, whereof the Secretary for the yere before shalbe one, and by question mynistred to the whole Company, they shall proceede to Election by houlding up of hands.

The elected person shall hold office for a year and take the oath appointed.

546. [p. 18] The office of the secretary who is to be chosen as aforesaid.

The said Secretary of this Company shalbe dilligent and attendaunt, at all tymes requisite, for matters towching the Company.

547. He shall obey the Commaundement of Maister President or his Deputy and the Assistaunts and fellowship, concerning the behalf or availes of the Company.

548. He shalbe of a curteous and honest behaviour to Maister President or his Deputy, and to the fellowship aforesaid.

549. He shall make due and true reporte of any thing belonging to his charge and office, when he shalbe required.

550. He shall write and register all Acts made in convenyent tyme after they be concluded.

551. He shall have Twenty pounds stipend a yere to be paide Quarterly by the Treasorer.

552. He shall register every Treasorers Accompt, being audited and underwritten by the Auditors, and shall have therefore Twenty shillings.

553. [p. 19] He may in the Pamphelet mend the phrase or Inditing by taking adding or altering any wordes, so as the meaning be not altered, and that the amendement be read at the next Courte, and be confirmed yf it be liked.

554. When any parson now being Apprentice, or which hereafter shalbe apprentice, shall clayme his freedome by Apprenticehood, the Secretarie shall enter into the Pamphelet the date of the Indenture, and nomber of yeres therein contayned, and shall thereof keepe a severall Booke, and shall have therefore twelve pence. Also he shall enter the Claymes of all such as requier the freedome either by Patrimony or by Redemption, and shall likewise have therefore twelve pence.

555. He shall keepe a booke of Inrolements of Indentures of Apprenticehood, either taken heere or certefied from any Cittie or Towne, and shall have for th'inrolement of any Indenture twelve pence.

556. At every Courte generall, or of Assistaunts, he shall reade at the end of the Courte that which passed that day, and at the next Courte he shall reade againe, that passed at the last Courte, ymediatly before the entring into the matters of the Courte, to th'intent it may be ratefied or disanulled as the Company shall finde occasion.

557. [p. 20] An act for choosing the beadle [is the same as **545**].

558. The office of the beadle.

The Officer called the Beadle shall geve his dilligent attendaunce uppon Maister President or his Deputy and their Commaundement, touching the businesses or affaires of the Company, shall observe and obey to his power.

559. He shall every Courte aswell of Assistaunts as generall keepe a note to the best of his power, who shalbe absent being lawfully warned, or who cometh late after three strokes of the hammer, and at the next Courte Deliver their names to the Treasorer.

560. [p. 21] He shall demaunde of every parson that maketh default at any Court generall, or of Assistaunts, or cometh late to either of them, such some of money as by the ordynance is due for his Default or absence.

561. And yf any parson (being Demaunded by the Beadle) doe refuse or doe not pay to hym such some of money as is due for his default or absence, he shall enforme the President or his Deputy or the Treasorer thereof.

562. He shall informe the President or his Deputy or the Treasorer, of all offences done, against any of the ordynaunces, whereof he shall have any knowledge.

563. And yf he shall conceale any offence which he knoweth to be done, against any of the ordynaunces, and doth not within fowerteene dayes after knowledg or Information thereof had, disclose and utter the same to the President or his Deputy or Treasorer, shall forfeit his office.

564. He shall have for his yerely fee or Sallary Twenty Marcks.

565. He shall monethly deliver to the Treasorer, all such somes of money, as he shall receave for absence or late coming to the Courte, and shalbe allowed for his collection three shillings and fowrepence in the pound, and so after the rate.

566. He shall have a fowrth part of all such bracks as he shall present, whereof the parson accused shalbe Condempned, and shall remayne with the Company.

567. [p. 22] For persons 'put in election' for any office. 'All parsons nomynated to supply any Roome or Office shall depart the Court, untill the Election be past.'

568. For removing the secretary and the beadle who were elected as aforesaid.

And yf such Secretary or Beadle which shalbe so elected as aforesaid fortune to Dye, or to be found insufficient to performe that which is expected, or of themselves will leave their Office or otherwise will absent themselves, whereby the business of the Company shalbe omytted, in such a Case it shalbe lawfull for the Company to make choise of some other to supply the Roome or Office of hym in whome the Default shalbe found, when and as often as neede shall require.

569. [p. 23] The ordinance for keeping courts, for fines, and for lack of appearance after due warning, for both the assistants and the generality.

570. It shalbe lawfull for the President or his Deputy for the Common weale and benifitt of the Company, or for any urgent cause, to call the Company together and keepe either a generall Court or a Court of Assistaunts, on any Day whatsoever (not being Sunday or any principall of solempne feast of any Evangelist or Appostle) to the which Court and Courts, every parson free of the Company being warned by the Beadle shall and is bound to come.

571. And yf any of the generallity being warned, doe not come to the generall Courte, having noe reasonable excuse to the contrary and so to be aiudged by the President or his Deputy, and the greatest number of the Assistaunts then present, shall forfeit for every tyme that he shall make default as aforesaid twelve pence.
572. And every one coming after the President be set, or his Deputy after three strokes given with the hammer, having no reasonable excuse, and adiudged as aforesaid, shall forfeyt sixpence.
573. And yf any shall departe the Courte, and have no leave of the President or his Deputy, shall forfeit sixpence.
574. And he that absenteth himself three Court dayes one after another without lycence or lawfull excuse, shall forfeit five shillings.
575. And every Assistaunt being warned, and not coming to the Court, but absenteth himself from the Court, and having no leave of the President or his Deputy nor reasonable excuse to the contrary, to be adiudged as beforesaid shall forfeit two shillings.
576. [p. 24] And coming late to the Court, having no reasonable excuse to be adiudged as aforesaid, shall forfeit twelve pence.
577. And every of the Assistaunts that shall absent himself three Court daies one after an other being lawfully warned by the Beadle, having no reasonable excuse to the contrary, and so adiudged as aforesaid, shall forfeit tenn shillings.
578. And every parson that shalbe warned to appeere upon a payne certen that shall make default of Apparaunce having no reasonable excuse to the contrary, and so adiudged, shall without favour pardon or myttigation pay the some and penaltie whereuppon he was warned, so the same exceede not Twenty shillings.
579. And that there shalbe present at every Court aswell of the Assistaunts as of the generality Thirteene Assistaunts at the least, or els nothing to be concluded at the Court, where such number shall lack.
580. And all things passed at any Court of Assistaunts, shalbe read at the end of the Court, and begyning of the next Court of Assistaunts, and likewise all things passed at a generall Court shalbe read at th'end of the Court, and begyning of the next generall Court.
581. All parsons commaunded by the President or his Deputy to depart the Court for any reasonable cause shall depart uppon payne to receave such Judgment and pay such fyne, as shalbe appointed and assessed by the greater parte of the Assistaunts then present at every such Court when any such contempt shalbe commytted.

582. [p. 25] For placing and setting of the assistants.

The Assistaunts shall sitt neere the President and his Deputie, as by the President and his Deputy they shalbe appointed. And yf any of the Society shall take uppon him to sitt in the Roome and place of the Assistaunts, He shall forfeit Twelve pence. Provided that every parson that is an Alderman, Justice of Peace in his Country, or hath borne Office of Maior in any Cittie or Towne Corporate, shall and may take place amongst the Assistaunts.

583. For setting and placing of the generality.

The Generallitie shall sitt next beneath the Assistaunts every one according to his calling and auncientry in the company namely such as have passed the Roome of Assistaunts, shall sitt highest and nearest the Assistaunts for the tyme being. And yf any question or curiosety do arise, or be offred, by any parsonn, for sitting or placing, Every such parson shalbe directed by the President or his Deputy, and shall sitt where he shalbe appointed, uppon payne every tyme to forfeit Twelve-pence, for refusing to sitt where hee shalbe appointed.

584. [p. 26] For direction and order of speech in court.

ffor avoyding of all confusion and superfluous speeches and talke in Courte, either Generall or of Assistaunts, it is ordred and enacted that such parson as first standeth up, shalbe first heard. And that no parson shall speake, while an other is speaking, nor yet one to an other, after silence is commaunded by the President or his Deputy, but shall give attentive eare to hym that is speaking: who (standing and uncovered) shall direct his speach to the President or his Deputy onely, without namyng any other person, and shall frame his speach but to the matter propounded or in question, neither shall any man speake but thrice to one matter, without Lycence of the President or his Deputy, uppon payne to forfeit every tyme that he shall offend contrary to this Act Twelve pence.

585. [p. 27] For decent speech in court.

It is ordred and enacted that no parson of this society shall in open Court use any unseemely or reprochfull speach, but shall in comely and quiet manner speake to the matter propounded. And yf any evill language be given that may breede offence, contrary to the meaning of this Act, and so adiudged by the Court, the party offending shall forfeit six shillings and eight pence, for every tyme that he shall offend.

586. For silence to be kept in court. 'If the President or his Deputy shall with the stroke of the Hammer, or otherwise commaund silence to be kept, the parson not obeying or speaking so, shall forfeit Twelve pence.'

587. [p. 28] That a party to a matter named in court shall absent himself and his father, son, brother and partner. 'Yf any matter be moved in Courte which may concerne any parson present in court, that party whome the matter concerneth, his father Sonne Brother and partiner shall depart the Courte so long as the matter is treated uppon'.

588. Against disclosing of matters passed in court.

Yf any Brother of this Society shall reveale or disclose any matters treated of or passed in any Courte, either Generall or of Assistaunts, to any parson, not being free of this Company, to the hurt or displeasure of any of this Company; the party so offending shall forfeit, for the first tyme six shillings eight pence, for the second tyme thirteene shillings fower pence, for the third tyme twentie shillings. And yf the disclosing of the secrets or speeches turne the whole Company to any hurt or displeasure, then he or they so disclosing shall pay such fyne as shalbe ceassed by the President his Deputy, Assistaunts, and generality. Or els shalbe Crost the Howse and loose the benifitt of his freedome of this Society forever.

589. [p. 29] The sums of money to be paid on admission by those named in the letters patent.

Every parson named in the letters patents (not being already sworne) clayming his ffreedome before the feast of Christmas next, and who hath right thereunto as a Marchaunt by auntient trade, shall pay at his admyssion to the Treasorer for the tyme being, to the use of the Company, six shillings and eight pence, and to the Secretary for entring his name twelve pence, and to the Beadle six pence, and shall take the Oath of a freeman by auntient trade. And all such as are named in the letters patents (not being already sworne) who have already paid to the use of the society Ten pownds a peece, shall severally pay to the Secretary (for entring his and their names) two shillings and to the Beadle twelve pence apeece, and shall take the Oath of freemen by Redemption. And all others whose names are inserted into the charter, who weare not either the sonnes or servaunts of freemen heretofore admytted by auntient trade, and have not paied their ffynes of tenn pownds a peece, to the use of the society, shall at their admyssions pay to the Treasorer the said some of Tenn powndes a peece, and to the Secretary for entring their names, two shillings and to the Beadle twelve pence, and shall likewise take the Oath of a freeman by Redemption.

590. [p. 30] For the admission of ancient merchants not named in the letters patent.

Every auncient marchaunt not named in the charter, who by the trewe intent and maning of the Chartre may lawfully clayme the freedome, either by birth or service, shalbe admytted, paying like fyne, as is taken of auncient Marchaunts, whose names are remembred in the letters patents, and taking the Oath appointed for a freeman by ancient trade.

591. An act that every freeman shall have a copy of his oath.

To th'entent that every ffreeman may be the more carefull to observe and performe his Oath, it is ordered and agreed, that the Secretary shall Deliver to every freeman, the trew Copy of the Oath mynistred unto him at his admyssion into this society, for which Copy it shalbe lawfull to the Secretary to Demaund and to take the some of six pence of every such freeman.

592. [p. 31] For the admission of mere merchants to be received by redemption.

Every parson and parsons being the king's subiects as now be or hereafter shalbe meere marchaunts and which by the lawes and statutes of this realme, may use the trade of marchaundize, from or into this realme of England, (except all Retailers, Artificers, Inholders farmours Comon marriners and handycrafts men. And also except all such as now be, or hereafter shalbe free of any speciall incorporation or Company of Marchaunts, trading by force of any act of Parliament, Chartre or letters Patents into any the parts beyond the Seas) shalbe receaved and admytted into this society by Redemption. So as they require it within one yere after the date of the Letters pattents, and pay Tenn powndes, or within the second yeere and pay Fyfteene pownds, or at any tyme after th'end of the said Two years and pay Twenty pownds to the use of the said society, and to the Secretary (for entring every of their names) two shillings, and to the Beadle twelve pence. And shall take the Oath appointed for a Redemptioner, to be receaved as aforesaid.'

593. [p. 32] An act of grace and favour for the admission into the freedom of those who have been mere merchants for the full term of seven years.

594. Whereas in and by the last Chartre graunted to this society the Company are required to receave into their freedom all and every parson and parsons being his Maiesties subiects, which then were or shalbe meere Marchaunts, and which by the lawes and statutes of this Realme may lawfully use the trade of Marchaundize from or into the Realme of England (excepting Retailers and such other parsons as in and by the said Chartre are mencioned). And whereas doubt and

84

question hath ben made, whether a man that hath ben a shopp keeper, and for the space of divers yeres hath given over his trade, who was not brought up in the trade of Marchaundize seaven yeres at the least as an apprentice, may be refused to be admytted into the freedome of this society, by the wordes of the said Chartre, the company being desyrous to carry an even and indifferent hand, and observing that by the lawes and Statutes of this realme, no man may use or exercise any manuell trade, or occupation (being farr inferior to the profession of a marchaunt) but such as have ben brought up therein seaven yeres at the least as an apprentice, Doe therefore at this Court upon full and deliberate consideration, order and agree, that every parson and parsons, which during the full space and terme of seaven yeres together, hath onely used or hereafter shall use, the trade of marchaundize, without keeping any shopp or using any other trade withall, [p. 33] but onely lyved as a meere marchaunt (Except all such as now be, or hereafter shalbe free of any speciall incorporation or Company of Marchaunts, trading by force of any act of Parliament, Chartre or letters patents, into any the parts beyond the Seas) shall and may from and after such tyme as he or they have or hath, or hereafter shall have onely used the trade of a meere marchaunt, during such full term of seaven yeres in forme aforesaid be admytted and received into the freedome of this society by Redemption for such fyne and fynes (according to the tyme they shall require the said freedome) as in and by the said Charter is lymited.

595. For the admission by redemption of those free of any other society of merchants.

Every parson and parsons being the kings subiects as nowe be, or hereafter shalbe free of any speciall incorporation or Company of marchaunts trading by force of any act of Parliament, charter or letters patents into any the parts beyond the Seas, (except all Retailers, Artificers, Inholders, farmors, Comon marriners and handicrafts men, who are specially excluded out of this incorporation) shalbe received and admytted into this society by Redemption, when they shall require the same. So as they offer and [p. 34] pay to Mr. President or his Deputy for the tyme being to the use of this society, at the tyme of his or their admyttaunce, such some and somes of money as is usually paid by others requiring to be admytted by redemption, into such other fellowshipp or Company, whereof such parsons so requiring to be admytted into this incorporation shalbe then free, or otherwise shall procure such and so many freedoms without fyne, for such and so many and the like nomber of this society (to be from tyme to tyme nomynated by the President of this society, and any fower or more of the Assistants for the tyme being) into such other fellowshipp or Company, whereof such parson or parsons so requiring to be admytted into this society shalbe then free. And paying to the Secretary (for entring every of their names) Two shillings, and to the Beadle twelvepence and shall take the Oath appointed for a Redemptioner, to be so received as aforesaid.

596. That no retailer or artificer etc. shall be received into the freedom. 'No Retailer, Artificer, Inholder, farmor, Comon marriner, or handycrafts man shalbe received or admytted into the freedom of this society for any fyne.'

597. [p. 35] The admission of sons and apprentices of redemptioners. 'The Sonne or Apprentice of a Redempcioner shall pay successively such fyne as his father or master paid, or ought to have paid, at the tyme of his admyssion.'

598. The term for which an apprentice shall be bound.

No man free of this Company shall after Michaelmas next Anno 1605 take any Apprentice to be bownde for any lesse terme then Eight yeres, nor the yeres of any apprentice shall end before he be of the age of fower and twenty years upon payne of Twenty pownde. Neverthelesse it shalbe lawfull to the Master of every such apprentice, at th'end of seaven yeares, to make his apprentice free of this society (yf the Apprentice shall faithfully serve, during the said seaven yeres), So as every such Apprentice shalbe then of the full age of fowre and twenty yeres.

599. [p. 36] The fine payable on the admission of an apprentice who has been set over.

Also yf any Apprentice by the Death of his Master with whome he was first bownd, or upon any other occasion be sett over, to any brother of the Company for the residue of his terme, He shall at his Admyssion into the freedome, pay such fyne as he should have done, by being made free by his first maister. And shalbe translated over by the consent of the Company, and his translation endorsed upon the back of the Indentur by the Secretary of this Company.

600. Those persons who may claim the freedom by patrimony.

All parsons clayming the freedome of this Company by Patrymony, shalbe borne meere English (that is to say) within the king's Domynions, or made a Denizen by acte of Parliament, and shalbe of the Age of Twenty and one yeres at the least.

601. [p. 37] Against the marriage of an apprentice during his term, or his using merchandise to his own use, etc.

Apprentice taken after this day (being the 30 day of August Anno domino 1605) marying before the expiration of his terme, or doing feate of Marchaundize to his owne use, without lycence of his master, or absenting himself willingly, contrary to the will of his master, by the space of two monethes, shall never enioy the freedome of the Company by Apprentizehood.

602. The apprentice to show his indenture and to bring his certificate.

An Apprentice clayming his freedome by Apprentizehood, shall shewe forth his Indenture in due forme made in Cittie, Borough or Towne Corporate, with a letter from his maister, (yf he be not present in Court) testefying that he hath well and truly served him as an Apprentize, according to the Ordynaunce.

603. [p. 38] Against an untrue certificate of the service of the apprentice.

If any parson shall at any tyme hereafter write Declare avowe or testefy, by his letter or otherwise, for the iust and true Service of his Apprentice, whereby such Apprentice shall attaine and enioye the freedome of this Company, and the testymony or declaration shall afterward be disproved, such a maister so offending shall forfeit to the use of the society Tenn poundes, and the Apprentize so fraudulently made free shalbe Disfranchised and Dismyssed out of the Company.

604. That every person shall confer with the secretary before he demand his freedom.

Every parson clayming or desyring his freedome by Patrymony, Apprentizehood, or otherwise, shall present himself two or three Daies before the Courte to the

Secretary, to the intent he may informe the Courte of such matters, as shalbe requisite in his admyssion, or els shall not be admytted at this Courte.

605. [p. 39] The form of indentures of apprenticehood.

And to the intent it may appeere at the taking of every Apprentice, whether it were ment he should be bownde for the trade of Spayne and Portugall or no, it is therefore ordayned and enacted, that in all Indentures of Apprentizehood, by which any apprentice shall clayme to be made free of this society, which shalbe made after Michaelmas next coming which shalbe anno Domino 1605 these wordes shalbe inserted, 'et mercatori Anglie mercantes in Hispaniam et Portugaliam' or in English, 'And Marchaunt of England trading into Spayne and Portugall' or to the like effect. Or els that Indenture of Apprentizehood and touching the freedome of this Company shalbe voide and of none effect.

606. For the freedom gratis. 'All parsons admytted into the freedome of this Company gratis, upon petition, and not named in the Charter shall enioy their freedom but for their owne parson onely.'

607. [p. 40] For the reading of letters and requests.

All Letters requests or writings directed to the President and Assistaunts shalbe openly published, at the next Court of Assistaunts to be holden after the delivery of them. And all letters, requests, or writings, directed to the President, Assistaunts and generallity, shalbe openly published at the next generall courte to be holden after the delivery of them, upon payne that every parson that shall neglect or hinder the performance thereof shall forfeit Twenty shillings, and such other fyne as such Courte, to whom the same respectively shalbe directed, shall order and appointe.

608. [p. 41] An act for the execution of ordinances.

Even as no comon weale, Company or fellowshipp can prosper or contynue without good acts ordynaunces constitutions and lawes, whereby we restrayne malefactors, and to punish offenders, Even so such Acts ordynaunces constitutions and lawes wilbe of smale force and effect, yf they be not (when occasion may serve) put in Due execution. It is, therefore for the better governement of this company ordayned and enacted, that yf any parson free of the same, shall transgress and breake any Act or ordynaunce made by comon consent of the Company, it shalbe lawfull for any parson to informe the President or his Deputy or Treasorer within every Devizion of the offence commytted, specially mencioning the tyme and place, and all other circumstaunces, which may manifest and playnely sett forth the matter. Which information or presentment the Secretary shall register in a Booke therefore to be kept, which booke he shall keepe secrett, and not shew to any parson, but to the President, his Deputy or Treasorer, nor shall by any meanes discover the name of the Presentor or informer.

609. [p. 42] The Treasorer shall by the officer commaund every parson presented to put in suerties for the some supposed to be forfeited, to aunswer to the matter presented, and to pay that he shalbe condempned in which sureties shall sett their hands to a booke therefore provided. And the parson so warned refusing, or not doing of yt, shall by vertue and force of our letters patents be commytted to ward by the President, or his Deputy and Assistaunts, untill he shall have accomplished this order, And refusing to go to ward being commaunded by the said President or his Deputy and Assistaunts or the more parte of them assembled shall forfeit to the use of the Company Twenty pownds.

610. Any parson presented and sent for and spoken with by the officer, to appeare at a Courte of Assistaunts, to aunswer to any offence presented against hym making default, and having no reasonable excuse to be allowed by the said Court shall forfeit Tenn shillings.

611. No parson condempned in a Courte of Assistants for any offence, shall sue for grace before the whole some condempned be paid to the Treasorer, nor then neither, except it be in Court of Assistants within three Courte dayes after the payment of the money, (absent money, or for late coming onely excepted).

612. [p. 43] No restitution shalbe made of any Brocke or somes of Money condempned (except it be tried by ballating whether any restitution shalbe or no). And it shall likewise be tryed by ballating what shalbe retorned.

613. No parson having sued for grace, and received his aunswer, shall solicite, for any further grace.

614. The party complayned on may purge himself by his Oath. But yf it shall after be fownde or tried, that he hath taken a wrong oath, He shalbe disfranchised out of the Freedome and liberties of this Company, as a parson periured.

615. The Presentor shall have the fowrth parte of that shall remayne to the Company.

616. [p. 44] An act to put in execution in the country all acts and ordinances made and to be made.

617. And for asmuch as the marchaunts of England trading Spayne and Portugall, lately incorporated, dispersed in so many Citties, Townes and places of the realme, as it would be very chargeable and troblesome to compell them to make their contynuall apparaunce heere, to aunswer to any matter obiected against them, for breach of any of the Privileges Acts or ordynaunces made, or to be made by the President Assistaunts and fellowshipp heere in London: And where for the more ease, and better governement of them out of the Citty, there are divers Deputies appointed in divers citties and townes within the Realme, it is therefore at this Courte concluded agreed and ordayned, that it shalbe lawfull for every Deputy and Assistaunt, appointed or to be appointed out of the Cittie of London, or the more parte of them, within their severall Lymitts and Jurisdictions, to put in execution all such Acts and Ordynaunces as are or shalbe made by the President Assistaunts and fellowshipp of marchaunts of England trading into Spayne and Portugall resident heere in London, and to punish all transgressors and offendors of them, or any of them, by fyne mulkte ymprisonment or otherwise, in such and as large manner and forme, as the President or Deputy and Assistaunts heerein London, may or ought to doe, by force of his Majesty's letters patents, or of any act or ordynaunce made or to be made by them. Provided alwaies that every such Deputy shall yerely the [p. 45] Munday before the Assention Day, make certificate to the President or Deputy here, under hys hand of all the proceedings within his Circuit the yere precedent, in such manner as the same shalbe registred in the Courte Book.

618. For enrolling of indentures of apprenticehood.

Every Indenture of Apprentizehood already made or taken within the Cittie of London, whereby the freedome of this society may be challenged, shalbe delivered to the Secretary to be by him enrowled before the feast of Christmas next ensuing (which wilbe Anno Domino according to the computation of the Church of England 1605). And also every other Indenture of Apprenticehood, which after this Day (being the 30 Day of August 1605) shalbe made or taken within the said Cittie of London, whereby the freedome of this society may be challenged, shalbe delivered to the Secretary, to be by him enrowled, within one yere next after the Date and making of every such Indenture upon the payne that the Master of every Apprentize shall forfeit for every Indenture already made, or hereafter to be made, that shall not be so enrowled, according to the true meaning of this Act the some of 10s. And that the Secretary shalbe allowed for every such enrowlement the [p. 46] some of 12d. And moreover that every Indenture of Apprentizehood, already made or taken, within any other Citty Borough or towne Corporate, whereby the freedome of this society may be challenged, shalbe delivered to the Clarck of that Devision respectively where yt was made, to be by him enrowled before the said feast of Christmas next ensuing. And also every other Indenture of Apprentizehood which after the said 30 Day of August, shalbe made or taken, within every Cittie Borough or towne Corporate whereby the freedome of this society may be challenged, shalbe likewise delivered to the Clarck of that Devision respectively where it was made, to be likewise by him enrowled within one yere next after the date and making of every such Indenture. Upon the like payne that the master of every Apprentice shall forfeit for every Indenture already made or hereafter to be made, that shall not be so enrowled according to the true meaning of this Act the some of 10s. And the severall Clarcks of every such severall devision, shall certefy to the Secretary of the society (resident in London) every yere the Munday after the Assension day, or oftener, all such enrowlements as they and every of them shall so severally take, to th'end, the same may also be so enrowled by the said Secretary. And that every such Clarck of every severall division, shall receave for every such enrowlement the some of 2s., whereof he shall retayne for his owne use 12d and the other 12d he shall send up hether to the said Secretary for his paynes, for enrowling the said Indenture here.

619. [p. 47] An act for dispensation notwithstanding the omission of the words 'merchants of Spain and Portugal' from apprentices' indentures, from 1585 until the feast of St. Michael the Archangel 1605.[1]

620. Forasmuch as during the tyme of the breach betweene our late soveraigne Lady Queene Elizabeth and the king of Spayne, divers parsons of this company being without hope of peace or reconciliation, did omytt out of their apprentizes Indentures the wordes 'Marchaunt of Spayne and Portugall' so that by the stricktnes of an auncient order no such parsons can clayme the benifitt of their freedome of Spayne and Portugall by any such service. It is Neverthelesse (upon full and deliberate Consideration) enacted concluded and agreed, that all such parsons as were or shalbe bownde to any freeman of this Company, at any tyme since the yere of our lord, One thowsand fyve hundreth Eighty fyve, untill the feast of Sainct Michaell th'archangell next ensuing, which shalbe Anno Domini 1605 shall and may be dispensed withall and be admytted into the freedome, Notwithstanding the omytting of the said wordes, so as they make iust proof of their service, and also make their clayme before the feast of Christmas next ensuing and so as the Indenture of every such Apprentize already bownde or to be bownd be [p. 48] enrowled with the Secretary before the said feast of Christmas next. And it is absolutely agreed that for all Indentures which shalbe made after the said feast of St. Michaell Th'archangell next ensuing, these words shalbe inserted 'Et Mercatori Anglie mercantes Hispaniam et Portugaliam' or in English 'and Marchaunt of England trading into Spayne and Portugall' or to the like effect. Or els that Indenture of Apprentizehood touching the freedome of this Company shalbe void and of none effect, as in an act before mencioned is laid downe and declared.

1. Michaelmas, 29 Sept.

621. An act for the allowance of provision for masters of ships.

Item in avoyding of all questions that may hereafter growe, what value in Marchaundizes may be allowed to the owners of Shipps, or other vessells fraighted for Spayne or Portugall, or any the Islands or Places comprehended within our privileges, for the necessary provision of the said Shipps or vessells. It is ordred and enacted that it shall not be lawfull to or for any owner of any Shipp or vessell, to be fraughted into any the places aforesaid being not free of our Company, to have transporte [p. 49] or carry in goodes wares or marchaundizes upon payne to forfeit 5s. for every pownd value that shalbe brought or transported contrary to this act. Provided allwaies that yf any owner shall hereafter send any Shipp or vessell into the places aforesaid, empty or unladen to seeke fraight onely and fynde none, that then in such case it shalbe lawfull for every such owner, his factor or Atturney to make retorne in Salt, paying the ordynary ympositions for the same, without incurring any penalty or payne. Provided also that yt shalbe lawfull for every master and marriner, to carry and returne such Portage, as they have ben accustomed to doe, viz. to the master, to the value of his wages, not exceeding Twenty Powndes, and for the marriner so much of his owne proper Goods as he may carry in his ordynary Chest, or in his Cabbyn, not disfurnishing himself of his Lodging, So as it exceede not the value of fyve pownds.[1]

622. [p. 50] No unfree son, servant or apprentice shall be sent into Spain etc. until he has taken his oath.

623. Item it is also ordayned and enacted, that no parson free of this society shall after the publication of this Act, send his sonne Servaunt or Apprentice (being not free of the Company) into Spayne or Portugall, or any the Islands comprehended within our priviledge, to doe any feate of Marchaundizes, or willingly suffer him so sent to doe any feate of Marchaundize there, before he have taken an Oath before the President or his Deputy in London, or before the Deputy under whose charge he is resiaunt, that he shall not Cullour Convey, nor take in charge, any the Goods wares and Marchaundizes of any parson, borne within the king's maiesties Domynions, to be transported or brought to or from any the Places aforesaid, contrary to the ordynaunces of this society, upon payne to forfeit to the use of this society, fyve powndes of lawfull money of England for every tyme that any such parson shall so be sent, contrary to the tenour of this Act.

624. [p. 51] An act against trading in partnership with foreigners, and setting a time to such as are not free to return their merchandise from Spain.

625. And it is agreed concluded and enacted, that every parson and parsons, that is or shalbe free of this society, which hath already ioyned with any Partner or partners not being free of the Company shall presently make relation thereof in writing to the Secretary of the Company, signifying with whome, and in what manner he hath so ioyned, upon payne, that every one that shall not performe the same (besides the infringing of his Oath) shall pay such fyne, as by a generall Courte shalbe agreed.

1. The right of portage, or allocation of private freight space to masters and seamen, was increasingly superseded by the direct payment of wages during the course of the 16th century. Here it seems to have lingered on as an alternative method of reimbursement or additional benefit (F. W. Brooks, 'A wage-scale for seamen 1546', *Eng. Hist. Rev.*, lx (1945), 244; H. D. Burwash, *English Merchant Shipping 1460–1540* (Toronto, 1947), 47–8).

626. Moreover, it is enacted and agreed that every parson and parsons not free of this company, which hath adventured any marchaundizes into Spayne or Portugall, or any places comprehended within our privilege, and also all such as have ioyned with any freeman shall have the favour and liberty of Six monethes viz. betweene this and the feast of Christmas next coming, for returning of their wares and marchaundizes from the said places. Provided allwaies that no such parson or parsons not being free, nor any whoe have ioyned with freemen, shall at any tyme or [p. 52] tymes from hensforth adventure any wares or marchaundizes outward, unto any the said places before mencioned. And moreover that after this Day noe parson or parsons, free of this fellowshipp shall ioyne, or deale as partener in occupying with any parson or parsons not free of the Company, nor with any Retailer, Artificer, Inhoulder, farmor, common marriner, or handycrafts man, of or for any goods wares or marchaundize to be transported or brought to or from Spayne or Portugall, or any place or places, comprehended within our privilege, upon payne to forfeit Twenty in the hundreth, to the use of the said fellowship. Provided allwaies that this Act shall not extend to any parson that doth occupy with any other being beyond the Sea, that may at his retorne enioy the freedome.

627. [p. 53] That no person free of the company shall be both a merchant and a retailer.

Forasmuch as in the letters patents lately graunted to us, whereby we are Incorporated and established a Society or fellowshipp of marchaunts of England, trading into Spayne and Portugall, There is a speciall exception that no Retailers, Artificers, Inholders, farmors Common Marriners or Handycrafts men, should be admytted into the sayd society. And forasmuch as not onely the meere marchaunts of the principall Citties and Townes of the Realme where marchaunts are, doe finde it inconvenient that a marchaunte should also be a Retayler, But also the Retailers in most places, which are not marchaunts but lyve onely by retaile, doe very much Complayne that the marchaunts which are also Retailers doe much hinder them in their trade and occupying, so as they are scant able to lyve.

628. The Company therefore aswell for the relief of the meere Retailer, As also for the reducing of a marchaunt into the right vocation and use of a marchaunt, After good deliberation doe by these presents decree ordayne and enact that from and after the feast of Sainct Michaell the archangell next coming, which shalbe Anno Domini 1605, no parson free of this Company which shall shipp or transport, or cause any goods wares [p. 54] or Marchaundizes to be shipped or transported, to or from Spayne or Portugall, or any the Islands Countries or Territories, comprehended within the said letters patents shall in any wise, during by all or any parte of such tyme, as he shall use or cause to be used any trade or traffique, to or from the said parts or any of them, use or exercise or cause to be used or exercised to his use Comodety or gayne, any handicraft or manuell occupation, or shall keepe any retailing, shopp, or use any retaile, or take any proffitt or comodety of any wares or marchaundizes, sould by retaile uppon payne of forfeiture of fyve shillings of the value of every pownde of such goods, wares, or Marchandizes so to be shipped or transported contrary to the true meanying of this Act. And in avoiding of all ambiguities and questions which may arise or growe upon the Definition of a Retailor and who is to be accoumted an Artificer or Retailor, it is by these presents declared ordayned and enacted that whatsoever parson or parsons doth or heereafter shall use or exercise any handicraft or manuall occupation, or doth or shall take any benifitt profit or comodety in use or exercise of any handicraft or manuall occupation or doth or shall by any manuell exercise,

91

alter or cause to be altered to his gayne or proffitt any goods wares or marchaundizes from the same Kynde nature or forme they were or shalbe brought in, shalbe [p. 55] Accoumpted and adiudged an Artificer. And it is further declared, ordayned and enacted that whatsoever parson or parsons shall use or exercise or directly or indirectly cause or procure any person to use or exercise any trade in buying and selling any goods wares or marchaundizes to his or their privat or partable accoumpt gayne or Comodety in manner and forme as is hereafter declared and defined to be a retailor shalbe accoumpted and adiudged a retailor. First he that keepeth an open shopp or warehowse in the streate, having a servaunt or servaunts attendaunt upon his wares, and usually selleth any wares to Chapmen by Retaile, shalbe accoumpted a Retailor.

629. He that Keepeth any Taverne or victualling howse whatsoever, shalbe accoumpted a Retailor.

630. He that selleth any marchaundize commonly sould by the hundreth, by any lesse waight then the hundreth, or any marchaundizes commonly sould by the pownde, by any lesse waight, then the Dozen pownde (Cloves, Mace, Synamon, and Nutmegge except) which may be sould by the half Dozen (and Powder of grane, granatha silke and other Silke, Cochenelia, Anele, Druggs Colours and perfumes also excepted, which may be sould by the Pownde or other wise, shalbe accoumpted a retailor. He that selleth Oyle by any lesse vessell then Pipe or hoggeshead or [p. 56] els in such Caske or vessell, as it shalbe brought over in, shalbe Accoumpted a Retailer. Raisons ffiggs marmalade and suckets may be sould by the peece box or barrell, and not be accoumpted a Retailor.[1]

631. He that selleth any kinde of wyne by any lesse measure, then the Butt, Pype, Hoggeshead or Terce,[2] or els in such Caske as it shalbe brought over in shalbe Counted a Retailor.

632. He that selleth any Ropes, Tarred or untarred, by lesse waight then the hundreth or the Coile, or lesse length then the peece, shalbe accoumpted a Retailor, Provided that upon the Coast, it shalbe lawfull to sell by the half hundreth.

633. Steele or Nailes may be sould by the Tonne or half Tonne, Barrell, or half barrell, or some of Nailes. And in the Countrey, Steele may be sould by the ffaggott wispe or barr, and not to be accoumpted a Retailor.[3]

634. He that selleth wainescotts by lesse nomber then the Dozen, Clough boord by lesse nomber then the hundreth, Deale boorde by lesse nomber then the Dozen, Sope ashes by lesse quantety then the last, Pitch or Tarr by lesse quantety then the Barrell, shalbe accoumpted a Retailor.[4]

635. He that selleth any kinde of Cloth, or other stuffe made of silke woole fflax or Hemp, by lesse measure then the peece or half peece, as it was made, or brought from beyond the Seas, not being Cut in England, shalbe accoumpted a Retailor.

636. [p. 57] The time in which the freedom of the company shall be claimed.

Every parson named in the last charter graunted to this society (being in England)

1. Grain powder, probably a form of kermes or alkermes, the scarlet dye made from dried insects; 'granatha' silk from Granada; anele, probably another form of dye or glaze; a pipe, a measure usually of 42 gallons; suckets, fruits preserved in sugar, either candied or in syrup.
2. A third of a pipe, or half a hogshead.
3. Faggot, a bundle of rods bound together, often weighing 120 lb.; a wisp, a similar but smaller bundle.
4. Clough board, a small size of split oak for barrel-staves and wainscots; soap ashes, burnt wood which provided the alkaline basis for soap.

shall clayme his and their freedome and pay such fynes and receave such oath, as according to the nature of their severall claymes and the true intent and meaning of the orders of this Company are lymited and appointed, within one yere next after the Date of the same charter viz. before the last day of May next ensuing, which shalbe anno Domino 1606. And yf any such parson be beyond the seas, then he shall make his clayme and demaund his freedome, and pay his fyne, and receave his Oath, within six monethes after his coming over into England. And also all and every other parson and parsons being in England not named in the Charter, and which are nowe Capeable of the said freedome, either by Patrymony or service, shall make his and their Claymes, and pay his and their fynes, within one yere next ensuing viz. before the last day of August, Anno Domino 1606. And if they be beyond the sea, they shall have six monethes liberty as aforesaid. And also every other parson and parsons which at any tyme hereafter, either by Patrymony or service may challeng the freedome of this society, shall make his and their claymes and pay his and their fynes within one yere next after the same respectively [p. 58] shalbe due unto them. And yf such parson be beyond the seas, then he shall have six monethes libertie after his returne into England as aforesaid. And if any such parson or parsons shall neglect, and shall not make his clayme, pay his fyne and receave his oath, within the tyme before severally and respectively lymytted, that then every such parson shall forfeit, and pay to the use of this society a fyne of Twenty shillings. And yf he or they shall neglect, and shall not make his and their clayme, paye his fyne, and receave his oath before the end of one other yere longer, then he shall pay a fyne of forty shillings. And yf he deferr it a third yere, then he shall pay a fyne of three powndes, being the greatest fyne that shalbe taken, notwithstanding he deferr his clayme never so long.

637. And yf the same fyne and fynes shall not be paide by hym or them who ought to have payd the same, that yet neverthelesse it shalbe aunswered and paid, by his and their Children, or Servaunts, before any of them shalbe admytted or receaved into the freedome of this society. Provided allwaies that this Act shall not extent to any Redemptioner nor to the sonnes or servaunts of any Redempcioner, but that they shall have libertie to clayme their freedome at their pleasures paying the fynes in that case lymitted and appointed. Neither shall it extend to the fyve honorable Earles named in the patent, Nor to the Lord Chief Baron, Mr. Attorney generall, Sir Danyell Dun, the three Clarcks of his Majesty's privy Counsaill, and the two Clarcks of his Majesty's signett and privy seale being likewise named in the charter, Nor to any that shall or may clayme the freedome by or under their rights.

638. [p. 59] An act that no child or apprentice of any usual trader before 1569, whose father or master was dead before the granting of the charter of 8 June 1577 by Queen Elizabeth, can or lawfully may challenge the freedom by virtue of the said charter.

Whereas at a generall Courte holden the 8 day of November 1577 it was concluded and ordered in these wordes viz.; Where question was moved at this Courte and intreated upon, for the admytting of such auncient Marchaunts, children and servaunts, whose fathers or maisters were usuall traders into Spayne or Portugall, before anno 1569 and neverthelesse Deade before the graunte of the letters patents. It was agreed concluded and adiudged by the whole Courte that it was not necessary that any such should be receaved or admytted, for that they be without the compasse of the expresse words of the said graunt, as by the sayd order may appeere. Which said opynion and resolution which was then concluded and agreed upon by the generall courte at that time, who were best acquainted with the true intent and meaning of the said charter, is now this Day (being the 30 of August 1605) confirmed and allowed, And ordred and enacted that the same shalbe observed accordingly. Provided alwaies that this act shall not extent or be pre-diudiciall to any parson whose name is inserted in the last Charter graunted by his majestie to this Society, Dated 31 Maii Anno regno Jacobi et cetera Tertio.

CHARTER OF 1605

(P.R.O., S.P. 14/21)

639. [p. 1] The copy of a charter granted by King James to the president, assistants and fellowship of the merchants of England trading into Spain and Portugal, 31 May 1605.[1]

James, by the grace of God, king of England, Scotland, France and Ireland, to all and singular admirals, captains, keepers of castles, customers, comptrollers, [etc.]

640. [p. 2] Whereas several charters have been granted by our progenitors unto our loving subjects the English merchants trading into Spain and Portugal, viz. one charter by Henry VIII late king of England (our progenitor of famous memory) bearing date at Westminster 1 September 1530, and another charter by our late dear sister Elizabeth late queen of England of famous memory, bearing date at Westminster 8 June 1577; and whereas we by our letters patent under our great seal of England bearing date at Westminster 30 March 1604 did confirm, ratify and allow the letters patent and charters aforesaid.

641. Forasmuch as sithence the said confirmation we have been informed by our council learned in our laws that there are divers misprisions and imperfections in the same letters patent and confirmation, and forasmuch as there is a firm peace concluded between us and our brother the king of Spain, and free liberty of trade and intercourse [p. 3] established between both our subjects; we knowing that no commerce or intercourse can be maintained or continue without order, and that the advancement of trade and traffic doth tend to the common good of the whole island, and the benefit and enriching of our loving subjects, have therefore and for divers other good causes and considerations us specially moving granted and declared, and for us our heirs and successors by these presents, we do declare, that our right trusty and right welbeloved cousins and councillors Thomas earl of Dorset[2] lord treasurer of England, Charles earl of Nottingham lord admiral of England, Charles earl of Devon, Henry earl of Northampton lord warden of our cinque ports, Robert earl of Salisbury our

---

1. In calendaring this document the language of the original has been used throughout but a number of repetitious words and phrases have been omitted.
2. Margin note, 'The names of such as are allowed to be of the Company; Earles 5, Speciall officers in service to his Majestie 7, names of London 237, names for Bristol 97, names for Exceter 45, names for Bridgwater 11, names of Yarmouth 2, names of Chester 4, names for Plymoth 12, names of Kingston uppon Hull 7, Marchauntes of Tiverton 14, Taunton 11, Charde 13, Totnes 43, names of Lyme 14, Barnestable 12, Southampton 8, Ipswich 15, in toto 557'.

principal secretary, and our trusty and welbeloved Sir Thomas Flemyng knight chief baron of our exchequer, Sir Edward Cooke [Coke][1] knight our attorney general, Sir Daniel Dun [Dunne] knight one of our masters of our requests, Sir William Waade [Waad] knight, Sir Thomas Smyth [Smithe] knight, and Sir Thomas Edmonds knight, three of the clerks of our privy council, Sir Thomas Lake knight one of the clerks of our signet, Sir Richard Martyn, Sir John Spencer, Sir Thomas Smyth [Smithe], [p. 4] Sir Robert Lee, Sir John Watts, Sir Thomas Cambell, Sir Christopher Hoddesdon [Hoddesden], Sir John Swynnerton [Swynerton], Sir William Romeney, Sir Henry Sackford, Sir Thomas Pullison, Sir William Bond and Sir Samuel Saltonstall knights, Richard Hale, Jerrard Gore the elder, Paul Banning [Banninge], Robert Chamberlen [Chamberlayne], Thomas Cordell [Cordall], John Barne, Robert Dow [Dowe], Henry Cletherowe, Thomas Wilford, George Holman, John Harby, John Newman, Michael Lock, Thomas Forman, Randle Mannyng [Manninge], Robert Cobb, George Collymere, Arthur Jaxon [Jackson], William Typper [Tipper], John Newton, William Cokayne [Cockayne], Richard Glascock, Richard Staper, Roger Howe, John Hawes, John Hall, Reginald Barker, William Salter, John Highlord, John Watson, John Castlyn, William Wilford, Hugh Ingram, Robert Bringborne, William Atkins, Oliver Stile, Nicholas Stile, Gregory Yong [Yonge], Thomas Alabaster [Allabaster], Anthony Pennystone [Pennyston], William Hareborne [Harborne], Hewyt Stapers, James Stapers, William Kevall, Jeffrey Davis [Davyes], John Bourne, Godfrey Wilson, John Allen, John Suragold, William Towreson, Clement Draper, William Jennyngs, Hugh Marsh, Richard Solda, George Hanger, John Dorrington, Thomas Altham, Isaac Jackson, Francis Dorrington, George Dorrington, Francis Barne, Richard Barne, [p. 5] Richard Gore, Jerrard Gore the younger, John Gore, William Gore, James Cambell, Robert Cambell, Thomas Cambell the younger, Robert Angell, [blank in both MSS] Alderley, William Addington, Andrew Banning [Banninge], Nicholas Ling [Linge], John Bate, George Benson, Nicholas Buckeridge, Simion Furner, Edmund Burton, William Carter, Richard Langley, Richard Colman, Robert Tipper, Roger Rogers, Henry Clytherow [Clitherowe] the younger, John Swynnerton the elder, Thomas Church, Raph Edmonds, William Evans, Nicholas Ferrer, Clement ffrier, Lawrence Greene, Roger Golding [Goldinge], John Harrold, Humphrey Hall, Leonard Haward, John Jowles, Robert Bowyer, Richard Wyche [Weeche], William Hangate [Hungate], Edward James, Bryan Janson, Phillip Jones, Jeffrey Kyrby [Kirby], Simon Lawrence, Nathaniel Marten [Martyn], Robert Savage, George May [Maye], John Newman the younger, Nicholas Oseley, Gyles Parslowe, Leonard Parker, John Rombridg [Romsbridge], Thomas Seracold, Thomas Southwick, Jarvis Elwes [Jervais Elwaies], William Speight, Philip Smyth [Smithe], Nicholas Smyth [Smith], Richard Shorter, William Stone, John Sherrington, John Stokeley, John Stronginarme, Robert Towreson [Towereston], Nicholas Towreson, James Wyche [Weech], Hugh Bourman, Francis Taylor [Tiler], John Apshawe [Aspshawe], John Worsopp, Gawen Walcott, William Wodder, William Wasteele [Wastle], Raph Weight [Weighte], William Dunscombe,

1. This and subsequent variant surnames are taken from the enrolment on the patent roll of 1605.

Nevill Davies, Francis Lamberd, George [p. 6] Samuell, Gyles Snode,
Robert Payne, Peter Beauvoyer [Beauvoy], William Harrison, Thomas
Trumball [Trumbell], Edward Davenant [Davenante], Thomas Dalby
[Dalbye], Robert Dawborne [Dawburne], John Hough, Robert Brooke,
James Wilford [Wilforde], William Wilford [Wilforde], Richard Ironside,
John Watts the elder, William Watts, Richard Watts, Jeffrey Watts, Thomas
Watts, John Watts the younger, John Hawes the younger, Thomas Cokayne,
George Sotherton, Francis Shawe, John Watson, Martyn Bond, George
Bond [Bonde], Robert Brooke, [blank in both MSS] Saltenstall, John
Merrick [Merick], John King [Kinge], Robert Jenny, Richard Cox [Coxe],
George Cotton, Thomas Owen, John Audley [Awdley], William Audley
[Awdley], Joseph Jackson, Francis Oliver [Olyver], Thomas Halwood
[Hallwood], Alexander Danger, William Walton, Henry Peyton, Thomas
Heaton, Leonard Parker, Thomas Honnyman, Phillip Honnyman, Roger
Combleton, Simon Bourman, John Cordale [Cordall], Richard Stephens,
Edward Barley, Robert Bell, John Potter, Bartholomew Graves, Thomas
Havers, Thomas Whetenhall, Humphrey Wymes [Wymies], Thomas
Waltham, William Palmer, John Cokayne, Thomas Boothby, Humphrey
Slany, Hugh Hamersley, Francis Cokayne, Roger Cokayne, Richard
Cokayne, Thomas Stills, William Bond, John Pulham, Jeremy Elwes
[Elweyes], Allen Thompson, James Flesher [Flusher], John Harby, William
Harby, William Chambre, Cavaliero Maycott [p. 7] alias Mackworth
knight, John Blunt [Blunte], Daniel Hills, Richard Waltham, John Morley,
James Wych [Wiche], Richard Wych [Wiche], Thomas Wych [Wiche],
John Apshawe [Aspshawe], and Humphrey Wotton, merchants of London,

642. William Vawer alderman of Bristol, William Cole sheriff of Bristol,
John Bolton, William Hopkins [Hopkines], Thomas Hopkins, William
Hicks, William Ellis [Ellys], John Hopkins, John Whitson, Thomas James,
John Barker, Matthew Haviland [Havilande], Robert Aldworth [Ald-
worthe], Abel Kitchin [Kytchin], John ffownes [ffawnes], John Aldworth
[Aldworthe], John Rowborrowe, John Roberts, Thomas Aldworth [Ald-
worthe], Thomas Pytt [Pitt], Henry Roberts, Lawrence Swetnam, Edward
Morris [Morries], Nicholas Hix [Hicks], Thomas Symonds, William Cole
in Corn street, John Browne, Roger Bowman [Boman], Christopher Cary,
John Sanford, John Angell, Robert Johnson, Thomas Whitehead [White-
heade], John Gittins, Edward Browne, John Wood [Woode], Richard
Barker, William Greves, Richard Powell [Pooell], Thomas Davy [Davie],
Thomas Pitt junior, George White in Corn street, Thomas Warden, Arthur
Hibbine, Robert Pentigrace, George Wilkins, Roger Hurt [Hurte], Francis
Doughty [Doughtye], Walter Spurwaie, William Slack, Daniel Baker, John
Barker the younger, Thomas Bramley [Brambley], William Ellis the younger,
Robert Haviland [Havilande], Edmond Camfford, William ffleete [ffleet],
[p. 8] William Pitt, Thomas Anthony, George Gough, Sampson Lorte
[Lort], John Haviland [Havyland], Thomas Walters, Phillip Ellis [Ellys],
Walter Ellis, William Mellyn [Mellin], John Aires, Thomas Wright
[Wrighte], Phillip Dickinson, John Griffith, Thomas Powell son of Richard
Powell, Thomas Leeke, Robert Smyth [Smithe], Robert Sheward, William
Angell, George White, John Guy [Guye], John Barnes, William Burrowes,

John Goning [Gonninge], John Merrick, John Bindon, Christopher Webbe, Walter Thomas, Morgan Reade, William Colston, George Lane, Richard Tegg [Tegge], Robert Owen, Walter Owfield [Owfeilde], Michael Quick, Edward Williams, John Langton, William Stanlack, Richard Winter, William Pynner [Pinner] the younger and Humphrey Fitzherbert, merchants of Bristol,

643. John Davy [Davie], William Martin, John Periam, John Hartwell, Nicholas Spiser [Spicer], Richard Harding [Hardinge], John Chapell [Chappell], John Lyvermore, John Trose, Richard Newman, Richard Perry [Perrie], John Sandy [Sandye], Valentine Tucker, Richard Dochester, John Elcott [Ellcott], John Sanford, Thomas Walker, Henry Hull, Walter Borro, Hugh Crossen, Alexander Jarmyn, John Larts, Jeffrey Welcham, Gilbert Smyth [Smithe], Robert Perry [Perrie], Richard Swette, Henry Swette, Thomas Blackiler [Blakiler], Oliver Taper, Samuel Alford [Alforde], Paul Trigge [Trige], Peter Cobelton, Thomas Pope, Robert Ellicote [p. 9], Thomas Martyn, Nicholas Martley, John Shore [Shere], Thomas Martyn [Martin] the younger, John Lambell, Gilbert Lambell, John Watkins, Christopher Spicer the younger, Nicholas Bewis [Bewys], Ignatius Jorden and Thomas Snowe, merchants of Exeter,

644. Alexander Jones, Henry Jones, Richard Godbeare, Amies Harvy [Harvye], John Beedoe, John Michaell, George Watts, Emanuel Buckine, Humphrey Black [Blacke], Robert Quirck [Quircke], Noah Randall merchants of Bridgwater, Somerset,

645. William Harebrowne and Humphrey Spencer merchants of Yarmouth, Norfolk,

646. Fulke Aldersey, William Aldersey, William Johnson and George Boys merchants of Chester,

647. Sir Richard Hawkins knight, John Trilany [Trylany], Robert Trilany [Trylany], James Bagge, Humphrey fformes, Walter Mathewes, Robert Rawlins [Rawlyns], Abraham Colmer, John Wadden, Robert Bragg [Bragge], William Carne, Matthew Bragg [Bragge], merchants of Plymouth,

648. John Groves, John Lister, John Lobbyn, Luke Thurscroste, John Barker, Richard Burgis, Thomas Bowmer, merchants of Kingston-upon-Hull,

649. Edward Amy [Amye], Nicholas Skynner, George Slee, John West [Weste], Thomas Amy [Amye], Henry Walrond [Walronde], John Walrond, Simon Land, Richard Prowse the elder, George Skynner [Skinner], Jonas Baker, Richard Slee, Edward Lewis, William Sheere [p. 10] merchants of Tiverton, Devon,

650. Thomas Fisher the elder, Thomas ffisher [ffysher] the younger, William Dare, John Clatlory [Clatlorie], William Leechland, Lewis Pope, Thomas

Gregory [Gregorye], Thomas Gobbyns [Gobbins], Henry Samwayes, Thomas Crocker, Thomas Manstedg [Manstedge], merchants of Taunton, Somerset,

651. Thomas Symmes, Henry Munday [Monday], Edward Munday [Monday], William Bourage [Bowrage], Jasper Pyne, Robert Tucker, Richard Sprake, John Day [Daye], John Hills, Osmond Walrond, Roger Leechland, Robert Granule [Granudle] and John Towker, merchants of Chard, Somerset,

652. William Duck [Ducke], Richard Lea, Christopher Wise, John Wise, Eustace Wise, Nicholas Wise, William Wise, Samuel Wise, Henry Every, Thomas Every [Everie], William Brooking [Brookinge], Christopher Brooking [Brookinge], Allen Brooking, Edward Gould, Richard Belfeild, Christopher Broderidg [Brodridge], Thomas Prestwood, Matthew Came, Richard Kellond, Christopher Kellond, John Kellond, Thomas Smyth [Smithe], Walter Smyth [Smithe], John Wakeham, John Warren, Leonard Blackhall [Blackyall], John Lary [Larye], William Squyre [Squire], John Kyttingall [Kittingall], Richard Marye, Gabriel Mary, Christopher Maynard [Maynarde], Thomas Dipford, John Shopley, Timothy Savary [Saverie], Phillip Holdich [Holdiche], Walter Dottyn [Dottin], Nicholas Strawe, Richard Savery [Saverie], Thomas Prideaux [Prideaux], Richard Leere [Lee], Richard [p. 11] Lary [Larye], Richard Newman merchants of Totnes, Devon,

653. John Hazard [Hayarde] the elder, Walter Harvy [Harvie], Robert Barnes, Richard Norris, Anthony Moone, John Hazard [Hayarde] the younger, Robert Hazard [Hayard], William Davy [Davie], George Plea, William Hill, Richard Bedford [Bedforde], William Barnes, Richard Coghan, John Norris, merchants of Lyme, Dorset,

654. William Gay [Gaye], John Salisbury [Salisburye], John Darracott, John Mewles, George Gay, Richard Dodderidge, James Beaple, Nicholas Downe, James Downe, Robert Dodderidge, Richard Beaple and Pentecost Dodderidg [Dodderidge], merchants of Barnstaple, Devon,

655. Francis Mills [Milles] esquire one of the clerks of our privy seal, John Cornish [Cornishe], William Nevey [Nevye], Robert Chambers, Thomas Bedford [Bedforde], Thomas Stoner, Peter Capelyn and Richard Dalby [Dalbye], merchants of Southampton, Hampshire,

656. Robert Cutler, John Clynch [Clynche], Walter Snelling [Snellinge], Richard Snelling [Snellinge], Robert Lymber [Limber] the elder, Edward Hunting, Edward Ryvett, William Cutler, Samuel Cutler, John Cutler, Roger Cutler, Jeremy Barber, James Tyllett [Tillett], Michael Cowdray and Christopher Cardinall, merchants of Ipswich, Suffolk, and their and every of their sons and apprentices whatsoever, and all and every other person and persons [p. 12] whose names are specified in the letters patent, granted by our late dear sister Queen Elizabeth, and their sons and their apprentices which have been bound by indenture to be free of the trade into Spain and have served according to such indenture eight years at the least, and also all such person and persons as have been admitted into the fellowship by the president, assistants and fellowship of merchants of Spain and Portugal sithence the granting of the letters patent of Queen Elizabeth, and their sons and apprentices which have been bound as is aforesaid, and have faithfully served or shall serve as aforesaid, and all and every other merchant and merchants, which shall hereafter from time to time be admitted or made free in such manner as hereafter in these presents is declared and specified, shall be one fellowship and one body corporate and politic in deed and in name, by the name of president, assistants and fellowship of merchants of England trading into Spain and Portugal.

657. And them by the name of president, assistants and fellowship of merchants of England trading into Spain and Portugal one body corporate and politic in deed and in name really and fully for us, our heirs and successors, we do erect, ordain, name, constitute [p. 13] and declare by these presents, and that by the same name of president, assistants and fellowship of merchants of England trading into Spain and Portugal they shall have perpetual succession. And that they and their successors by the name of president, assistants and fellowship of merchants of England trading into Spain and Portugal be and shall be at all times hereafter one fellowship and one body corporate and politic, and capable in law to have, purchase, receive, possess, enjoy and retain manors, messuages, lands, tenements, liberties, privileges, franchises, jurisdictions and hereditaments of whatsoever kind, nature and quality they shall be of, to them and their successors in fee and perpetuity or otherwise for term of life or years.

658. And also to give, grant, alienate, let, assign and dispose manors, messuages and hereditaments. And to do and execute all and singular other acts and things whatsoever by the same name, and that they and their successors by the name of president, assistants and fellowship . . . may sue and be sued, plead and be impleaded, answer and be answered, defend and be defended in whatsoever court and places and before whatsoever judges and justices and other persons and officers whatsoever of us, our [p. 14] heirs and successors, within this our realm of England in all and singular actions.

659. And that the president, assistants and fellowship may have a common seal to serve for all the causes and businesses of them and their successors, and that it shall and may be lawful to the president, assistants and fellowship the same seal at their will and pleasure to break, change and make new, as to them shall seem expedient.

660. And further we do ordain that there shall be from henceforth forever one of the fellowship to be elected and appointed in such form as hereafter in these presents is expressed, which shall be called the president of the fellowship of merchants of England trading into Spain and Portugal.

661. And [p. 15] for the better execution of this our will and grant in that behalf we do assign, nominate, constitute and make our welbeloved Thomas Wilford to be the first and present president of the fellowship by virtue of these our letters patents, to continue in the office from the date of these presents, until the Monday next before the feast of the Ascension next coming, and from thence until another of the fellowship shall in due manner be chosen and sworn unto the office, according to the ordinances and provisions hereafter in these presents expressed and declared, (if Thomas Wilford shall so long live).

662. And further we do grant that from henceforth forever there be of the fellowship threescore and one men of the best and most honest persons of the fellowship (whereof thirty of them at the least shall be dwelling and inhabiting in the cities, towns and places of this realm of England out of the city of London) the which [p. 16] threescore and one men shall be called assistants and chief councillors of the fellowship for all things, matters, causes and business of the fellowship and the good rule, state and government of the same touching or concerning. And that they may and shall be from time to time assistants and aiders to the president, or to his deputy or deputies for the time being in all causes and matters touching or concerning the fellowship.

663. And also we do assign and make our welbeloved Sir Robert Lee,[1] Sir John Watts, Sir John Swynnerton, Sir William Romeney knights, Richard Staper, Thomas Cordall, Robert Chamberleyn [Chamberlen], William Cokayne [Coken], John Newman, John Harby, Andrew Bannyng [Banninge], Nicholas Lyng [Lynge], Arthur Jackson, John Dorrington, John Bate, Robert Savage, Edward James, Robert Bowyer, John Castlen, Symion ffurner, John Newton, William Towreson [Towerson], Nicholas Stile, Thomas Owen, Richard Wych [Wich], Robert Cobb [Cobbe], George Cullymore [Collymer], George Hanger, Lawrence Greene, Thomas fforman [ffarman], citizens of London,

664. John Whitson, William Ellis, John Hopkins, Thomas James, citizens of [p. 17] Bristol; Nicholas Spicer, William Martyn [Marten], Thomas Walker and Walter Boro, citizens of Exeter,

665. Phillip Holdich [Holdiche] and John Shopley, merchants of Totnes; Fulke Aldersey and William Aldersey, merchants of Chester; Richard Dodderidge and James Beaple, merchants of Barnstaple; Robert Hussard [Hussarde], merchant of Lyme; Sir Richard Hawkins knight and John Trylany [Trelany], merchant of Plymouth; Alexander Jones, merchant of Bridgwater; John Clynch [Clynche] and Walter Snelling [Snellinge], merchants of Ipswich; William Harebrowne and Humphrey Spencer, merchants

---

1. Margin note, 'The names of the 61 Assistants, viz. of London 30, of Bristoll 4, of Exceter 4, of Totnes 2, of Chester 2, of Barnestable 2, of Lyme 1, of Plymoth 2, of Bridgwater 1, of Ipswich 2, of Yarmouth 2, Kingstone upon Hull 3, of Southampton 3, of Taunton 1, of Chard 1, and the secretary of the fellowship for the tyme being, in toto 61'.

of Yarmouth; John Groves, John Lister and John Lobbyn, merchants of Kingston-upon-Hull; John Cornish, William Nevey and Robert Chambers, merchants of Southampton; Thomas Fisher the elder, merchant of Taunton; Thomas Symms [Symmes], merchant of Chard and the secretary of the fellowship for the time being, to be the first and present assistants and chief councillors of the fellowship to continue in the office of assistants and chief councillors of the fellowship from the date of [p. 18] these presents until the Monday next before the feast of the Ascension next coming, and from thence until they or threescore and one others of the fellowship shall in due manner be chosen and sworn unto the said office according to the ordinances and provisions hereafter in these presents expressed and declared.

666. And further we will and grant by these presents for us our heirs and successors unto the presidents, assistants and fellowship that it shall and may be lawful to and for the president, assistants and fellowship for the time being, or the most part of them present, at any public assembly commonly called the general court held for the fellowship (the president of the fellowship being always one) from time to time to elect one of the fellowship to be deputy unto the president, which deputy shall and may from time to time in the absence of the president execute and exercise the office of president of the fellowship in such sort as the same president ought to do, and shall continue in the office only during the pleasure of the president, assistants and fellowship, and to be removed when the president, assistants and [p. 19] fellowship or the greater part of them present at any general court shall think fit.

667. And furthermore for the greater increase and advancement of trade and traffic, and for the enriching of our loving subjects being mere merchants, we do command the president, assistants and fellowship that they and their successors shall from time to time, and at all times hereafter, admit and receive into their fellowship, and to be free of the same, all and every such person and persons, being subjects of us our heirs or successors, as now be or hereafter shall be mere merchants and which by the laws and statutes of this our realm, may lawfully use the trade of merchandise from or into our realm of England, (except all retailers, artificers, innholders, farmers, common mariners and handicrafts men, and also except all such as now be or hereafter shall be free of any special incorporation or company of merchants trading by force of any act of parliament, charter or letters patents into any the parts beyond the seas) so as such person or persons (except before excepted) require [p. 20] to be free of the fellowship, within one year next after the date of this our present grant, and shall offer and pay to the president or his deputy at the time of his or their admittance the sum of £10 for his freedom in that behalf, and that they shall also admit and receive into their fellowship, and to be free of the same, all and every such person and persons being subjects of us, our heirs or successors, as now be or hereafter shall be mere merchants, and by the laws and statutes of this realm may lawfully use the trade of merchandise, from or into our realm (except all retailers and all such free of any special incorporation) so as such person or persons (except before excepted) having neglected to be made free as is

102

aforesaid, within the first year, shall require to be free of the fellowship within one year next after the end of that first year and shall offer and pay to the president [p. 21] or his deputy for the time being at the time of his or their admittance the sum of £15 for his freedom in that behalf.

668. And that they shall also admit and receive into their fellowship and to be free of the same, all and every such person and persons being subjects of us, our heirs and successors, as now be, or hereafter shall be mere merchants, and which may lawfully use the trade of merchandise (except all retailers and all such free of any special incorporation) so as such person or persons (except before excepted) having neglected to be made free within the said two former years, shall require to be made free at any time whensoever after the end of the said two years next coming after the date of this our present grant, and shall offer and pay to the president of the fellowship or his deputy at the time of [p. 22] his or their admittance the sum of £20 for his freedom in that behalf.

669. And we are nevertheless pleased and contented, and do also for us, our heirs and successors, straightly charge the president, assistants and fellowship that they and their successors shall from time to time and at all times hereafter, admit and receive into their fellowship and to be free of the same, all and every such person and persons now being, or which hereafter shall be subjects of us our heirs and successors, as now be or hereafter shall be free of any special incorporation or company of merchants trading by force of any act of parliament, charter or letters patents, into any the parts beyond the seas (except all retailers, artificers, innholders, farmers, common mariners, and handicrafts men whom we do especially exclude out of this incorporation) which at any time or times hereafter shall require to be free of the fellowship, and shall offer and pay to the president of the fellowship or his deputy for the time being, at the time of his or their admittance such sum and sums of money as is usually paid by other persons requiring to be admitted [p. 23] by redemption into such other fellowship or company whereof such person or persons so requiring to be admitted into the incorporation of president, assistants and fellowship of merchants of England trading into Spain and Portugal shall be then free, or otherwise shall procure such and so many freedoms without fine for such and so many and the like number of the incorporation of president, assistants and fellowship trading into Spain and Portugal (to be from time to time nominated, by the president of the fellowship, and any four or more of the assistants for the time being) into such other fellowship or company, whereof such person or persons so requiring to be admitted into the incorporation by these presents granted shall be then free.

670. And our will and pleasure is, and we do will and grant unto the president, assistants and fellowship that all and singular such sum and sums of money as at any time or times hereafter shall be due, received or paid, for or in respect of any admittance [p. 24] or admittances into the incorporation of president, assistants and fellowship by virtue and force of these presents

103

shall from time to time be employed and bestowed to and for the use and behoof of the president, assistants and fellowship for and towards the bearing and defraying of the common charges of the same.

671. And we do will and grant, that if any of the said person or persons, being a mere merchant or merchants, and which for any sum or sums of money or other considerations, might or ought to be admitted into the corporation of president, assistants and fellowship according to the true intent and meaning of these presents (except retailers, artificers and handicraftsmen) shall upon reasonable request and upon payment or tender of such sum and sums of money, or performance of such other considerations as is aforesaid, be refused by the president, assistants [p. 25] and fellowship to be admitted or made free of the fellowship contrary to the true intent and meaning hereof, then we for us, our heirs and successors, do grant that every such person and persons so being refused shall be free of the fellowship and a member of the incorporation.

672. And further know ye that we for the relief and benefit of all such widows whose husbands are or shall happen to be of the said incorporation or fellowship do grant that all and every the widows of any such persons whose husbands now are, or hereafter shall happen to be of the incorporation or fellowship, during the time only of such their widowhood, shall and may lawfully use and exercise trade and traffic into Spain and Portugal, and also shall and may during the time of such their widowhood take apprentices to serve in and for the same trade, and shall also have and enjoy all such liberties, privileges and immunities as their or any of their husband or husbands might or ought to have had and enjoyed by virtue of these our letters patents [p. 26] in as ample and beneficial manner and form as their or any of their husband or husbands lawfully could or might have done, anything before in these presents to the contrary thereof notwithstanding.

673. And further of our especial grace we do grant to the president, assistants and fellowship of merchants that the president and his successors, or his deputy or deputies, with the assent and consent of the assistants or the greatest part of them then present for the time being, may and shall have power, to name from time to time one or more of the fellowship to be their consul or consuls, or governor or governors in the parts of Spain and Portugal, and that the consul or consuls, governor or governors so named together with six others or more of the most discreet merchants of the fellowship for the time being, to be elected by the consul or consuls, governor or governors, for his or their assistants in that place, where the consul or consuls, governor or governors in the parts [p. 27] of Spain and Portugal shall then be resident, shall have full power and authority to govern in the said dominions within the limits to them, by the president and assistants of the fellowship resident in England, prescribed and assigned, or the greater part of them then present, all and singular merchants our subjects and of our heirs and successors, as well of the fellowship as others which be not of the fellowship and their factors, agents and servants trading merchandise in Spain or Portugal, and to administer unto them full speedy and expedite justice in all and every their causes, plaints and contentions amongst them in the dominions of Spain and Portugal, and to pacify, decide and determine all and all manner of questions discords and strifes amongst them in any of the realms of Spain and Portugal, moved or to be moved, for the better government of the merchants in Spain and Portugal, for the time being, and to do and execute all things which by the president or his deputy and assistants of the fellowship or by the more part of them then present, shall be to the said consul prescribed and commanded, according to the statutes [p. 28], acts and ordinances of the fellowship, so as any of the orders and ordinances, directions or constitutions so to be prescribed be not to the hindrance of the trade and traffic of any of the fellowship, behaving him or themselves duly and orderly as becomes good merchants of the fellowship without any fraudulent or disorderly attempt or practice.

674. And furthermore we do grant to the president, assistants and fellowship of merchants that they or the greater part of them (whereof the president for the time being or his deputy to be one) from time to time and at all times hereafter shall have authority and power yearly and every year on the Monday next before the feast of the Ascension, or at any time within twenty days after that day, to assemble and meet together in some convenient place, within the City of London or within three miles of the same, to be appointed from time to time by the president or in his absence by the deputy, and that they being so assembled, it shall be lawful to and for the president, assistants and fellowship of merchants [p. 29] or the greater part of them which then shall happen to be present (whereof the president of the fellowship or his deputy for the time being to be one) to elect and nominate one of the assistants or fellowship which shall be president of the fellowship for one whole year, from thence next following, and from thence until another of the assistants or fellowship shall in due manner be chosen and sworn into the said office, which person being so elected and nominated to be president of the fellowship before he be admitted to the execution of the office, shall take his corporal oath at that or the next general court to be holden before the last president his predecessor or his deputy, and the greater part of the assistants of the fellowship then present that he shall from time to time well and truly perform the office in all things concerning the same, and that immediately after the oath so taken, he shall use the office of president of the fellowship for one whole year next following and from thence until another of the assistants or fellowship shall in due manner be chosen and sworn unto the office according to the true meaning of these presents.

675. We do grant to the aforesaid president, assistants and fellowship [p. 30] that if it happen the president at any time before a new election of another president to die or for any just or reasonable cause to be discharged or removed from his office, that then it may be lawful to the assistants and fellowship aforesaid one other of themselves to choose and prefer to be president of the fellowship, and that he so chosen and preferred shall have and exercise that office, during the rest of the same year and from thence until another of the assistants or fellowship shall in due manner be chosen and sworn unto the office, he first taking a corporal oath in form aforesaid, and thus as often as the case shall so happen.

676. And that if it happen the deputy of the same society at any time before a new election of another deputy to die or to be discharged or removed from his office, that then it shall be lawful to the president, assistants and fellowship or the greater part of them then present, one other of themselves to choose and prefer to be deputy of the fellowship and that he shall have and exercise that office and continue in the same as aforesaid, he first taking a corporal oath in form [p. 31] aforesaid, and thus as often as the case shall so happen.

677. And further we will and grant unto the president, assistants and fellowship that it shall and may be lawful to and for the president or his deputy, assistants and fellowship for the time being yearly at the time of the election of the president as is aforesaid, or the greater part of them, which then shall happen to be present (whereof the president of the fellowship or his deputy for the time being to be one) to elect and nominate threescore and one of the best and most discreet and honest persons of the fellowship (whereof thirty at the least shall be dwelling and inhabiting in the cities, towns and places of this realm of England out of the city of London) to be assistants of the same fellowship for one whole year, from thence next following and thenceforth until a new election of assistants of the same fellowship, which persons being so elected and nominated to be assistants of the fellowship, before they be admitted to the execution of their offices shall take a corporal oath before the president or his deputy and ten other of the assistants at the least of the same fellowship, being their last predecessors, [p. 32] that they and every of them shall well and faithfully perform their offices of assistants in all things concerning the same, and that immediately after the oath so taken, they shall and may execute and use their offices of assistants for one whole year from thence next following, and until a new election be made of the assistants of the same fellowship.

678. And further we will that the assistants be from time to time aiding, counselling and assisting unto the president or his deputy in all causes matters and things touching or concerning the fellowship.

679. And furthermore we ordain and grant to the president, assistants and fellowship that whensoever it shall happen one or more of the threescore and one assistants for the time being to die, or from his place of assistant to absent himself, or for any just and reasonable cause to be discharged or amoved, that then and so often it [p. 33] shall be lawful to the president and other assistants of the fellowship then overliving or remaining, or to the greatest part of them then present, one other or more of the fellowship into the place or places of the assistant or assistants so happening to be dead, discharged or moved, to choose, name and prefer, and that he or they so chosen and preferred first having taken a corporal oath before the president, and greatest part of the other assistants of the fellowship then present,

106

shall be of the number of the threescore and one assistants and thus as often as the case shall so require.

680. And furthermore we do grant to the president, assistants and fellowship that it shall and may be lawful to and for the president or his deputy or deputies, and to the assistants and fellowship and their successors, for the time being, from time to time forever to assemble themselves, for or about any the matters, causes, affairs or business of the fellowship in any place or places for the same convenient, within our city of [p. 34] London or elsewhere within our realm of England, and there to hold court for the fellowship and the affairs thereof.

681. And that also it shall and may be lawful to and for them, or the more part of them (whereof the president for the time being or his deputy to be one) to make ordain and establish statutes, laws, constitutions and ordinances, so as the laws and constitutions be not contrary, repugnant or derogatory to any treaties, leagues, capitulations or covenants between us, our heirs and successors, and any other prince or potentate made or to be made, nor tending to the hindrance of the trade and traffic of any of the fellowship, behaving him or themselves duly and orderly as becometh good merchants of the fellowship, without any fraudulent or disordered attempts or practices, as well for the good rule and government of the president, assistants and fellowship as of all and singular other subjects of us, our heirs and successors intermeddling or by any means exercising merchandise, in the realms of Spain and Portugal or either of them.

682. And the same statutes, [p. 35] laws, constitutions and ordinances so had and made, to put in use and execute accordingly, and at their pleasure to revoke or alter the same or any of them as occasion shall require, and that the president, assistants and fellowship so often as they shall make any such laws, constitutions, orders or ordinances in form aforesaid may lawfully ordain, limit and provide such pains, punishments and penalties by imprisonment of body, or by fines and amercements, or by all or any of them, upon and against all offenders contrary to such laws, constitutions, orders and ordinances, or any of them, as to the president, assistants and fellowship (the president or in his absence his deputy being always one) shall seem necessary requisite or convenient, for the observation of the same laws, constitutions, orders, and ordinances. And the same fines and amercements shall and may levy, take and have to the use of the president, assistants and fellowship without impediment of us, our heirs or successors, and without any accompt therefore to us, our heirs [p. 36] or successors, to be rendered or made. All and singular which laws, constitutions, orders and ordinances so as aforesaid to be made, we will to be observed, performed and kept under the pains and penalties therein to be contained (so as the same laws be not contrary or repugnant to the laws and statutes of our realm).

683. And also we do grant to the president, assistants and fellowship and their successors that the president or his deputy or deputies and assistants, or the more part of them for the time being then present, may and shall have full and whole power and authority from time to time to assess and set reasonable and convenient sums of money as well upon the merchandise to be transported or carried out of this our realm of England or dominions of the same into Spain and Portugal or to the islands of the said realms towards the south or west belonging, as also upon all other merchandise to be transported out of the realms of Spain and Portugal and the said islands in or to this realm of England and dominions of the same or elsewhere, and upon every ship laden with the said [p. 37] merchandise, as to them shall seem requisite and convenient for the common profit and sustentation of the necessary and reasonable stipend and other charges of the fellowship and corporation.

684. And further we do grant to the president, assistants and fellowship that if any of the fellowship reasonably warned by the officer or officers of the fellowship to come and appear at any court, assembly or congregation by the president or his deputy shall not come, nor shall appear at the hour or place appointed, having no just cause of excuse in that behalf, or if any of the fellowship or any other of them, which shall use trade of merchandise in the said realms, shall refuse to pay or shall not pay the sums of money so to be assessed and set upon their merchandise or ships as beforesaid, or if any shall offend or do against the advancement of the said trade and traffic, and the common profit of the privileges or liberties of the fellowship in and by these presents to the [p. 38] president, assistants and fellowship granted, or against any statutes acts and ordinances by the president or his deputy or deputies and assistants or the more part of them made or hereafter to be made.

685. Or if any person or persons whatsoever by any means directly or indirectly or by way of complaint, or by any other cautel, device, consideration or intelligence, with any foreign prince, potentate or magistrate, or with any stranger born, attempt to break violate or make void these our privileges, or any of them, or any article in these presents contained, to the president, assistants and fellowship, whether it be within this realm of England or elsewhere, that then and so often it shall be lawful to the president or his deputy and to the assistants, or to the more part of them then present, and their successors for the time being, such obstinate offenders and evil doers to chastise and correct by imprisonment or otherwise by fine, amercement or other reasonable punishment, according to the quality of the fault or offence, as by the president for the time being or to his deputy, and to the assistants, or to the more part of them, for the time being then present, shall be [p. 39] ordered and adjudged.

686. And for that divers persons our subjects being not brought up in merchandise or use of traffic, but altogether ignorant and inexpert as well in the order and rules of merchandise as in the laws and customs of the realms of Spain and Portugal, and in the customs, usages, tolls and values of moneys, weights and measures, and in all other things belonging to merchandise very necessary, through their ignorance and lack of knowledge do commit many inconveniences and absurdities (as we are informed) to the offence of us and our dear brother the king of Spain, we willing to prevent and meet with such inconveniences and intending to further and help the expert and exercised merchants in their lawful and honest trade, and to establish good order and government in the said trade, of our ample and abundant grace do grant unto the president, assistants and fellowship of merchants that they, and such only as be or shalbe of this incorporation or free of this fellowship, shall enjoy the whole entire and only trade and traffic [p. 40] and the whole entire and only liberty, use and privilege of trading and trafficking and using the feat and trade of merchandise, by and through all the parts of Spain and Portugal, from the town of Fuenterrabia in the kingdom or province of Biscay along the coast of Spain or Portugal or either of them unto Barcelona and in all the islands adjoining or appertaining to the said realms, towards the south or west part thereof.

687. And therefore we command all the subjects of us, our heirs and successors, of what degree or quality soever they be, that none of them directly or indirectly do visit haunt frequent or trade, traffic or adventure by way of merchandise into or from any the parts of Spain or Portugal or either of them from the town of Fuenterrabia unto Barcelona, neither within any islands adjoining or appertaining to the said realms, towards the south or west part thereof, other than the president, assistants and fellowship [p. 41] and such particular persons as be of that fellowship, their factors, agents, servants and assigns, upon pain not only to incur our indignation, but also to pay such pains and amercements and also to suffer imprisonment and other pains due to the transgressors of the statutes of the fellowship. Any law, statute, custom or ordinance heretofore made or put in use to the contrary thereof in any wise notwithstanding.

688. And further of our more plentiful grace we will and grant to the president, assistants and fellowship that the president, deputy and assistants, as also the consul or consuls, governor or governors, him and their assistants for the time being, or the more part of them then present, all and singular the subjects of us, our heirs and successors, not being of the fellowship which in the said dominions or any of them shall attempt to use merchandise [p. 42] in the said places and kingdoms contrary to the force and tenor of these presents, to punish them according to their statutes and ordinances, and freely and lawfully constrain and compel them that they shall desist their attempts by fines, mulcts, imprisonments and other pains. And that all and singular forfeitures levied and collected, for the violation or not observing of any acts, statutes or constitutions by the president or his deputy and the assistants made or to be made shall be levied by distress, or any other lawful way or mean, and employed to the use and behalf of the president, assistants and fellowship.

689. And further we straightly charge and command all and singular customers, comptrollers and collectors of customs, poundage and subsidies, and all other officers within our port and city of London and elsewhere unto whom it shall appertain, that they their clerks or substitutes, shall not take entry of any goods wares or merchandises to be transported into Spain or Portugal, or make any agreement for any custom, [p. 43] poundage or other subsidy for any such goods, but only of such person and persons free of the fellowship by virtue of these our letters patents.

690. And for the better and more sure observation thereof, we will and grant that our treasurer and barons of our exchequer for the time being by force of these presents or the enrolment thereof in the court of exchequer, at all and every time and times hereafter, at and upon the request of the president, assistants and fellowship, their attorney, attorneys, deputy or assigns shall and may make and direct under the seal of the said court one or more sufficient writ or writs, close or patent, unto every or any of our customers or other officers, commanding them thereby that they nor any of them at any time or times hereafter, shall take entry of any goods, wares or merchandises to be transported into Spain or Portugal, or make any agreement for any custom, poundage or other subsidy for any such wares with any person or persons [p. 44] whatsoever, other than with or in the name of the president, assistants and fellowship, or with or in the name of some person or persons free of the fellowship, by virtue of these our letters patents, willing hereby and straightly charging and commanding all and singular admirals, vice-admirals, justices and all and singular other our officers, ministers, liegemen and subjects whatsoever, to be aiding, favouring, helping and assisting unto the president, assistants and fellowship, and to their officers, agents and ministers in executing and enjoying the premises.

691. And our further will and pleasure is that all and every person and persons as by virtue and force of these presents shall be admitted and made free of the corporation of president, assistants and fellowship shall at the time of his and their admittance before the president or his deputy and four of the assistants take his and their corporal oath and oaths for his and their good behaviour in the fellowship, and for other things to be done and [p. 45] performed as heretofore hath been accustomed.

692. And moreover we do by these presents appoint that the sons and apprentices of all and every person and persons of this fellowship, as well those that were made free by virtue of the letters patent granted by our dear sister Queen Elizabeth or by virtue of our late confirmation or by virtue of this present charter, shall at the time of their admittance into the fellowship satisfy and pay such sum and sums of money severally and respectively to the use of the fellowship as the fathers and masters of such sons and apprentices severally and respectively did pay at the time of their several admissions.

693. And also before the president or his deputy for the time being shall take such oath or oaths for his and their good behaviour in the fellowship, and for doing and performing such other matters as hath been heretofore used as the president or his deputy and the assistants then present, or the greater part of them, shall think fit and convenient.

110

694. And further we will and do grant to the president, assistants and fellowship [p. 46] that the president or his deputy and the assistants or the more part of them being present at any general court, shall and may from time to time put out of the fellowship any of the fellowship for faults, offences and evil government committed against any act, statute or ordinance of the fellowship for their good government made or published, or to be made or published. And that all such persons so excluded from thenceforth shall by no means intermeddle or use any trade of merchandise or traffic there with the fellowship.

695. And further we do grant to the president, assistants and fellowship that they and their successors forever hereafter shall have one sage, fit and discreet person in form hereafter in these presents expressed and specified, to be named and chosen, which shall be the secretary of the fellowship.

696. And for the better execution of this our grant, we do of our special grace [p. 47] appoint the aforenamed Richard Langley to be the first and present secretary of the fellowship, to have, hold, exercise and enjoy the office of secretaryship by himself or his sufficient deputy or deputies for and during the term of the natural life of Richard Langley, with all and as large fees, profits, commodities and emoluments, and as fully, beneficially and amply as any other secretary to any other company of merchants, fellowship or corporation of this our realm hath, occupieth or enjoyeth, or may lawfully have for or in respect of the execution of any such office. And after the decease or surrender of Richard Langley, then we do by these presents give full power and authority to the president, deputy and assistants or the more part of them then present to elect and choose from time to time the secretary of the fellowship to have such continuance and allowance and in such manner and form as to them or the more part of them shall be thought fit and convenient, which Richard Langley or his sufficient deputy or deputies and such other person and persons as shall be so chosen [p. 48] to be secretary shall take his and their corporal oath before the president or his deputy and some of the assistants that he and they shall honestly and faithfully execute the office during such time as he or they shall use and enjoy the same in all points as a faithful assistant and secretary of the fellowship ought to do.

697. And furthermore we do grant to the president, assistants and fellowship that the president or his deputy and assistants or the more part of them then present may and shall have full power and authority at their will and pleasures from time to time to assign such and so many other officers and ministers, as well within our city of London, and in all other places of our realm of England or other our dominions, as also in the said parts beyond the sea, and every of them as to the president or his deputy and assistants for the time being, or the greater part of them shall seem expedient for the doing and executing of [p. 49] all the affairs and business pertaining to the fellowship, as also to receive, gather and levy by distress or other lawful way or means, all sums of money and amercements of all and every person as well of the fellowship being, as also of all and every other persons which shall attempt to use and exercise any trade of merchandise in the realms or dominions of Spain or Portugal, and shall be condemned and found culpable for their evil government or offence, against these our letters patent or any statute, act or ordinance by the president or his deputy or deputies and assistants for the time being or the greater part of them made or to be made by virtue of these our letters patent.

698. And further we do straightly charge and command all and every mayors, sheriffs, all and every other our officers and ministers and of our heirs and successors, to support, assist, aid and help the president or his deputy or deputies and the assistants of the fellowship in executing [p. 50] the statutes and to punish the offenders and transgressors until they be fully satisfied according to the penalties and fines by the statutes appointed.

699. And if it shall happen the president or his deputy or deputies upon just cause, to commit any of the fellowship of merchants or any other the subjects or lieges of us, our heirs or successors to any gaol or prison for any offence against the statutes or any of them done or committed, then we will and command, and do grant to the president, assistants and fellowship that from time to time all and every wardens and keepers of all such gaols shall receive into their custody all and every persons so to him sent by the president or his deputy or deputies and the assistants or the more part of them, and there safely keep them at the cost and charges of the offender or offenders without any enlargement until by the consent and [p. 51] assent of the president or his deputy or deputies or their successors he or they shall be dismissed, released or enlarged, and that neither we neither our heirs or successors by any means shall remit or release such offender or offenders out of prison under bail or mainprize without the assent of the president, his deputy or deputies for the time being, and until the offenders shall obey and satisfy the president or his deputy and assistants according to the statute and ordinance aforesaid, and shall pay such and so many fines, penalties, forfeitures and amercements as by the president or his deputy or deputies or assistants or the more part of them as he or they for such offence or contempt shall be adjudged to pay. All and every which pains, fines, forfeitures and amercements shall be gathered, received and levied, to the use of the president, assistants and fellowship.

700. And furthermore we command all and every officers, mayors, sheriffs, [etc.] and all and every other ministers [p. 52] lieges and subjects of us, our heirs and successors whatsoever that they from henceforth be helping, aiding, favouring and assisting the president and his deputy or deputies and assistants of the fellowship and also their factors, substitutes, deputies and servants and their assigns and every of them, in executing and enjoying the promises as well upon the land as upon the sea, from time to time whensoever they or any of them shall thereto be required.

701. And further we have granted and given licence to the foresaid president, assistants and fellowship to have, receive and purchase to them and their successors forever, as well of us, our heirs and successors, as of all other our subjects and lieges, or of any person or persons whatsoever, any manors, messuages, lands, tenements, parsonages, tenths, rents, reversions, services and other possessions, revenues or hereditaments whatsoever, (not being holden of us, our heirs or successors, in chief or by knights service [p. 53] nor of us, our heirs or successors, nor of any other person or persons in chief or by knights service, without the special licence of us, our heirs and successors, or without the licence of the lord or lords of whom the same lands or hereditaments are holden). So as the said manors, messuages, lands and services or any other possessions, revenues, and hereditaments do not exceed the value of 100 marks by the year, the statute of mortmain, or any other act, statute, ordinance, provision or restraint thereof to the contrary heretofore made or any other thing, cause or matter in any wise notwithstanding.

702. And moreover we will, and for us, our heirs and successors, grant by these presents to the president, assistants and fellowship of merchants that these our letters patent and all and singular grants, donations, gifts, articles, clauses, sentences and words whatsoever in the same contained and declared shall be adjudged, taken and interpreted as well before us, our heirs and successors, as our council and the [p. 54] council of us, our heirs and successors, in the court of Star Chamber as also before the justices of us, our heirs and successors, of our court of the king's bench and common pleas, and before the treasurer, chancellor and barons of the exchequer of us, our heirs and successors, or in whatsoever other courts of us, our heirs and successors, and in all other places within the dominions of us, our heirs and successors, most beneficially graciously and most in the favour of the president, assistants and fellowship and of their successors for the time being and of every one of them, and of the servants and apprentices of them, and of every one of them, and chiefly for the great profit and commodity of them, and most amply, strongly and liberally against us, our heirs and successors, any prerogative, preeminence, law, custom or act of parliament or any other thing, cause or matter whatsoever before this time had ordained, made, set forth, provided or used to the contrary thereof in any wise notwithstanding.

703. And we will and do grant to the president, assistants and fellowship [p. 55] that they have and shall have these our letters patent under our great seal of England, in due manner made and sealed, without any fee or fine great or small in our hanaper or elsewhere to be taken, paid or done to our use in any manner of wise for the same, although express mention of the true yearly value or certainty of the promises or of any of them or of any other gifts or grants by us or any of our noble progenitors or predecessors, to the president, assistants and fellowship before this time made in these presents is not made, or any statute, act, ordinance, provision, proclamation, commandment or restraint to the contrary thereof made ordained or provided, or any other thing, cause or matter whatsoever it be in any wise notwithstanding.

704. In witness whereof we have caused these our letters to be made patent, witness ourself at Westminster the one and thirtieth day of May, in the third year of our reign of England, France and Ireland, and of Scotland the eight and thirtieth, per breve de privato sigillo.

ADDITIONAL DOCUMENTS

i. Articles of trade, 1604 (B.M. Harl. 295 ff. 216–20)

705. A note of all such matters as the English merchants trading Spain and Portugal do most humbly offer to the consideration of the lords and others of the king's majesty's most honourable privy council, to be considered of in the treaty of amity between our king's most excellent majesty and the king of Spain.[1]

706. Firstly that all former grants and privileges granted by the predecessors of the king of Spain to the English merchants may be ratified and confirmed.

707. That none of his majesty's subjects or their ships, goods or merchandise shall be molested, arrested, detained or compelled to answer at law by the king of Spain or his subjects for any offences committed in the late queen's day or before the signing of the treaty.

708. That the king's subjects may be free to enter and trade in any port or haven in the dominions of the king of Spain, and not restrained to any kingdom, dominion, place or port, but able to trade where they find themselves best treated and most commodious for the sale of their merchandise.

709. That no subject of any nation shall be allowed to take legal action against Englishmen in Spanish courts, nor sequester their persons, ships or goods, for any ships, goods or treasure formerly seized, on land or water, but to be brought to justice in England.

710. That all restraints by proclamation or pragmatic against the import of any particular types of goods into Spain shall be abolished; thereafter English merchants shall be free to import goods and merchandise wrought, made and dyed in England, as well as all types of goods made in any other country whatsoever, as amply and freely as they did before 1584. They should pay the import and export duties levied in that year, no more.

711. That English merchants who freight their ships to carry goods to any of the dominions of the king of Spain, may reload them back again without molestation or interruption, or any composition made with the officers or subjects of the king of Spain for the same.

1. There is a similar document in S.P. 94/10 ff. 191–3. They may safely be identified with the articles drawn up by Wilford and read out at the general court on 24 May 1604 (see above, **31**). Both are followed by further documents amplifying the general requests made here concerning the powers of the Inquisition.

712. All Englishmen committed to the galleys or other prisons, for any cause except debt, to be released.

713. That the king's subjects may regain the house and land belonging to it at San Lucar de Barrameda, and enjoy it in as ample a manner as they did before the late restraint, and that fugitives, who are Englishmen and enemies to his majesty, and all others may be removed.[1]

714. That English merchants may be free to keep their houses and warehouses to themselves, as Spanish merchants are at liberty to do in England, and that they shall not be compelled to keep their books of account in Spanish. No *alcaide de sacas* or any other officer may enter their houses or studies, or take away any books, papers or accounts.[2]

715. If any subjects of the king of England should die in the dominions of the king of Spain, then the local English consul with three or four of the assistants, (or in their absence three or four English merchants of good credit) should administer the estate of the deceased, taking an inventory of his goods, wares, books and other things, and certifying its accuracy. The Inquisition and any other Spanish official or subject shall not meddle with the matter, under any custom, law or pretence whatsoever.

716. That English merchants shall not be molested in their persons, ships or goods, or in any other way, for any trade or traffic to Barbary or Turkey. They should be free to trade there without any interference or restraint.[3]

717. That English merchants shall not be molested by the Inquisition before they land their goods, but shall be free to land them in any port within the dominions of the king of Spain without interference. The Inquisition shall not search or examine Englishmen for any books or about any services they have held at sea, nor whether they be Christians according to the romish religion. The possession of any such books, or participation in such services at sea, shall not be prejudicial to any Englishman.

718. That Englishmen shall not be forced to land their goods against their own wishes, and that they shall pay no dues except for goods landed and sold.

719. That it may be lawful for English merchants to nominate from time to time one or more consuls and such other officers as they shall think fit,

1. See above, pp. xxx–xxxi and below, **738**.
2. The *alcaides de sacas* were customs officials whose particular task was to prevent the export of gold and silver from the realm (R. B. Merriman, *The Rise of the Spanish Empire in the Old World and the New*, vol. ii *The Catholic Kings* (New York, 1936), 42). They seized merchants' accounts in order to ascertain the sum realised by their imports, and then forced them to export Spanish goods of equivalent value, rather than return their profit in specie.
3. See above, p. ix and below, **744**. The Spaniards objected to English trade with Turkey on the grounds that trading with the enemies of Spain was universally forbidden (S.P. 94/18 f. 174).

being natural-born subjects of the king of England; those so elected shall have power to assemble themselves and to make laws to govern such of his majesty's subjects as shall be resident in the dominions of the king of Spain. No Spanish officials shall meddle in these matters.[1] If any disputes should arise between England and Spain, English subjects should have at least six months warning, for the disposal and transporting of their goods and persons out of the country without impeachment or interruption.

720. If any English merchant shall ship prohibited commodities out of Spain, then only the guilty party shall incur penalties and then only on the prohibited goods. The ship and the goods loaded on it by other merchants shall not be molested or forfeited.

721. All English goods confiscated since the king's majesty was proclaimed king of England, by virtue of any edict put out by the king of Spain and the archduke or either of them, shall be restored or satisfaction given for the same. Any customs duties or deposits paid since the king was proclaimed, that are over and above the ancient and usual customs and duties, shall likewise be restored and all bonds taken for the same delivered and discharged.

722. If any Englishman shall marry a subject of the king of Spain, then it may be lawful for them, their children or any of them separately, to come into England and to bring their goods, wares and other things belonging to them, without any let or interruption.

ii. Petition to the lord treasurer, 1604
(B.M. Cott. Nero B i f. 296)

723. The petition of the Spanish Company to the earl of Dorset, lord treasurer of England.[2]

That whereas in one of the articles between England and Spain, prohibiting the carrying over of wares of Holland and Zeeland to them, that more heed may be taken that no deceipt follow through the likeness of the wares, it is provided that the merchandise to be brought or carried out of England, Scotland and Ireland to the dominions of the king of Spain and the archdukes shall be recorded in the register of the town or city, and sealed with the seal from whence they shall be brought.

724. Forasmuch as the petitioners are desirous to observe the true intent of the articles, they do most humbly desire your good lordship's resolution, whether a certificate from the president of our company or his deputy under the seal of our company, that the said goods are registered and sealed, will be a sufficient testimonial in the courts of Spain to defend us from all

---

1. Another hand has added, 'As was granted by Henry VIII and Charles V'.
2. The petition was discussed at the general court of 7 Sept. 1604 (see above, p. xxxv, **81** and below, **748**).

trouble there, for such goods as carry any likeness with the goods of Holland and Zeeland.

725. And forasmuch as there be divers vintners, retailers and shopkeepers prohibited by our charter, which presume to adventure into Spain, and being without government will destroy the trade; the petitioners do most humbly desire your lordship's most honourable letters to the officers of the custom-house, that none be suffered to enter their goods unless they be certified by the president, his deputy, or treasurer of our company that they be free of our society; and we as we have been already bound to your good lordship and the rest of the honourable commissioners, for your lordship's care of us, will etc. . . . .

726. Endorsement by Dorset, 1 September 1604.
Memorandum: Daniel Dun and Sir Thomas Edmonds to consider of this point, for to me it seems just and reasonable that the president and company of the Spanish merchants by whom the said goods are levied and provided are able by their common seal to testify the same.

iii. Letter from Sir Charles Cornwallis, 1605 (B.M. Harl. 1875 ff. 217–19)

727. Sir Charles Cornwallis, in Valladolid, to Mr. Thomas Wilford, president of the Spanish Company.[1]

Sir, my purpose in staying Owsley here grew never out of any desire I had to serve myself of him for any business concerning my own employment, having brought with me one very able and sufficient for that purpose. But finding that his majesty's subjects that trade hither, had and were likely to find here at the first settling of the intercourse many difficulties and questions, and Owsley well experienced in the country and not ignorant of the course of traffic, I was willing for my better enabling to do them a service in such businesses as should occur to procure his stay here and to charge myself with him and a man to attend him, only to follow their occasions.

728. I have accordingly employed him in many of those general negotiations that have touched the traffic here; I have at my charge sent him divers times to the court when it has been many miles distant from this town, and there continued him for divers days whereby I obtained what was desired in sundry things very beneficial and an answer to the rest.

729. I expected a more liberal performance towards him for his travails because in your letters to me you promised it, I looked for a more kind acceptance of my own industries for you because it was more than I owed you, for in so long a time as I have been here until now very lately, neither was I required nor instructed nor so much as saluted by any of you; what I have done for you and what I have endeavoured appears in such papers

---

1. The letter was read out at the court of assistants on 5 Dec. 1605 (see above, **501**).

as in September last I addressed to the lords of the council and yourself by letters from Owsley have also had understanding of them.

730. In your late letter to him you wrote that you marvel I would take upon me to bestow the office of consulship by naming and appointing whereof were granted by his majesty to you of the company. If you would name anyone to whom I had made grant of any such office without exception of your allowance when you should be made a company, you might build your marvel upon some foundation; if in the meantime I gave allowance to one of Lisbon who had exercised the place before and was recommended to me by at least twenty of the best traders then residing in that city, by your favour it is not so much to be wondered at, as that you, having so long time past obtained his majesty's grant, have not until now very lately made it known to me, or any other here to my knowledge, that your company was established, neither sent hither any writings conducing to the obtaining of the king here the confirmation of your privileges nor given any order to any of your traders or factors to hold correspondence with one for any advertisements, as I know by some of the lords of the council you were directed, neither yet taken or sent any order hither for making of consuls or any officers that might here set orders or give directions to the traders.[1]

731. My charge and my duty it is when I came hither to protect you as subjects to the king I serve, and mine own desire is to do any service within my power to you all, in regard you are my countrymen, and men of worth who understand what appertains to wise and civil courses.

732. But I must, as well in regard of my place as of your own good, desire you will hereafter show more care of what concerns you than hitherto I have been made acquainted with, and so with my very hearty commendations to yourself and the rest of the company I leave you.

iv. Petition to the privy council, 1606
(P.R.O. S.P. 14/16 no. 118)

733. To the lords of the privy council.[2] We his majesty's dutiful and faithful subjects, the English merchants trading Spain and Portugal, do in all humbleness present to your good lordships' most honourable and grave considerations, divers injuries offered to us in Spain and Portugal the same being so grievous and intolerable that unless reformation be had therein we shall be driven to forsake the country and give over trading thither. And therefore we most humbly pray your lordships to recommend our petition in that behalf to the king's most excellent majesty; and we shall

1. For the case of Rowland Mailart, see above, p. xxxviii and **295**.
2. The document is slightly damaged in places. The drawing up of the petition is mentioned at the final court of 2 Jan. 1606 (see above, **509**). There is a similar list in S.P. 94/12 f. 199.

ever (as duty binds us) pray to almighty God to preserve his most excellent majesty and your good lordships.

734. First for matters of religion, upon false and slight accusations our servants and factors are threatened to the Inquisition, and also they practise to entrap our servants and factors by questioning with them upon points of religion, and thereby to draw them into the danger of their Inquisition. As namely about January last one William Watson, a young man and servant to Mr. Roger How a merchant of London, coming newly over into Spain to a town called Faro,[1] and passing in the street, a *canonigo* or churchman called him; and presently after a little conference a procession came by, to which the said Watson made the same reverence that the *canonigo* did. The procession being passed, the *canonigo* demanded of Watson, (being in a house, and only one or two present) whether we had that order in England et cetera. Watson asked what it was and what he meant; the *canonigo* said it was a procession and they prayed to saints for rain, and demanded what they in England thought; who answered in Latin, that no saint though never so holy was never able to save himself, much less another, without the mercy of Jesus Christ and so they pray directly to Jesus Christ and no other.

735. For these words he was the next day convented before a bishop and reproved for the same, and so far that time discharged. But about nine months after, namely in October last, for the same words so spoken he was committed to prison, into a loathsome dungeon with irons, and after set upon a mule and bound with irons and chains, and carried to Evora, and threatened to be burned; and was by them persuaded to change his religion and to be new christened, or else to be brought up in a monastery. And because he would not yield thereto, God knows in what misery he remains; and not so contented, they practise not only to confiscate all his goods, but also the goods of all others consigned to him.[2]

736. And one Nicholas Moone, servant to Francis Oliver, a merchant of London, seeing a procession coming along, did before it came near him, pass aside into a street with a purpose to have gone away. But one pursued him, using opprobrious words to him, and demanded the cause of his passing down the street; who answered that by the articles of the peace he might lawfully do so. And yet he was committed to prison for the same.

737. They will not permit any books of prayer to be used in private amongst ourselves, notwithstanding they are not so restrained here in England, but have their masses to common, (as is generally reported). And some of them dispute and maintain their opinions upon the Exchange, as merchants of good account will approve and witness.

738. They have got possession of a house in San Lucar which was built

1. Actually in the Portuguese Algarve.
2. Further details concerning the case were set out in a letter to Roger How from John Watson the prisoner's brother (S.P. 94/12 f. 118).

by the English nation and have there placed English fugitives, Jesuits and seminarians, enemies to our king and country. And for their maintenance have and do constrain our factors and servants to charge our account with a quarter per cent inward and a quarter per cent outward; and many other exactions they lay upon us, which we dare not deny to pay, for fear of the Inquisition, for if they be any way contradicted or denied their demands some wicked person or other will unjustly accuse us to the Inquisition whereby we are committed.[1] And when we are in prison none dare speak for us, neither shall we know our accuser nor know when to come to our answer.

739. By a charter granted by King Henry VIII to our company, and confirmed and allowed by Charles the emperor, we have authority to elect consuls; and by the twenty-fourth article of the late treaty, these privileges are revived.[2] And yet we have intelligence that the king of Spain will not admit any to be consuls there, but a continual dweller within his kingdom and one of their religion, which we may not by any means endure.

740. In the time of the wars between England and Spain there was a new imposition raised of three per cent by express words to defend the coast from the English ships, the which notwithstanding the peace they still continue and enforce us to pay the same. Also there is lately imposed in the Canaries a new exaction, amounting (besides the custom) for some goods to almost ten per cent, and divers other grievous exactions in other places.

741. We are exceedingly molested by several visitors; one sort coming aboard our ships for books and exact [? eight shillings] for every visitation; and in every port we put in we are soon visited [missing] called visitors of [missing] they be sued to come aboard, will defer their coming five [missing] to our great charges and hindrance. And for their [missing]. And if they find anything to their liking it may not be denied them; and our ships lying in the open road they put aboard a man to remain over us, under colour that there shall be no ballast or rubbish thrown overboard, to whom we give ryalls of plate,[3] and meat and drink every day.

742. And after they have thus visited us then may we bring our packs to land, yet the same shall not be opened but at their pleasure, and a familiar of the Inquisition must then be present to see that there be no books, neither can we be masters of our own goods but they are carried to the custom houses, where they are so cast up and down that there grows great loss in the sale thereof.

743. In Spain they do not admit us to reload our own ships if any of their own nation do demand the freight, pretending they have a proclamation from the king's father with preeminence not only to take away the freight from strangers' bottoms but also in discretion of the justice to force us to

1. See above, pp. xxx–xxxi, and **713**.
2. See above, p. xxxiv and **431**.
3. The Spanish *real*.

pay more freight in their Spanish ships, than we have agreed for with the masters of ships of our own nation. They knowing this advantage and the danger which we run in case the Hollanders should take our goods in their shipping, with many other inconveniences which they know would befall us, oftentimes they take advantage of his proclamation and thereby compel us to our great charge to compound with them, as by experience has been proved in San Sebastian in the province of Guipuzcoa and we fear every day more and more to be molested with the advance [missing]. The remedy of which would [missing].[1]

744. If any of us bring any commodities from Barbary they will not suffer us to bring the same into Spain, without great rewards given to their officers, pretending that we ought not to trade into any the kingdoms conquered by the king of Spain, of which the said Barbary is parcel.[2]

745. In September last a mean fellow caused the justices to stay an English ship in San Sebastian upon a false suggestion that she had in her fourteen or fifteen thousand ducats to be brought for England, whereupon all the merchandise that was in her was unloaded, searched and no money found; the ship likewise searched and broken up in many places, wherein the merchants and owners received loss and damage, at the least £500, and know no way to be recompensed.

746. A western bark going directly from Newfoundland (where she took fish) and arriving at Lisbon, they did confiscate both ship and goods, and committed the mariners to the galleys without any offence by them given, where they still remain for anything we hear to the contrary.

747. A mean justice will command the master of a ship to shoot his ordnance and spend his powder; if the master refuse he is committed to prison. Also they will take away their ships' barks and use them at their pleasure; and if they be denied some complaint or other will be made to the Inquisition.

748. Our goods arriving in Spain, let us make never so good proof that they are not the goods of Holland and Zeeland, they will not be satisfied but seize upon them.[3] And one Mr. Bowyer of London, sending over commodities of the value of £160 made at Norwich, the same were seized as Flemish stuff, albeit divers in Spain affirmed that the same was made here. And albeit since then a certificate was sent over under the seal of London upon the oaths of them that made the same in England and certified from

---

1. This paragraph replaces one which has been crossed through. It complains that English merchants loading English ships in Biscay are constrained to pay one *real* for every bag of wool, and that before the loading could begin a proclamation was made that if Spanish vessels were available they were to be loaded in preference to the English merchants' own ships. This in turn put English goods at risk since Dutch privateers often attacked Spanish shipping. In Galicia the English were restricted to La Coruña and Bayona, in contravention of article 16 of the treaty which allowed them to trade wherever they wished.
2. See above, p. x and **716**.
3. See above, p. xxxiv and **81**, **723–6**.

the custom house that the custom was paid here, and also a letter from the Spanish ambassador resident here, yet all this nothing prevailed but the goods are detained. And such exactions are there required for bonds and certificates of loading our goods in England, that it is not to be endured, and upon every slight suggestion they arrest us under colour of the eleventh article. And therefore we humbly pray his majesty and your good lordships to be a mean either for the annihilation of the said eleventh article, or for some better usage thereupon, otherwise we shall be continually molested without excuse,[1] and the rather because the Spaniards have of late given a toleration to Hollanders to bring corn into Spain; and the archdukes' own subjects and the Flemings, do daily carry the goods of Holland and Zeeland into Spain without molestation.

749. Also Mr. Edward Davenant a merchant of London, in May last having for his factor at Seville one Stephen Payne, and also his apprentice Henry Savill there at the same time, the tenth of May, the said Stephen fell sick and in his sickness sent for two notaries, one of the which made an inventory of all things being in his possession, and the other made a writing testifying that all in his possession were the goods of Edward Davenant (except some small things certainly named belonging to a friend or two of his). After which viz. the seventeenth day of May Stephen Payne died having before delivered both goods and account to Henry Savill the apprentice; within two days after his death the friars began a suite with Henry Savill claiming all the said goods to ransom prisoners, and the *santa cruzada*.[2] Later in July last imbarred [missing] of four, and for ought we can learn [missing] charge of Edward Davenant [missing].

750. Your lordships have heretofore had notice of the great cruelty offered in the city of Messina in Sicily to our ship and the people in the same.[3]

751. These and a number more, which would be tedious to lay down, are wrongs and injuries only offered to particular citizens of London, there being a number more such injuries offered to divers merchants of other cities and towns, to divers masters of ships and mariners which we have heard in general, but the particulars we have not enquired after, which we will do if your lordships command; and therefore are unwilling to trouble your lordships with the same, humbly craving pardon for this our boldness, because we are assured that [missing] lordships [missing] desirous of the same.

1. Among the complex regulations of the treaty of 1604 were provisions against both the import of Dutch goods and the export of Spanish goods to the rebel provinces. Certificates of origin had to be provided for imports, and securities given for exports that they would not be unloaded in Holland and Zeeland. The merchants were expected to obtain certificates of unloading from local magistrates and on the production of these in Spain, their securities were released; but the system was so intricate that the possibilities of error and corruption were endless.
2. A tax originally levied under the papal *bulla de la cruzada* against the Moors, which became a permanent source of revenue (Merriman, *The Catholic Kings*, 132).
3. This and other cases concerning English merchants in Sicily are set out in S.P. 94/13 ff. 144, 87 and S.P. 94/12 f. 9.

v. *Opinions concerning the charters, 1606*
(B.M. Harl. 295 ff. 211–212v)

752. The difficulties which have arisen in the charters of the merchants trading to Spain.[1]

[The document reviews the grants previously made to the company by Henry VIII, Charles V and Elizabeth, with particular attention to the latter.] This charter [of 1577] was used until the embargo, from which time they had no use of their charter until 1604, when a confirmation was granted of the said charters under the great seal by virtue of a general warrant granted to the lord chancellor. And upon that confirmation they entering into use again, complaints against the charter were made by merchants not free, pretending the same to be grievous; wherefore it pleased the lords of the council to refer the consideration thereof to the lord chief baron and the attorney general and others, to consider first of the validity of the charter; and if it were needful to obtain a new charter, to consider how far it might be convenient for the common good of the trade to have a new charter. Hereupon it was certified that there were imperfections in the former charter, as well in the form of words of the incorporation as also for the non-user. And thereupon the charter now in question was by order from his majesty drawn and granted as it now stands.

753. In the charter there are 557 by express name admitted to be free; and by general words all their sons and apprentices and all others named in the charter of 1577 and their sons and apprentices also. And commandment is further therein given to admit over and above the said number mere merchants not being retailers et cetera desiring the same, paying if they require it the first year £10 and if they require it the second year £15 and desiring it after two years £20. And if they be free of other companies then they are to procure one freedom for another, or to pay as much as they take of others to be made free in their companies etc., their sons and apprentices to pay as their fathers did before, as appears more at large by the breviat.

754. Exceptions are now taken to this charter; first that it is an impediment to free trade contrary to the statute of 1497.[2]

755. Response: they answer that it is no further impediment than is given by all other companies since made, viz. the Merchant Adventurers, the Russia Company, the Eastland Company, the company of Tripoli[3] which

1. The document is probably best dated to the early months of 1606 during the parliamentary attack on the company.
2. 12 Hen. VII cap. 6, entitled 'Merchant Adventurers' which decreed that all Englishmen might trade freely to the coasts of Holland Zeeland Flanders and Brabant, and the places adjoining, for a fee of ten marks. Although cited here as an act in support of free trade the statute is more usually regarded as a milestone in the development of the Merchant Adventurers' monopoly.
3. The Levant Company, first incorporated in 1581, which established one of its earliest consuls at Tripoli (Wood, *History of the Levant Company*, 11–15).

have notwithstanding been erected and continued to the good of the commonwealth.

756. Objection: that whereas mariners do now increase by fishing at Newfoundland, if they should be restrained to sell their fish in Spain they should be discouraged to go fishing, and so navigation decay.

757. Response: it is answered they shall not hereby be restrained for that the merchants trading for Spain will buy their fish from them yearly to the value of £40,000 and will bear the hazard of the venting the same again in Spain, so that they shall have no less cause to fish than they now have, which the merchants think to be the more convenient because the fishers now thrusting into every port of Spain without order do but glut the market and cannot make the best of the commodity and yet hinder the merchant.[1]

758. Objection: the Scots and Irish are left at liberty and only the Englishman restrained by this corporation.

759. Response: it is no otherwise in this than in the other companies.

760. Objection: it is over chargeable in respect of admittance money viz. for that they which come in by redemption should pay the first year £10 the second £15 the third et cetera £20 and their children and servants hereafter for ever in like sort.

761. Response: it is answered that the greatness of the charge that the company has undergone and is yearly to undergo cannot be conveniently discharged otherwise, and the good which does and will grow thereby will be to the benefit of all such as shall be admitted, and therefore that the same ought not to seem burdensome to them. Besides, that they take not more than other companies it is apparent, because they are content to admit one for another out of any company of mere merchants.

762. Objection: that none are to be admitted but mere merchants, which is against the liberty of all other subjects.

763. Response: it is said that herein the direction of 1563 has been followed because by that statute order is taken that none may exercise any mystery etc. but such as have been apprenticed to it.[2] If it shall please your lordships to change anything in this charter it is wished rather to be done by order than by a new charter, because this charter is approved in Spain and therefore suite must be made anew for confirmation if a new one should be made again, which would be a discredit to the company and benefit to none. Besides, the company of Tripoli since made will thereby encroach upon this company.[3]

1. See above, p. xlv.
2. 5 Eliz. cap. 4, statute of artificers.
3. The Levant Company received a new and permanent charter on 14 Dec. 1605 (see above, p. xlix).

INDEX

Roman numerals printed in italics refer to pages of the Introduction: Arabic numerals refer not to pages but to the numbered paragraphs of the text.

Accounts:
  of consuls, 373, 382
  of deputies, 264
  of merchants, 714, 738, 749
  of treasurers, *xxix*, 34, 66, 72–3, 146, 170
  of treasurers in outports, *xx*, 314
  see also Spanish Company, accounts
Adderley, William, 75
Addington, William, 641
Admirals, 639, 690
  vice-admirals, 690
Adriatic, *xlix*
Africa, *ix*, 468
Agents, *see* Factors
Aires, John, 642
Alabaster, *see* Allabaster
Albert, archduke of Austria, *xxix*, *xxxiii*, 468, 721, 723, 748
Alcaides de sacas, 714
Alderley, Mr., 641
Aldermen, 582
  of Bristol, 642
  of London, 2, 20, 28, 44, 49, 54–5, 71, 75, 87, 145, 191, 194, 203, 208, 216, 220, 227, 240, 242, 280, 339, 363, 412
Aldersey:
  Fulk, 23, 160, 646, 665
  Thomas, *xi*
Aldington, William, 641
Aldworth(e):
  John, 642
  Richard, 366
  Robert, 642
  Thomas, 642
Alford(e), Samuel, 643
Alicante, Spain, *xlix*
Allabaster (Alabaster), Thomas, 4, 11, 20, 40, 64, 223, 641
Allen, John, 641
Altham:
  Thomas, 38, 641
  Thomas, jnr., 38
Alum, *xxvi*
Alva, duke of, *x*
Ambassadors, 54; *see also* Cornwallis, *Sir* Charles; Howard, Charles; Tassis, Juan Baptista de
Amherst, John, 279

Amy(e):
  Edward, 649
  Thomas, 649
Andalusia, Spain, *vii*, *ix*, *xx–xxii*, *xxvii–xxviii*, *xxx–xxxi*, 467, 469
Andalusia Company, *viii*, *xxi*, *li*
  charter, *viii*, 3, 7, 14, 641, 738, 753
Andirons, *xvi*
Andrewes (Androwes), John, 490
Anele [? dye *or* glaze], 630
Angell:
  John, 642
  Robert, 54, 641
  William, 642
Anthony, Thomas, 642
Antwerp, Belgium, *vii–viii*
Anwell, *see* Lewes, Robert
Anys:
  Dunstan, 195, 379
  William, 195, 379
ApJohn, John, 26
Apprentices, *xxxvi*, *xl*, *xlii*, 8, 43, 60, 67, 78, 175, 209, 245, 313, 415, 554, 594, 597–9, 601–3, 605, 618, 622–3, 638, 656, 672, 692, 702
Apshawe (Aspshawe), John, 43, 641; (? another), 641
Apsten, Mr., 463
Archdale, Richard, 330
Armada, *xxviii–xxix*
Armourers, 221
Artificers, *xii*, *xvi*, 44, 153, 157, 263, 514, 592, 595–6, 626–8, 667, 669, 671
Ashprington, *see* Asperton
Aspshawe, *see* Apshawe
Asperton [? Ashprington, Devon], 461
Assurance policies, *xxiii*, *xli*, 275
Atkins (Atkyn), William, 450, 614
Attorney-general, *xvi*, *l*; *see also* Coke, *Sir* Edward; Yelverton, *Sir* Henry
Attorneys, 621, 690
Auditors, 72, 170, 250, 537–43, 552
Audley (Awdley):
  John, 348–50, 641
  William, 641
Austria:
  archduchess of, *see* Isabella Clara Eugenia

Austria (*contd.*)
　archduke of, *see* Albert
　Don John of, *see* John
Awdley, *see* Audley
Ayamonte, Spain, *x*, 467, 469
Azores, *xliii*, 345; *see also* Islands

Backhouse:
　Nicholas, 220
　Rowland, 220
Bagg(e), James, *xlii*, 23, 160, 249, 274, 281, 286, 307, 318, 647
Baker:
　Daniel, 642
　George, 487
　Jonas, 649
　Thomas, 487
Ball:
　Henry, 149, 189
　Nicholas, 274
　Thomas, 228
Ballast, 741
Banbury, earl of, *see* Knollys, William
Banning (Banninge, Bannyng):
　Andrew, *xxx*, 2, 4, 6, 20, 28–9, 33, 36, 46, 69, 72, 75, 79, 83, 85, 89, 110, 191, 193, 238, 286, 318, 325, 339, 353, 358, 362, 368, 378, 392, 403, 412, 414, 641, 663
　Paul, *xxx*, 3, 4, 11, 75, 188, 641
Barbary, *ix–x*, *xxix*, *xxxiv*, 716, 744
Barber, Jeremy, 656
Barcelona, Spain, *xiii*, 474, 686–7
Barker:
　John, jnr., 642
　John, of Bristol, 23, 160, 176, 642
　John, of Hull, 648
　John, of Ipswich, *xvii*, *xx*, 242
　Reginald, 641
　Richard, 642
　Robert, 379
　William, 54
　William, of Ipswich, 379
Barley, Edward, 641
Barnaby, John, 172
Barnes (Barne):
　Francis, 4, 11, 20, 85, 641
　Sir George, 240
　John, 641
　John (? another), 642
　Richard, 240, 641
　Robert, 653
　William, 653
Barnstaple, Devon, *xvii*, *xlii*, 10, 158, 160, 281, 299, 307, 654, 665
Bate (Bates), John, 4, 6, 11, 13, 20–21, 28, 33–4, 52, 65, 69, 72, 79, 93, 100, 110, 113, 191, 201, 212, 215, 223, 225, 234, 252, 271, 282, 284, 412, 420, 459, 465, 481, 493, 641, 663

Battery, beaten metal wares, *xlix*
Bayona, Galicia, *x*, *xliii*, 345, 348, 372, 433, 473
Bayona, isles of, *x*
Beaple:
　James, 654, 665
　Richard, 654
Beauvoy (Beauvoyer), Peter, 641
Beavoir, Abraham, 381
Bedford(e):
　Thomas, 655
　Richard, 653
Beedoe, John, 644
Belfeild:
　Ralph, 221
　Richard, 652
Bell, Robert, 641
Benson, George, 55, 641
Bermudas, *xlvi*
Berrisford, George, 488
Bewis (Bewys), Nicholas, 643
Bilbao, Spain, 408
Bindon, John, 642
Biscay, Spain, *xxiv*, *xliii*, 345, 347, 372, 433, 472, 502, 686
Bishop, Portuguese, 735
Black, Humphrey, 644
Blackhall (Blackyall), Leonard, 652
Blackiler (Blakiler), Thomas, 643
Blackwall, London, *xxvii*
Blanck, *Sir* Thomas, 149
Bland, Gregory, 203
Blount, Charles, earl of Devon, 637, 641
Blunt (Blunte), John, 641
Boards:
　clough, 634
　deal, 634
Bodenham, Roger, *xiii*, *xxi*
Boile, Michael, 219
Bolton, John, 642
Boman, *see* Bowman
Bond(e):
　George, 641
　Sir George, 149
　Mrs. Margaret, 203
　Martyn, 238, 247, 271, 286, 318, 325, 339, 353, 358, 362, 368, 378, 392, 403, 412, 420, 444, 453, 465, 481, 493, 500, 505, 641
　Nicholas, 149
　William, 149, 641
　Sir William, 641
　William, alderman, 203
Books, religious, 717, 737, 741–2
Boornford, William, 274
Boothby, Thomas, 217, 223, 242, 250, 280, 641
Boro (Borro), Walter, 643, 664
Bostock, Thomas, 4, 65, 79, 93, 98, 136, 238, 247, 273, 286, 325, 339, 353, 358,

362, 368, 378, 392, 403, 420, 481, 493, 500
Boston, Lincs., 158
Bourage (Bowrage), William, 651
Bourman (Boureman):
 Hugh, *xxxviii, xliv*, 151, 350, 406–9, 421, 433, 440, 467, 469, 502, 641
 Simon, 43, 151, 351, 641
Bourne, John, 641
Bowman (Boman), Roger, 642
Bowmer, Thomas, 648
Bowrage, *see* Bourage
Bowyer:
 Francis, 75
 Robert, 4, 6, 11, 13, 20–21, 52, 69, 85, 93, 113, 116, 127, 155, 174, 178, 186, 191, 201, 212, 225, 271, 284, 318, 325, 339, 392, 403, 481, 505, 641, 663, 748
Boyle, James, 219, 273
Boys, George, 646
Bragg(e):
 Matthew, 647
 Robert, 647
Bramley (Brambley):
 Thomas, 11, 75
 Sir Thomas, 447
Brand, Josias, 334
Brass, *xvi*
Brazil, *xxviii*
Bridgwater, Som., 158, 160, 289, 292, 644, 665
Bringborne, Robert, 641
Bristol, *viii, xii, xvii–xviii, xxv, xli, xliii*, 10, 15, 23, 119, 122, 124, 158, 160, 176, 286, 292, 318, 320, 389, 642, 664
Broadhempston, Devon, 461
Broderidg (Brodridge), Christopher, 652
Bromley, Robert, 227
Brooke:
 John, 13
 Percival, 119, 122, 124, 128
 Robert, 641
 Robert, jnr., 139, 149, 329, 641
Brooking(e):
 Allen, 652
 Christopher, 652
 William, 652
Brown(e):
 Edward, 642
 John, 642
Brussels, Belgium, *xxxiv*
Buckeridg(e), Nicholas, 75, 641
Buckfould, Richard, 447
Buckine, Emanuel, 644
Bucking, Robert, 289
Buffeild, John, 221
Burge (Burgh), Thomas, 8, 150
Burghley, lords, *see under* Cecil
Burgis, Richard, 648

Burgundy, France, 468
Burrowes, William, 642
Burton, Edmond, 77, 641

Cacaca, marquis of, *see* Perez de Gusman, Alonso
Cacafuego, ship, *xxiv*
Cadiz, Spain, *vii–viii, xlix*
Cage, John, 172, 331
Calais, France, *vii*
Calfskins, *xix*
Cambell:
 James, 641
 Robert, 641
 Sir Thomas, 11, 20, 85, 172, 341, 641
 Thomas, jnr., 641
Cambric, 278
Came, Matthew, 652
Camfford, Edmond, 642
Caminha, Portugal, 471
Canary Isles, *xliii*, 345, 740; *see also* Islands
Candler, Richard, *xli*, 235, 275
Canonigos, 734
Cape-merchants, 376
Caplyn (Capelyn):
 John, 188
 Peter, 655
Captains, 639
Cardiff, Glam., 158
Cardinall, Christopher, 150, 656
Cargoes, *vii, xxxv*, 156–7, 442, 689–90; *see also* Merchandise
Carlill, Lawrence, 244
Carne, William, 647
Carpet, *xl*, 183
Carrowe, Thomas, 276
Carter, William, 641
Cary, Christopher, 642
Castile, 40:
 constable of, *see* Velasco, Juan de
 king of, *xxix*
Castle, William, 204
Castles, keepers of, 639
Castlyn (Castelyne, Castelyn, Castlen), John, 72, 79, 85, 87, 100, 110, 247, 476, 481, 500, 505, 641, 643
Castro Marim, Portugal, 471
Cater, William, 55
Cecil:
 Robert, 1st viscount Cranborne & 1st earl of Salisbury, *xxxvi–xxxvii, xli, xlvii*, 97, 107, 111–12, 164, 166, 388, 395, 422, 436, 438, 637, 641
 Thomas, 2nd lord Burghley, 97
 William, 1st lord Burghley, *xi, xiii–xiv, xxv, xxvii*
Certificates:
 for customers, *xxxiv–xxxv*, 267, 724, 748
 of deputies, 617
Chace, Thomas, 347

Challenger (Challener), John, 380
Chamberlen (Chamberleyn, Chamberlayne), Robert, 6, 11, 20, 36, 39, 46, 52, 69, 83, 85, 110, 119, 127, 135, 155, 178, 186, 191, 212, 225, 252, 271, 339, 362, 420, 444, 453, 481, 641, 663
Chambers, Robert, 655, 665
Chambre, William, 641
Chancery, 7
Channel Islands, *x*
Chapell (Chappell, Chaple), John, 124, 643
Chapmen, 628
Chard, Somerset, 162, 412, 444, 651, 665
Charles V, emperor, 427, 468
Charter-parties, *xlviii*
Chester, *xvii–xx*, *xli*, 10, 23, 158, 160, 646, 665; *see also* Merchant Venturers of Chester
Chichester, Sussex, 158
Chipiona, Spain, *vii*
Church, Thomas, 91, 641
Church of England, 618
Cinnamon, 630
Clatlory (Clatlorie), John, 650
Cletherowe (Clitherowe, Clytherow):
  Christopher, 74
  Henry, 72, 74, 641
  Henry, jnr., 641
Cloths and stuffs, *xxvi–xxvii*, *xxxi*, *xlix*, 635
Clothworkers' Company, members, 38, 50, 172, 228, 242, 328, 495
Cloves, 630
Clynch, John, 160, 238, 242, 246, 271, 307, 654, 665
Clytherow, *see* Cletherowe
Cobb(e):
  Nathaniel, 188
  Robert, *xxx*, 2, 4, 6, 11, 13, 20–21, 28, 34, 36, 46, 52, 54, 69, 72, 75, 100, 119, 127, 135, 141, 155, 174, 178, 186, 188, 191, 252, 271, 318, 378, 392, 403, 412, 420, 453, 481, 505, 641, 663
Cobelton, Peter, 643
Cobham, *Sir* Henry, *xiv*
Cochineal, *xxv–xxvi*, 630
Cockayne, *see* Cokayne
Cofradias, *vii*
Coghan, Richard, 653
Coinage, *viii*, *xlix*, 376, 741, 745
Cokayne (Cockayne, Cokaynes, Coken):
  Francis, 641
  John, 641
  Richard, 641
  Roger. 641
  Thomas, 641
  William, 4, 6, 11, 13, 18, 20–21, 31, 34, 40, 46, 64, 85, 105, 113, 115, 119, 122, 124, 127, 141, 145, 191, 205, 225, 234,

253, 274, 282, 286, 289, 318, 362, **481,** 488, 641, 663
  William, jnr., 488
Coke (Cook), *Sir* Edward, *xxxiii*, *xxxvi*, *l*, 95, 101, 104, 107–8, 116, 637, 641, 753
Cole:
  William, 642
  William, of Corn Street, Bristol, 642
Coles, William, 274
Colfox, Charles, 289
Collaton, *see* Culleton
Collet, Peter, 203, 365
Collymere (Collymore, Collymer, Cullimore, Cullymore):
  George, 2, 4, 6, 11, 13, 20–21, 28, 36, 46, 52, 69, 83, 85, 100, 110, 188, 201, 271, 273, 378, 392, 403, 420, 444, 447, 453, 465, 641, 663
  Roger, 273
Collyns, Edward, 172
Colman (Coleman), Richard, 25, 58–9, 133, 139, 199, 252, 641
Colmer:
  Abraham, 647
  John, 227
Colours, 630
Colston, William, 642
Colthurst, Henry, 227, 457
Colyton, *see* Culleton
Combes, John, 172
Combleton, *see* Gomeldon
Commissioners:
  for fruit, *xxvii*
  for 1604 treaty, *xxxiii*, 725
  of crown, *x–xi*
Commodities, *see* Alum; Andirons; Anele; Boards; Brass; Calfskins; Cambric; Cloths; Cloves; Copper; Cordage; Corn; Currants; Drugs, Figs, Fireshovels; Fish; Flax; Flemish stuffs; Foodstuffs; Fruit; Grain powder; Gunmetal; Hemp; Hides; Kermes; Latten; Lead; Leather; Lichen; Mace; Metals; Nails; Nutmeg; Oil; Ordnance; Perfumes; Pitch; Raisins; Ropes; Salt; Sherry-sack; Silk; Skins; Soap-ashes; Spices; Steel; Suckets; Tar; Tin; Tobacco; Tongs; Vellum; Wainscots; Wax; Wines
Common cryer, *see* ApJohn, John
Common Pleas, court of, 702
Companies, *see* Trading companies
Composition for wines, etc., *xlvi*, 459, 482, 484, 486
Compounder for sweet wines, 484
Condado, Spain, 467, 469
Consulado, *see* Seville
Consuls, *vii–ix*, *xii–xiii*, *xx–xxi*, *xxxi*, *xxxiv*, *xxxvi*, *xxxviii*, *xliii–xlvi*, *xlviii*, *l*, 62, 96, 164, 166, 223, 295–6, 344,

128

352, 354, 367, 369, 370–3, 376, 382,
386–7, 390, 416, 426, 430, 432, 434,
436, 467–75, 502–3, 506, 673, 688, 715,
719, 730, 739
Cook, *see* Coke
Cooper:
  Benjamin, 276
  Isack, 276
  John, 366
Copper, *xv, xlix*
Cordage, *xlix*
Cordale (Cordall, Cordell):
  John, 641
  Thomas, 247, 641, 663
Corn, *xxi, xxvii, xxxii, xlv, xlvii*, 478, 748
Cornish(e), John, 655, 665
Cornwallis (Cornewallis, Cornwalleis,
  Cornwalleys, Cornwallys):
  Sir Charles, *xxxvii–xxxix, xliv, l*, 112–
    13, 116–17, 184, 194, 223, 251, 293,
    295–6, 405–7, 422, 436–40, 501–2, 727
  Sir William, *xxxvii*, 116
Coruña, La, Spain, *xxiv*
Cotton, George, 641
Couchman, John, 188
Council of State, 438
Counsel, legal, 486
Court, royal, *xi, xxvi*, 96
Cowdray, Michael, 656
Cox(e):
  Edward, 172
  Richard, 329, 641
  Robert, 289, 381
Cranborne, viscount, *see* Cecil, Robert
Criste, Robert, 329
Crocker, Thomas, 650
Crofts, *Sir* James, *xiv, xxvi*
Crosmer, Bertrand, 164, 166
Crossen, Hugh, 643
Culleton (? Collaton *or* Colyton), Devon,
  489
Cullimore, Cullymore, *see* Collymere
Culverwell, Richard, 399
Currants, *xlix*
Cushions, *xl*, 182
Customs:
  in England, *viii, xii, xx, xlvii, l*, 157, 384,
    510, 689, 690, 748
  in Spain, *vii–ix, xxxiii*, 710, 718, 721, 742
  bonds, 721, 748
  comptrollers, 157, 639, 689
  officers, *xxxv–xxxvi, xli*, 81, 122, 144,
    156, 180, 217, 442, 463, 639, 689–90,
    725; *see also* Needham, George
Cutler:
  John, 656
  Robert, 656
  Roger, 656
  Samuel, 656
  William, 656

Cutlers, 221

Dade, John, 243
Dalby (Dalbie, Dalbye):
  Richard, 227, 655
  Thomas, 78, 88, 641
Danger, Alexander, 641
Dare, William, 650
Darracott, John, 654
Dartmouth, Devon, *xlv*, 461
Davenant (Davenante, Davenatt):
  Edward, 78, 88, 241, 335, 641, 749
  John, 241
Davis (Davies, Davys):
  Jeffrey, 34, 351, 641
  John, 221, 353, 368
  Nevill, 6, 13, 34, 65, 641
Davy (Davie):
  John, 643
  Thomas, 642
  William, 653
Davys, *see* Davis
Dawborne, Robert, 329, 641
Dawks, William, 149
Dawkyns, Phillip, 449
Day, John, 651
Dent:
  Francis, 150
  John, 55, 150
Deptford, London, *xxvii*
Deputies, Western, *xlii–xliii*, 281–2, 297–
  305, 308
Derby, earl of, *see* Stanley, Henry
Devereux, Robert, 2nd earl of Essex, *xxvi*
Devon, 332, 455, 489, 497, 649, 652, 654
Devon, earl of, *see* Blount, Charles
Dickins (Diggins), Nicholas, 143, 451, 456
Dickinson, Phillip, 642
Diggins, *see* Dickins
Dipford, Thomas, 652
Dochester (Dorchester), Richard, *xlii*, 160,
  223, 281, 307, 463, 643
Doddridge (Dodderidg, Doderidge):
  John, 332, 455
  Pentecost, 654
  Richard, 654, 665
  Robert, 654
Dorchester, Dorset, 330; *see also* Dochester
Dorrington:
  Francis, 641
  George, 641
  John, *xxxvii*, 2–4, 6, 11, 20, 28–9, 31, 34,
    36, 40, 46, 52, 64–5, 69, 81, 83, 85, 93,
    98, 105, 113, 115, 117, 119, 122, 124,
    127, 141, 145, 148, 155, 163, 168, 174,
    178, 191, 201, 205, 212, 225, 234, 238,
    250, 253, 282, 325, 339, 353, 358, 362,
    368, 392, 403, 453, 455, 459, 465, 481,
    493, 500, 505, 641, 663
Dorset, 487, 653

Dorset, earl of, *see* Sackville, Thomas
Dorset House, London, 157, 397
Dottin (Dottyn), Walter, 652
Doughty, Francis, 642
Dow(e):
  Robert, *xxvii*
  Robert (? another), 11, 641
Downe:
  James, 654
  Nicholas, *xlii*, 160, 281, 307, 654
Drake, *Sir* Francis, *xxiii–xxv*
Draper, Clement, 641
Drapers' Company, members, 54, 74, 77,
  89, 91, 171–2, 221, 273, 289, 330, 447
Drugs, 630
Duck(e), William, 652
Dudley, Robert, earl of Leicester, *x–xi*,
  xiv, *xxvii*
Dun (Dunne), *Sir* Daniel, *xxxiv–xxxv*, 34,
  81, 95, 101, 104, 637, 641, 726
Dunscombe:
  George, 381
  William, 641
Durham:
  Baldwyn, 446
  Baldwyn, jnr., 446
Duties, *see* Customs
Dyers, *l*

East India Company, *xxx*, *xl*, 342–3
Eastland, *xv–xvi*, *xlix–l*
Eastland Company, *xvi*, *xxvii*, *xl*, *xlviii*,
  208, 280, 462, 756
Eaton (Heaton), Thomas, 139, 641
Edmonds (Edmunds, Edmundes):
  Ralph, 54, 641
  Sir Thomas, *xxxiv–xxxv*, 34, 81, 95, 101,
  104, 637, 641, 726
Edward III, 459
Edward IV, *xvi*
Egerton, Thomas, 1st baron Ellesmere,
  xxx–xxxi, 1, 3, 96–7, 108, 753
Elcott (Elkott), John, 643
Elizabeth I, *ix–x*, *xvi*, *xviii*, *xx*, *xxii–xxiv*,
  xxviii–xxix, *xxx*, *xxxv*, *xxxvii*, *xxxix*,
  li, 60, 96, 236, 428–9, 438, 484, 620,
  638, 640, 656, 692, 707, 753
Elizabethan settlement, *viii*
Ellesmere, *Lord*, *see* Egerton, Thomas
Ellicote, Robert, 643
Ellis (Ellys):
  Phillip, 642
  Walter, 642
  William, 642, 664
  William, jnr., 642
Elwes (Elwaies, Elweyes):
  Jarvis, 641
  Jeremy, 641
Embargoes, *ix*, *xi–xii*, *xxii-xxiii*, *xxviii*,
  721, 753

Emden, Germany, *xii*
English nation, 166–7, 453
Englishmen, *ix*, *xxii*, *xxxvi–xxxvii*, 167,
  641, 681, 701, 709, 712–13, 717–18,
  759
  mere, 600
Entries of cargo, *see* Cargoes
Erick, John, 290
Estepona, Spain, 474
Essex, earl of, *see* Devereux, Robert
Evans, William, 54, 641
Every (Everie):
  Henry, 652
  Thomas, 652
Evora, Portugal, 735
Exchange, *xli*, 275, 737
Exchequer:
  barons, *xxxvi*, *xli*, 442, 702
  court, *xii*, 95, 441–2, 690
  treasurer, 702
Exeter, Devon, *xvii–xviii*, *xx*, *xxxii*, *xli–*
  xlii, *xlvi*, 10, 23–4, 124, 158, 160, 281,
  289, 299–300, 307, 461, 463, 642, 664;
  see also Merchant Adventurers of
  Exeter
Exiles, *see* Fugitives
Exports:
  from England, *ix*, *xvi*, *xxvii*, *xxxii*, *xlix*,
  65, 68
  from Spain, *xxii*
  re-exports, *xii*, *xvii*, *xlix*; *see also*
  Commodities
Eyton, Edmund, 289

Factors, *vii*, *xiv*, *xxviii*, *xxx*, *xxxvii*, *xl*,
  xlvi, 376, 468, 621, 673, 687, 700, 730,
  734, 738, 749
Farington, Thomas, 136
Farman, *see* Forman
Farmers, *xlv*, 153, 157, 263, 478, 592,
  595–6, 626–7, 667, 669
Faro, Portugal, 734
Farrar (Ferrer), Nicholas, 38, 641
Fayrefaix, Thomas, 400
Feild, John, 227
Ferrer, *see* Farrar
Figs, 630
Fines, *see* Spanish Company, entry fines,
  fines
Fireshovels, *xvi*
Fish, *xxxii*, *xlv–xlvi*, 477, 748, 757–8
Fisher:
  John, 239, 457
  Thomas, 650, 665
  Thomas, jnr., 650
  William, 239, 457
Fishermen, *xlvi*
Fishmongers' Company, members, 228,
  276, 330, 366
Fitzherbert, Humphrey, 642

Flanders, *xii*

Flax, *xlix*

Fleet(e), William, 642

Fleming (Flemyng), *Sir* Thomas, *xli*, 104, 108, 144, 441, 637, 641, 753

Flemings, *viii*, *xii*, 748

Flemish stuffs, 748

Flesher (Flusher), James, 139, 641

Foodstuffs, *xxii*

Forman (Farman), Thomas, 11, 79, 119, 127, 135, 141, 476, 641, 663

Fornes, Humphrey, 642

Fowlks (Fulke), Augustine, 54, 172

Fownes, John, 642

Frampton, John, *xi*

France, *x*, *xvii*, *xxix*, *xlvi*, *xlix*, 1, 129, 438, 468–9, 639, 704

Franklyn, Emanuell, 228

Free trade, *xxxi*, *xliv–xlvi*, 755

Freedom; Freemen, *see* Spanish Company

Freeman:
  Thomas, 136
  William, 136

Friars, 749

Frier, *see* Fryer

Fruit, *xxvii*, *xxxii*

Fryer (Frier), Clement, 89, 641

Fuenterrabía, Spain, *xiii*, 472, 686–7

Fugitives, 713, 738

Fulke, *see* Fowlks

Furner, Symion, 85, 87, 100, 119, 135, 137, 412, 453, 465, 493, 500, 641, 663

Galicia, Spain, *x*, *xiv*, *xliii*, 472–3

Galleys, 712, 746

Gamage, Anthony, *xii*

Gamyng, William, 332

Garrard, George, 450

Garrett:
  Anthony, 240
  John, 365
  Samuel, 240

Gay(e):
  George, 654
  William, 654

Germany, *xv*, *xlix*

Gibraltar, 467–9
  lord of, *see* Perez de Gusman, Alonso

Girdlers' Company, members, 54, 75, 188, 242

Girling:
  Thomas, 277
  William, 277

Gittins, John, 642

Gloucester, 158

Gobbyns (Gobbins), Thomas, 60

Godbeare:
  Richard, 644
  William, 329

Goddard, *Sir* Richard, 11

Golden Hind, *xxiv*

Golding(e), Roger, 641

Goldsmiths' Company, members, 74

Gomeldon (Combleton), Roger, 89, 641

Goninge (Gonninge), John, 642

Goodlacke, Christopher, 414

Gore:
  Jerrard, 75, 447, 641
  Jerrard, jnr., 641
  John, 641
  Richard, 11, 641
  William, 4, 641

Gough, George, 642

Gould, Edward, 652

Governors, *see* Consuls

Grain, powder of, 630

Granule (Granudle), Robert, 651

Granvelle, Antoine Perrenot de, *Cardinal*, *xxviii*

Graves, Bartholomew, 641

Greene:
  John, 400
  Lawrence, *xliii*, *xlviii*, 3–4, 20, 46, 49, 52, 100, 113, 116, 135, 141, 148, 155, elected treasurer, 169; 178, 182–3, 186, 198–9, 201, 204, 212, 225, 239, 243, 249, 292, 318, 322, 325, 334, 337, 339, 362, 378, 392, 394, 407–8, 412, 415–16, 420, 440, 442, 444, 450, 459, 465, 481, 486, 491, 493, 500, 505–8, 641, 663
  Robert, 329
  William, 221

Greenewell, William, 462

Greenewood, John, 221

Greenwich, London, 112, 166

Gregory(e):
  Phillip, 349
  Thomas, 650

Grent, Edward, 243

Gresham, *Sir* Thomas, *xiv*, *xli*, 275

Greves, William, 642

Greville, *Sir* Fulke, *l*

Griffith, John, 642

Groce, William, 449

Grocer, king's, 485

Grocers, *l*

Grocers' Company, members, 49, 54, 74–5, 91, 171–2, 274, 288, 329, 342, 366, 379, 381, 401, 414, 449–50, 457

Groves, John, 648, 665

Guadalquivir, Spain, *vii*, *xxviii*

Guernsey, *xi*, 381

Guinea, *ix*

Guipuzcoa, Spain, 743

Gunmetal, *xvi*

Gusman, Alonso Perez de, *see* Perez de Gusman, Alonso

Guy(e), John, 642

Guybon, Gregory, 457

Haberdashers' Company, members, 74–5, 221, 228, 240, 289, 329, 333, 379–80, 447, 490
Haberdashery, *xxvi, xlix*
Hale:
  John, 274
  Richard, 149, 274, 641
Hall:
  Humphrey, 641
  John, 11, 34, 53–4, 641
  John, jnr., 53
Halwood (Hallwood), Thomas, 641
Hamburg, Germany, *xii, xv, xlix*
Hamersley:
  Hugh, 236, 379, 641
  Hugh, snr., 236, 379
Hamford, Humphrey, 457
Hammer, used in court, 559, 572, 586
Hampshire, 654
Hanaper, royal, 703
Hancock, William, 495
Handicrafts men, 153, 157, 263, 514, 592, 595–6, 626–7, 667, 669, 671
Hanger, George, *xxix*, 2–4, 6, 8, 11, 13, 20, 21, 28, 31, 34, 66, 69, 72–3, 85, 100, 127, 135, 141, 148, 150, 155, 178, 191, 201, 205, 212, 223, 225, 238, 250, 253, 271, 282, 286, 307, 318, 325, 339, 353, 368, 378, 392, 403, 420, 440, 444, 453, 465, 481, 493, 500, 505, 641, 663
Hanson, Thomas, 172
Harburne, *see* Hareborne
Harby (Harbie):
  John, 3–4, 11, 20, 31, 36, 38–9, 52, 135, 137, 148, 174, 238, 250, 325, 339, 353, 378, 493, 500, 641, 663
  John (? another), 641
  William, 641
Harding(e), Richard, 643
Hardy, Robert, 489
Hareborne (Harebrowne, Harburne):
  William, of London, 641
  William, of Yarmouth, 160, 225, 227, 231–2, 276, 493, 645, 665
Harrison, William, 138, 214, 223, 234, 247, 250, 282, 307, 353, 368, 455, 459, 641
Harrold, John, 641
Hartwell, John, 643
Harvy (Harvie, Harvye):
  Amies, 644
  Walter, 653
Harwood (Haward, Harward), Leonard, 54, 172, 641
Haward, *see* Harwood
Hassall, Percival, 399
Hassard (Hayard, Hazard):
  John, snr., 160, 653
  Robert, 653
Havers, Thomas, 641
Haviland (Havilande, Havyland):

John, 642
Matthew, 641
Robert, 642
Haward, *see* Harwood
Hawes:
  James, *xii–xiv, xxxvii*
  John, 6, 13, 20–21, 28, 34, 87, 331, 641
  John, jnr., 641
  Robert, 11
Hawkins, *Sir* Richard, 647, 665
Hawser, 376
Hayard, Hazard, *see* Hassard
Heath, Nicholas, 399, 457
Heaton, *see* Eaton
Hemp, *xlix*
Henry VIII, *viii*, 426–7, 429, 468, 640, 739, 753
Hewett, William, *xiv*
Heydon, John, *xiv*
Hibbine, Arthur, 642
Hicks (Hickes, Hix):
  Nicholas, 642
  William, 642
Hides, *xv*
Higgins, Thomas, 160, 394
Highlord (Highelord), John, *xlix*, 6, 11, 20, 28, 36, 39, 641
Hill:
  Edmond, 171
  Edmond, jnr., 171
  William, 171
  William, of Lyme, 653
Hills:
  Daniel, 139, 641
  John, 651
Hix, *see* Hicks
Hobby, Richard, 279, 333
Hoddesden (Hoddesdon), Christopher, 641
Holdich(e), Phillip, 652, 665
Holland, Bartholomew, 172
Holland, 81, 723–4, 748
  goods and wares, *xxxiv*, 81, 723–4
  merchants, 743, 748
  see also United Provinces
Hollworthy:
  John, 273
  Richard, 273
Holman, George, 641
Holmes, Leonard, 227, 231, 233, 276, 491
Honnyman:
  Phillip, 149, 641
  Thomas, 149, 509
Hopkins (Hopkines, Hopkyns):
  John, 642, 664
  Thomas, 642
  William, 642
Horton, Lawrence, 222
Hough, John, 641
Household, royal, *xxvi, xlvi*, 482, 484

controllers, *xxvi*, 482
treasurers, 482
Howard:
Charles, earl of Nottingham, 97, 116, 637, 641
Henry, earl of Northampton, 97, 637, 641
John, 203
Thomas, 1st earl of Suffolk, 97
How(e), Roger, 3–4, 6, 11, 18, 27, 30, 34–5, 42, 45, 51, 57, 64–5, 68, 74–7, 79–81, 84, 88, 89–92, 98, 100, 105–6, 113, 116, 119, 122, 124, 128, 139, 146, 163, 168–9, 205, 207, 214–15, 223, 234, 238, 241, 250, 271, 282, 286, 307, 318, 325, 335, 339, 353, 358, 362, 368, 378, 412, 444, 453, 459, 465, 493, 500, 505, 641, 734
Howell, John, 24
Howse, Richard, 172
Hukeley, Thomas, 149
Hull, Henry, 643
Hull, Yorks., *xvii*, 10, 158, 160, 249, 648, 665
Humffrey, John, 414
Hungate, William, 91, 641
Hunting, Edward, 656
Hurt(e), Roger, 642

Imports, *xv, xxiii, xxv–xxvi, xlix*
Impositions, *viii, xxx–xxxi*, 436, 738, 740–1; *see also* Spanish Company, impositions
Imprisonment, 682, 685, 687–8, 699
Ingram, Hugh, 641
Innholders, 153, 158, 263, 514, 592, 595–6, 626–7, 667, 669
Inquisition, *viii, xx, xxxiv*, 715, 717, 733, 737, 742, 747
Interlopers, *xi–xiii, xvii, xxxvi*, 153, 157, 360
Ipswich, Suffolk, *xvii*, 10, 150, 158, 160, 238–9, 242, 246, 271, 307, 379, 458, 656, 665
Ireland, *viii, xxii, xxiv, xxxvi*, 1, 129, 438, 468–9, 639, 704
Ironmongers' Company, members, 74, 91, 172, 341
Ironmongery, *xlix*
Ironside, Richard, 641
Isabella Clara Eugenia, archduchess of Austria, 468, 748
Isam:
Henry, 328
Nathaniel, 328
Islands, the (i.e. Azores, Canary, etc.), *xxvi*, 468, 524, 623, 628, 686–7

Jackson (Jaxon):
Arthur, *xlii–xliii, xlix*, 2, 4, 11, 20, 31, 34, 40, 46, 52, 64–5, 79, 83, 93, 98, 100, 105, 113, 115, 119, 122, 124, 127, 141, 145, 148, 155, 163, 168, 186, 207, 212, 223, 238, 249, 271, 286, 318, 320–2, 327, 332, 389, 420, 440, 444, 463, 465, 481, 493, 500, 641, 663
Isack, 641
Joseph, 4, 242, 641
Jacobb, Mr., and his deputy, 484
James I, *xxvi, xxix–xxx, xxxiii, xxxvi–xxxvii, xxxix, xlvi*, 7, 95–6, 108, 112, 120–1, 136, 138, 145, 157, 209, 296, 321, 386, 407, 416, 422, 429–30, 434, 437, 439, 468–9, 484, 501, 510, 512, 514, 516–17, 519, 521–4, 600, 623, 638–9, 705, 715, 719, 721, 727, 730–1, 733, 738, 748, 753
James:
Edward, 4, 20, 36, 38–9, 46, 52, 65, 69, 72, 119, 122, 124, 127, 129, 141, 148, 191, 201, 205, 212, 225, 252, 271, 286, 318, 325, 339, 353, 368, 392, 403, 444, 493, 641, 663
John, 38
Sir Roger, 44
Thomas, 642, 664
Janson, Bryan, 89, 641
Janveryne, Mr., 360
Jarmyn, Alexander, 643
Jaxon, *see* Jackson
Jennings (Jennyngs):
Henry, 289
William, 4, 13, 20–21, 28, 36, 38, 46, 52, 87, 100, 641
Jenny, Robert, 4, 149, 641
Jerez de la Frontera, Spain, *xxvii*
Jesuits, *xxxi*, 738
John, *Don*, of Austria, *xxii*
Johnson:
Henry, 495
Robert, 642
William, 646
Joiners' Company, members, 276
Jolles, *see* Jowles
Jones:
Alexander, 160, 292, 644, 665
Henry, 644
Phillip, 91, 641
Jorden, Ignatius, 643
Jowles (Jolles), John, 145, 216, 223, 363, 641
Justices, 690, 702
of the peace, 582, 658
in Spain, 743, 745, 747

Kellond:
John, 652
Richard, 652
Kerby (Kirby, Kyrby), Jeffrey, 4, 75
Kermes dye, *xxv*

Kerwyn, George, *xiv*
Kevall, William, 641
King(e), John, 641
King's Bench, 702
King's Lynn, *see* Lynn
Kingsbridge, Devon, 461
Kingswear, Devon, 461
Kirby, *see* Kerby
Kitchin (Kytchin), Abel, 642
Kittingall, *see* Kyttingale
Knight's service, 701
Knollys, William, 1st earl of Banbury, 482, 485
Kynnersley, Henry, 228
Kyrby, *see* Kerby
Kytchin, *see* Kitchin
Kyttingale (Kittingall), John, 652

Lake, *Sir* Thomas, *l*, 637, 641
Lambell:
  Gilbert, 643
  John, 643
Lambert (Lamberd), Francis, *xliv*, 348, 433, 473, 641
Land, Simon, 649
Lane:
  George, 642
  Ninus, 380
Langham, John, 278
Langley, Richard, *xxx, xxxvi, xl, xlv, lxiii*, 3, 8, 9–10, 25, 57, 59–60, 67, 98, 116, 119–20, 127, 131, 133, 135, 139, 141, 146, 148, 153, 155, 163, 173–4, 178, 180, 186, 191, 198, 201, 212, 223, 234, 238, 253, 269, 271, 282, 284, 310, 318, 325, 339, 358, 362, 378, 392, 403, 407, 420, 440, 444, 453, 455, 477, 481, 486, 493, 505, 507, 544, 641, 665, 696
Langton, John, 642
Larts, John, 643
Lary (Larie, Larye):
  John, 652
  Richard, 652
Latten, *xv*
Lawrence:
  Simon, 74, 641
  Simon, jnr., 74, 245
Lawyers, *xxx, xxxv*, 497; *see also* Attorneys; Counsel, legal
Lea (Lee):
  Hugh, *xlv*, 348–9, 390, 433, 471, 506, 508
  Richard, 652
Lead, *xxvii*
Leate, Nicholas, 341
Leather, *xvi*
Leathersellers' Company, members, 228, 278
Lee, *Sir* Robert, *xxx*, 2, 4, 6, 11, 13, 16, 20–21, 28, 34, 36, 55, 83, 119, 127,

155, 186, 339, 362, 412, 641, 663; *see also* Lea; Leere
Leechland:
  Roger, 651
  William, 650
Leeke, Thomas, 642
Leere (Lee), Richard, 652
Leicester, earl of, *see* Dudley, Robert
Lennox, duke of, *see* Stuart, Ludovick
Letters:
  from the Spanish Company, *xx, xxxiv–xxxv, xxxvii, xxxix, xli–xlii*, 10, 15, 63, 80, 121, 163, 176, 179, 223, 231, 249, 251, 281, 292, 296, 360, 400, 406, 440, 441, 502, 730
  to the Spanish Company, *xxxvii–xxxix, xlii*, 15, 23, 62, 94, 98, 101, 111, 144, 164, 167, 184, 194, 248–9, 251, 292–3, 388–90, 395–8, 460–1, 463, 482–5, 496, 501, 607, 727–32
  other letters, *xxxix, l*, 81, 100, 103, 156–8, 163, 386, 407–8, 416–17, 422, 434, 436–9, 725
Letters of credit, 410
Letters of mark, *xxiii, xxviii*
Letters patent, *see* Spanish Company, charters
Levant, *xiii, xxix–xxx, xlix*
Levant Company, *xxxvii, xlviii*, 756, 764
Levies, *see* Impositions
Lewes *alias* Anwell, Robert, 187
Lewis, Edward, 649
Licences to trade, *x, xix, xxii*
Licensing system, *xxii*
Lichen, *xxv*
Limehouse, London, *xxvii*
Ling (Linge, Lyng, Lynge), Nicholas, 11, 20, 28–9, 34, 36, 46, 69, 79, 85, 93, 100, 110, 119, 127, 135, 141, 148, 155, 168–9, 174, 178, 191, 201, 212, 223, 225, 238, 250, 271, 286, 307, 325, 339, 353, 358, 362, 368, 392, 412, 420, 444, 465, 493, 505, 641, 663
Lisbon, Portugal, *xxviii, xxxi, xxxviii, xliii–xliv, xlix*, 345, 349, 371, 390, 433, 471, 506, 730, 746
Lister, John, 160, 249, 648, 665
Liverpool, Lancs., *xix–xx*
Lobbyn, John, 648, 665
Lock, Michael, 641
Lockwood, Nicholas, 228
London, City, *vii–xiv, xvii–xxii, xxiv–xxviii, xxx–xxxii, xxxvi–xxxvii, xli–xliv, xlvi–li*, 3, 22, 26, 44, 71, 158, 194, 216, 220, 263, 273, 276, 280, 286, 290, 294, 302–3, 318, 321, 325, 329–30, 354, 379, 397, 412, 414, 444, 459, 476, 484, 528–9, 618, 623, 641, 662–3, 680, 689, 697, 734, 736, 748–9, 751
  aldermen, *see* Aldermen

chamberlain, *see* Wilford, Thomas
citizens, 459
livery companies, *see under individual companies*
lord mayors, *xiii*, 26
merchants, *viii, x, xiii, xvii, xix, xxxi, xxxvi, xli–xlii, xlvi–xlviii, l–li*
streets:
Fenchurch St., 278
Lime St., *xxvii*
see also Dorset House; Middle Temple
Long, John, *xli*, 441
Lort(e), Sampson, 642
Low Countries, *see* Netherlands
Lyme Regis, Dorset, *xlv*, 160, 653, 665
Lymer, Robert, 150
Lynch, Edward, 203
Lyng, *see* Ling
Lynn, Norfolk, *xvii*, 10, 159–60, 189, 228, 248, 273, 277, 400, 450, 457, 487
Lyvemore, John, 643

Mace, 630
Mackworth, *see* Maycott
Madeira, *see* Matheres
Madrid, *xiv, xxxi*
Mailart, *see* Maylard
Malaga, Spain, *xliii–xliv, xlix*, 345, 351, 372, 433, 474
Man:
Edward, 487
John, 487
Manning (Mannyng), Randall, 641
Manstedg(e), Thomas, 650
Mariners, *xxviii, xlv*, 143, 263, 451, 595–6, 621, 627, 669, 757
Matheres (? Madeira), 345
May(e):
Richard, *xxviii*, 25, 245
Richard (? another), 75, 90
Maycott *alias* Mackworth, Cavaliero, 641
Maylard (Mailart), Rowland, *xxxviii–xxxix*, 295, 730
Maynard(e), Christopher, 652
Mayors, 448, 582, 698, 700; *see also* London, City, lord mayors
Medina Sidonia, dukes of, *xx, xxxi, xxxiii*, 416, 425, 434–5, 438–9, 470; *see also* Perez de Gusman, Alonso
Melcombe Regis, Dorset, 448, 498
Mellyn (Mellin), William, 642
Mendoza, Bernardino de, *xxiii–xxv*
Mercers' Company, members, *xi*, 54, 75, 78, 171–2, 219, 240, 243, 273, 275, 328, 379, 399, 414, 446, 457
Merchandise, *ix–x, xv–xvi, xix–xx, xxii–xxiii, xxvi–xxviii, xxxiv–xxxv, xliv–l*, 65, 81, 122, 153, 156–7, 180, 263, 265, 301, 330, 373–4, 376, 383–4, 468, 477–8, 503, 510, 517, 523, 594, 601, 621, 623–4, 626, 628, 630, 681, 683–4, 686–90, 694, 697
prohibited merchandise, *xxi*, 720
Merchant Adventurers, *vii, x–xvii, xxiv–xxvi, xxxii, xl, xlviii–xlix, li*, 220, 222, 280, 756
Merchant Adventurers of Exeter, *xvii, xlvi*
Merchant Staplers, *vii, x*, 208, 280
Merchant Tailors' Company, members, *xiv*, 38, 55, 74–5, 78, 89–90, 172, 228, 241–3, 273, 365, 380–1, 415, 447
Merchant Tailors' Hall, *xxxix*, 122–3
Merchant Venturers:
of Bristol, *xviii*
of Chester, *xviii–xix*
Merchants, foreign, *viii, xxiv*
Merchants, mere, *xvi, xix, xxxv, xlvii, l*, 55, 77, 91, 136, 175, 187, 204, 209, 221, 228, 243, 263, 276, 278, 290, 330, 342, 366, 381, 400, 449–50, 461, 491, 592–4, 627, 667, 668, 671, 754, 763
Merrick (Merick):
John, 641
John, of Bristol, 642
Mershe, *Sir* John, *xi–xiv, xviii*
Messina, Sicily, 750
Metals, *xvi*
Mewles, John, 654
Michaell, John, 644
Middle Temple, *xlv*
Middle Temple Hall, 477
Milford Haven, Pembroke, 158
Mills (Milles), Francis, 655
Mokett (Mockett), John, 47, 448
Monday, *see* Munday
Monopolies, *see* Patents
Moone:
Anthony, 653
Nicholas, 736
Moore, John, 54
Morley, John, 641
Morocco, straits of, *ix*, 467, 469
Morris (Morries):
Edward, 642
John, 329
Morse, William, 289
Moxey, John, 414
Muffett, Peter, 244
Munday (Monday):
Edward, 651
Henry, 651
Munslow, Mr., *xxvi*
Munster, Ireland, *xxiv*
Muscovy, *see* Russia
Myldmay, Robert, 401

Nails, 631
Needham:
Arthur, 447
George, *xxvi–xxvii*

Netherlands, *x*, *xxii*, *xlix*; *see also* United
Provinces
Nevey (Nevye), William, 160, 225, 227,
233, 360, 441, 463, 655, 665
New world, *viii, xxiii–xxv*
Newcastle-upon-Tyne, Northumberland,
xvii, 10, 158, 161
Newfoundland, *xxxii, xlv*, 746, 757
Newman:
John, 4, 11, 20, 52, 56, 69, 74–5, 83, 85,
93, 100, 127, 141, 148, 155, 168–9,
174, 178, 191, 225, 252, 271, 286, 318,
325, 339, 362, 378, 392, 412, 419, 444,
453, 465, 481, 493, 500, 505, 641, 663
John, jnr., 74, 641
Richard, 276
Richard, of Exeter, 643
Richard, of Totnes, 652
Newton:
Henry, 328
John, *xxxix, xlii–xliii, xlv, xlvii*, 54,
119, 122, 124, 127, 141, 148, 155, 171,
174, 178, 186, 201, 205, 207, 212, 214,
223, 224, 238, 239, 245, 249–50, 253,
270, 282, 284–5, 291, 307, 317, 320–2,
324, 327–9, 332, 337, 389, 414, 440,
443, 452, 459, 463–4, 477, 480, 486,
492, 499, 504, 641, 663
John, jnr., 171
Newton Bushel, Devon, 461
Niebla, earl of, *see* Perez de Gusman,
Alonso
Norfolk, 400, 645
Norris:
John, 653
Richard, 653
Northampton, earl of, *see* Howard, Henry
Northumberland, earl of, *see* Percy,
Henry
Norwich, Norfolk, 491, 748
Notaries, 749
Nottingham, earl of, *see* Howard, Charles
Nutmeg, 630

Oil, 630
Oliver, Francis, 139, 641, 736
Ordnance, *xxi*, 747
Osborne:
Edward, *xii–xiii*
Peter, *xi*
Oseley (Osely), Nicholas, *xxxvii–xxxix*,
50, 184, 194, 223, 251, 405, 406, 439–40,
501–2, 641, 727–9
Outports, *xii, xvii–xx, xxxi, xxxiv, xxxvi,
xli–xliii, xlv–xlvii, l–li*, 22–3, 63, 121,
158–60, 234, 533–69; *see also*
Accounts, of treasurers; Deputies,
Western; Ports, privileged
Owen:

Robert, 642
Thomas, 89, 119, 122, 124, 135, 137,
141, 148, 155, 174, 186, 191, 201, 212,
271, 284, 318, 325, 378, 403, 412, 444,
453, 481, 493, 641, 663
Owfield(e), Walter, 642

Pallavicini family, *xxxvi*
Palmer, William, 152, 347, 641
Paris, *xxviii*
Parke, Zachary, 457
Parker, Leonard, 4, 75, 641
Parkyn, William, 457
Parliament, *xxx–xxxii, xxxv, xxxvii,
xxxix, xlvii*, 24, 477, 592, 594–5, 600
acts of, *xlvi, l*, 592, 594–5, 600, 667, 682,
701–3, 755, 764
bills of, *xxxiii, xlvi*, 7, 40
committees of, *xxxiii, xlv–xlvi*, 471
house of Commons, *xxx–xxxiii, xxxvi,
xlvi*
house of Lords, *xxxiii, xlvi*
members, *xxxi–xxxiii, xlv–xlvii*
Parslowe, Gyles, 75, 85, 87, 100, 353, 368,
641
Parsons, Fr. Robert, *xxxi*
Partnerships, *xl, xlviii*, 153, 624–5
Pasages, Spain, *l*
Patents, *xxv–xxvi, xxxi–xxxii, xxxvii,
xlv–xlvi, xlvii–li*
Patronage, *xli*, 144, 166, 387, 395–8, 463
Payne:
Robert, 641
Silvanus, 279
Stephen, 749
William, 227
Peacock:
Robert, 288
Robert, snr., 288, 329
Peele, Nicholas, 13, 20–1, 34, 36, 46, 52, 83
Pennystone, Anthony, 641
Pentigrace, Robert, 642
Percy, Henry, 9th earl of Northumberland,
97
Perez de Gusman, Alonso, duke of
Medina, *vii*, 424, 468
Perfumes, 630
Periam, John, 643
Perry (Perrie):
Richard, 643
Robert, 643
Peshall, Edmond, 149
Peter, John, 289
Petit lodagie money, 376 & n
Petitions, *viii–ix, xi, xxv, xlvii*, 439
Pewterers' Hall, *xxvii, xxxii, xxxix, xl*, 12,
27, 34–5, 45, 51, 68, 82, 84, 92, 99, 109,
118, 126, 134, 140, 147, 153, 174, 177,
182, 185, 189, 200, 211, 223, 237, 270,
285, 306, 317, 324, 338, 357, 361, 368,

377, 391, 402, 411, 419, 443, 452, 464, 480, 492, 499, 503
Peyton, Henry, 139, 641
Philip II, *viii–x, xxii–xxiv, xxxiii*, 60, 620, 743
Philip III, *xxix, xxxiii–xxxiv, xxxvi–xxxvii, xxxix*, 41, 54, 112, 295–6, 407, 409, 416, 434–5, 437–9, 468, 641, 686, 705–8, 711, 715, 717, 721–2, 730, 739, 744
Phipps, Humphrey, 276
Pilotage, 376
Pinner, *see* Pynner
Piracy, *xxiii, xxviii*
Pitch, 634
Pitt (Pytt):
  John, 288
  Richard, 288
  Thomas, 642
  William, 642
Plate, *xlvi*; *see also* Coinage
Plea, George, 653
Plomer, Henry, 463
Plymouth, Devon, *xvii, xxiv, xli–xlii*, 10, 23, 158, 160, 249, 274, 281, 286, 299, 307, 318, 414, 647, 665
Pooell, *see* Powell
Poole, Dorset, 158, 487
Pope:
  Lewis, 650
  Thomas, 643
Popham, *Sir* John, *xlviii*
Portage, 621
Ports, privileged, *xvii–xli*, 10, 63, 121, 159, 320
  in Spain, 708, 717, 758
Portugal, *vii–xii, xiv–xv, xvii–xviii, xx, xxii, xxiv–xxv, xxviii, xxxv–xxxvi, xlv–xlvi, xlix*, 3–734 *passim*
  king, *xxix, xxxvii*; *see also* Sebastian I
  markets, *x*
  merchants, *xxv*
  ports, *xxix*
Potter, John, 641
Powell (Pooell):
  Richard, 642
  Thomas, 642
Pragmatics, 710, 721, 743
Presentments, 534, 608, 610, 614–15
Prestwood, Thomas, 652
Prideaux, Thomas, 652
Primage, 376
Prisons, 699, 712, 735–6, 738, 747; *see also* Imprisonment; War, prisoners of
Privateers, *ix, xv, xix, xxviii–xxx, xxxii*
Privy Council, *xii–xiii, xvi–xxvi, xxix–xxxi, xxxiii–xxxv, xl, xlvi, l*, 31, 34, 40, 94, 98, 101–3, 138, 206, 386, 509, 641, 702, 705, 730, 733, 748, 753, 759, 764

Processions, 734, 736
Provisions for ships' masters, 621
Prowse, Richard, 649
Puerto de Sta Maria, Spain, *vii–viii*
Pulham, John, 641
Pullison (Pullyson), *Sir* Thomas, *xii–xiii, xvi*, 13, 20–1, 34, 36, 46, 54, 69, 83, 85, 89, 128, 227, 340, 641
Purveyance, 459, 486
Pyne, Jasper, 651
Pynner (Pinner), William, 642
Pytt, *see* Pitt

Quays, *xxvi–xxvii*
  Customhouse quay, *xxvi–xxvii*
Quick, Michael, 642
Quirck(e), Robert, 644

Raisins, 630
Ramridge (Rombridg, Romsbridge), John, 54, 203, 247, 350, 641
Randall, Noah, 644
Rawlins (Rawlyns), Robert, 647
Reade, Morgan, 642
Religion, matters of, *viii, xx–xxii, xxiv, xxxi, xxxiv*, 717, 734–5, 739; *see also* Books, religious; Church of England; Services
Retailers, *ix, xii, xvi, xviii–xix, xxxv, xl–xli, xlvii*, 44, 78, 96, 153, 157, 209, 263, 265, 515, 592, 594–6, 626–35, 667–9, 671, 725, 754
Retailing, 175, 221, 228, 243, 258, 278
Reynolds (Reynoldes), Richard, 245, 284, 329
Richard II, *xvi*, 459
Roberts:
  Henry, 642
  John, 642
Robinson, John, *xxvii*
Rogell, Roger, 447
Rogers, Roger, 641
Rolls, master of the, *xvi, xix*
Romaging, 376
Rombridg, *see* Ramridge
Romeney (Romeny, Romney), *Sir* William, 6, 11, 20, 31, 40, 64, 69, 71, 81, 85, 98, 100, 105, 113, 116, 119, 122, 127, 133, 135, 141, 145, 191, 225, 339, 353, 641, 663
Romsbridge *see* Ramridge
Ropes, 632
Rota, Spain, *xxvii*
Rowborrowe, John, 642
Roye, John, 330
Rumbald, Francis, 228
Russia, *xlix–l*
Russia Company, *xxxii*, 756
Rye, Sussex, 160, 394
Ryvett, Edward, 656

137

Sack, *see* Sherry-sack
Sackford, *Sir* Henry, 641
Sackville, Thomas, 1st earl of Dorset, *xxxv, xli,* 97, 156–7, 163, 388, 395, 637, 641, 723, 726; *see also* Dorset House
Sailors, *see* Mariners
St. George, brotherhood of, *vii–viii, xiii, xx–xxi, xxx–xxxi, xxxiii–xxxiv, xxxviii, xlviii*
chapel, *vii–viii, xxi*
chaplains, *xxxi*
St. George's day, *vii–viii, xxi, xxx*
St. Jean de Luz, France, *x*
Salcombe, Devon, 461
Salisbury, earl of, *see* Cecil, Robert
Salt, 621
Saltenstall, Mr., 641
Salter, William, 641
Salters' Company, members, 55, 228, 331
Saltingstall (Saltonstall):
Sir Richard, *xiii,* 43
Sir Samuel, 641
Samuell (Samnell), George, 13, 25, 641
Samwayes, Henry, 650
San Lucar de Barrameda, Spain, *vii–ix, xiii, xx, xxx–xxxi, xxxiii, xxxviii, xliii–xliv, xlviii,* 345, 350, 370, 409, 416, 424, 433, 467–70, 713, 738
San Sebastian, Spain, *l,* 408, 743, 745
San Miguel, Azores, 345
Sandwich, Kent, 158, 161
Sandy(e):
John, 643
Robert, 342
Sandyll (Sendall), Thomas, 160, 189, 284
Sandys, *Sir* Edwin, *xxxiii*
Sanford:
John, of Bristol, 642
John, of Exeter, 643
Santa cruzada, 749
Savage, Robert, 13, 20–1, 28, 34, 36, 46, 49, 69, 83, 85, 100, 119, 127, 135, 148, 155, 174, 191, 201, 225, 238, 271, 286, 325, 339, 358, 362, 420, 453, 465, 481, 493, 641, 663
Savary (Savarie, Savery, Saverie):
Richard, 652
Timothy, 652
Savill, Henry, 748
Scotland, 1, 129, 321, 468–9, 639, 704
Seals, *xiii,* 438, 448, 637, 690, 704, 748
great seal of England, *xxxviii,* 3, 7, 120, 129, 157, 321, 405, 468, 703, 753
Sebastian I, *ix*
Seminaries, *xxxi,* 738
Sendall, *see* Sandyll
Seracold, Thomas, 54, 641; *see also* Suracold
Servants, *xv, xxxvii,* 397, 401, 455, 468, 523, 622–3, 628, 637–9, 673, 687, 734, 738
Services, religious, 717
Seville, Spain, *vii–viii, x, xiii, xxiii–xxiv, xxviii, xxxi, xxxviii, xliii–xliv,* 345, 350, 370, 433, 467, 469–70, 749
cardinal-archbishop, *xxxi*
consulado, xxiv–xxv
Shaw(e):
Francis, 328, 641
Leonard, 328
Shawcroft, William, 242
Sheere, William, 649
Shere, *see* Shore
Sheriffs, 642, 698, 700
Sherratt, William, 488
Sherrington:
John, 75, 641
William, 279, 333, 490
Sherry-sack, *xxvi*
Sheward, Robert, 642
Ships and vessels, *vii, ix, xxii–xxviii, xl, xlviii, l,* 373, 382, 621, 683–4, 707, 709, 711, 716, 720, 740–1, 743, 745; named, *see Cacafuego; Golden Hind*
shipbuilding, *xlv*
ship's company, 376
ships' masters, 143, 376, 382, 621, 743, 747, 751
ships' owners, *xxii,* 382, 621
Shopkeepers, *xxxv, xlvii,* 96, 144, 209, 594, 725
Shopkeeping, 125, 217, 278
Shopley, John, 652, 665
Shore (Shere), John, 643
Shorter:
Richard, 74, 641
Salaman, 273
William, 74, 273
Sicily, 750
Signet, 438, 637
clerks of, 641
Silk, 650
Skeggs, Edward, 221
Skinner (Skynner):
George, 649
Nicholas, 649
Skinners' Company, members, 38, 53–4, 75, 188, 221, 226, 244, 274, 289, 399, 414, 488
Skins, *xv; see also* Calfskins; Hides
Skybow, John, 329
Skynner, *see* Skinner
Slack, William, 642
Slany, Humphrey, 139, 641
Slee:
George, 649
Richard, 649
Smyth (Smythe, Smith, Smithe):
Gilbert, 643

138

Nicholas, 75, 641
Phillip, 74, 641
Phillip, jnr., 74
Robert, 642
Simon, 229
Simon, jnr., 229
Thomas, 652
Sir Thomas, 11, 641
Sir Thomas, clerk of privy council, 637–41
Snelling(e):
  Richard, 656
  Walter, 656, 665
Snode (Snoade), Gyles, 247, 250, 641
Snowe, Thomas, 643
Soame, *Sir* Stephen, *xlix*, 194, 208, 280
Soap-ashes, 634
Solda, Richard, 641
Solicitor-General, *xvi*; *see also* Dodderidge, John
Somers, *Sir* George, *xlv–xlvi*
Somerset, 644, 650–1
Somerset, Edward, earl of Worcester, 97
Sotherton, George, 641
Southake (Southwick), Thomas, 54, 641
Southampton, Hants., *viii*, *xvii*, *xli*, 10, 144, 158, 160, 225, 227, 232–3, 291, 360, 441, 463, 498, 655, 665
Southwick, *see* Southake
Sozar, John, *xli*, 496
Spain, *vii–xiii*, *xv*, *xvii–xviii*, *xx–xxv*, *xxviii–xxx*, *xxxiii–xxxix*, *xliii–li*, 3–764 *passim*
Spanish authorities, *xx–xxi*, 711, 714–15 719, 744
  court, *xliv*, 409, 728
  crown, *vii*, *xxix*; *see also* Charles V; Philip II; Philip III
  dominions, *xxiii*, *xxviii–xxix*
  economy, *viii*
  embassy, *xxiv*
  language, 495–6, 509, 714
  law, *ix*, *xxxiii*, 468, 686, 707, 709, 722
  loading regulations, *ix*, *xxii*, *xxv*, *xxxiv*
  market, *xxxv*
  merchants, *xxv*, 714
  navigation laws, *xxii*, *xxviii*, *xxxiv*
  shipping, *xxii*
  silver, *xxiv*
  subjects, *xii*, *xxiv*, *xxxiii*
Spanish Company:
  accounts, *xx*, *xxix*, 34, 66, 72–3, 146, 170, 182, 198–9, 250, 264, 292, 314, 322, 336, 373, 382, 416, 442, 486, 513, 535–43, 552
  acts, *xii*, *xv*, *xxvii*, *xl*, *xlii–xliii*, *l*, 256–8, 269, 301, 305, 311, 320–1, 332, 345, 356, 359, 367, 418, 426, 468, 510, 517, 521, 523, 526–638, 673, 681–2, 684, 687–8, 694, 697–9, 719

arms, 80, 421
assemblies, *xxxvi–xxxix*, 9, 14, 92, 96, 99, 101, 109, 115, 123, 168, 174–5, 177, 184–5, 187, 192, 337, 510, 684
assistants, 10–703 *passim*, 715
certificates, miscellaneous, *xxxiv*, 267, 617, 724, 728
certificates of fitness, 263, 276, 313, 448, 450, 491, 602–3
charges, 3, 7, 34, 40, 42, 98, 106, 116, 146, 168, 170, 182–3, 292, 304, 322, 360, 368, 394, 408, 416, 442, 455, 459, 486, 507–8, 519–20, 670, 683, 753
charters:
1577, *xii–xiv*
1603, *xxx–xxxiii*, 7, 10, 14, 34, 96
1605, *xxxv–xxxvii*, 108, 129, 321, 430, 639–704; *see also* Andalusia Company, charter
committees, *x*–497 *passim*
courts general, *xx*–694 *passim*
courts in the outports, *xlii*, 199, 301, 305, 320
courts of assistants, *xxvii*–576 *passim*
entry fines, *xvi*, *xx*, *xli–xlii*, *xlviii*, 33, 38, 42, 49, 54–5, 57, 59, 74–7, 88–91, 133, 138–9, 149–52, 171–2, 187–8, 203–4, 210, 216–17, 219–21, 226–30, 239, 241–5, 264, 273–4, 276–7, 280, 284, 288–90, 304, 328–31, 335, 341–2, 365–6, 379–81, 399–400, 414–15, 441, 446–51, 457–8, 463, 487–8, 491, 495, 589, 591–2, 594–5, 597, 599, 618, 636–7, 667–71, 692, 754, 761
fees, *xxxiv*, *xxxix*, *xliv*, 9, 16, 25–6, 42, 62, 198–9, 251, 336–7, 406, 409, 506, 508, 542, 551–2, 564–6, 696
fines, *xv*, *xl*, 153, 252, 265, 304, 359, 418, 510, 531–2, 539, 560–1, 569, 571–5, 578, 581–6, 588, 603, 607, 609–12, 617–18, 621, 623, 625–6, 628, 636–7, 682, 685, 687–8, 698–9
freedom, *xxxvi*–761 *passim*
freemen, *xvii*–754 *passim*
impositions, *xxx*, *xliv*, *xlvii*, 3, 181, 268, 310, 355, 367, 373–4, 382–4, 426, 436, 468, 503, 621, 683–4, 688, 697, 738 740–1
indentures, *xlii*, 8, 59–61, 67, 256, 313, 380, 354–5, 599, 602, 605, 618–20; *see also* Apprentices
letters, *see* Letters
oaths, 33–696 *passim*
petitions,
  made by the company, *xvi*, *xxiv*, *xlvi*, 81, 422–36, 438, 456, 509, 723–6, 733–51
  made to the company, *xli–xlii*, 235, 275, 451, 496, 498, 606–7, 613
  other petitions, *viii–ix*, *xi*, *xxv*, *xlvii*, 439

139

Spanish Company (*contd.*)
  president, *xiii*–726 *passim; see also* Wilford, Thomas
  privileges, in Spain, *vii–viii, xxix, xxxi, xxxiii–xxxiv, xxxvii–xxxix,* 112, 117, 153, 223, 251, 416, 421, 423, 431, 434, 438–9, 468, 470, 510, 515, 706, 730, 739
  property, *vii, xx–xxi, xxiii, xxv, xxxi, xxxiii,* 424, 713–14, 738
  seal, *xxix, xxxiv–xxxv,* 80, 249, 321–2, 327, 467, 469, 475, 659, 724, 726
  secretary, *xl,* 3, 9, 25, 153, 521, 529, 544–57, 568, 589, 591–2, 595, 599, 604, 608, 618, 620, 625, 695–6; *see also* Langley, Richard; May, Richard
  treasurer, *xxxii, xl, xliii,* 18, 169, 336–7, 519, 522, 530–7, 551, 559, 561–3, 565, 589, 608–9, 611, 725; *see also* Greene, Lawrence; Hanger, George; Howe, Roger; Watts, *Sir* John
Speight, William, 55, 651
Spence, John, 495
Spencer:
  Humphrey, 645, 665
  Sir John, 4, 149, 242, 340, 641
Spicer (Spiser):
  Christopher, 643
  Nicholas, 643, 664
Spices, *xvi, xlvi,* 459, 482, 486
Sprake, Richard, 651
Spurwaie, Walter, 652
Squyre (Squire), William, 652
Stade, Germany, *xlix,* 397
Stafford, *Sir* Thomas, *xxviii*
Stanlack, William, 642
Stanley, Henry, 4th earl of Derby, *xix*
Staper (Stapers):
  Hewitt, 196, 641
  James, 641
  Richard, *xlix,* 4, 6, 11, 20, 36, 39–40, 46, 52, 64, 85, 110, 127, 155, 172, 178, 191, 195, 223, 225, 238, 271, 276, 339, 353, 362, 641, 663
Star Chamber, 702
Starkey, Thomas, *xii–xiii,* 227
Stavely, Paul, 227
Staverton, Devon, 461
Steel, 663
Stephens, Richard, 149, 641
Stile (Style):
  Nicholas, 11, 87, 119, 212, 215, 238, 362, 403, 453, 457, 500, 641, 663
  Oliver, 11, 641
  Thomas, 274
Stills, Thomas, 641
Stokeley:
  John, 89, 172, 250, 641
  Thomas, 172
Stone, William, 4, 13, 75, 250, 641

Stoner:
  Peter, 291
  Thomas, 291, 655
Stowe, John, *xxiv*
Strachey, John, 149
Stradling, John, 289, 292
Straits, *see* Morocco, straits of
Strangers, 167, 356, 367, 510
  Merchant strangers, *xxv*
Strawe, Nicholas, 652
Stronginarme, John, 89, 641
Stuart, Ludovick, 2nd duke of Lennox, 62
Style, *see* Stile
Suckets, 630
Suffolk, 656
Suffolk, earl of, *see* Howard, Thomas
Summonses, 252, 354
Suragold (Suragold, '*alias* Seracold'), John, 76, 641
Sureties, 30, 169, 531, 609
Sussex, downs, *l*
Sweene, Mr., 127
Sweete (Swette):
  Henry, 24, 643
  Richard, 643
Swetnam, Lawrence, 642
Swynnerton (Swynerton):
  Sir John, 199, 122, 124, 145, 155, 191, 641, 663
  John, snr., 641
Symcotts, Jon, 172
Symms (Syms, Symmes):
  Richard, 204
  Thomas, 412, 444, 651, 665
Symonds:
  Thomas, 399
  Thomas, of Bristol, 642

Tallow, *xv, xlix*
Taper, Oliver, 643
Tar, 634
Tassis, Juan Baptista de, *xxxvii,* 54, 223, 509, 748
Taunton, Somerset, 162, 329, 650, 665
Taverns and victualling houses, 629
Taxes, 112
Taylor (Tayler, Tiler, Tyler), Francis, 54, 641
Tedcastle, John, 447
Tegg(e), Richard, 642
Teignmouth, Devon, 461
Terceira, Azores, *xxviii*
Tessemond, Thomas, 491
Thomas, Walter, 642
Thompson, Allen, 13, 415, 641
Thurscroste, Luke, 648
Thurston, William, 228
Tiler, *see* Taylor
Tillett, *see* Tyllet
Tin, *xxvii*

Tipper (Typper):
  Robert, 641
  William, *xxv–xxvi*, 641
Tiverton, Devon, 649
Tobacco, *l*
Toll-bills, *xlviii*
Tongs, *xvi*
Topsham, Devon, 455, 497
Tor Bay (Toore), Devon, 461
Totnes, Devon, 162, 461, 652, 665
Towerson (Towreson, Towereston, Toureson):
  Nicholas, 641
  Parnell, 89, 414
  Robert, 141, 226, 641
  William, 4, 20, 53, 69, 72, 83, 119, 122, 127, 135, 145, 148, 155, 163, 178, 186, 191, 212, 223, 225–7, 234, 282, 414, 453, 500, 505, 641, 663
  William, jnr., 53
Towker, John, 651
Trade:
  illicit, *x, xxi, xxix, xxxii, xxxvii, xlv*
  triangular, *xxxii, xlv–xlvii*
  see also Free trade
Trading companies, *xxxi, xxxvii, xl, xlvi, xlviii*
  joint stock, *xxx–xxxi, xl, xlviii, xlix–l*
  regulated, *xi, xxiv, xlviii, l*
  see also under individual companies
Traves, Edward, 149
Treasure, 709
Treaties, *xxix*, 112, 681
  of 1604, *xxxi, xxxiii–xxxiv, xxxvii, xlix*, 31, 34, 63–5, 81, 468, 641, 705, 707, 723–4, 736, 739, 748
Trigge (Trige), Paul, 643
Trilany (Trylany):
  John, 647, 665
  Robert, 647
Tripoli Company, *see* Levant Company
Troops, *xxiv*
Trose, John, 643
Trumball (Trumbell), Thomas, 641
Trylany *see* Trilany
Tucker:
  Robert, 651
  Valentine, 643
Turkey, 717
Turner, George, 25
Tyler, *see* Taylor
Tyllet (Tillett), James, 656

United Provinces, *xxxiv*; *see also* Flanders; Holland; Zeeland

Valencia, Spain, *xliv*, 164, 166, 345, 352
Valladolid, Spain, *xxxi, xxxvii*, 295, 727
Vawer, William, 642

Velasco, Juan de, *xxxiii–xxxiv*, 40
Vellum, *xxxvi*, 129
Verreyken, Louis, *xxix*
Victualling houses, *see* Taverns
Vigo, Spain, *x*
Villars, William, 149
Vintage, *xxiii*
Vintners, *l*, 725
Virginia Company, *xlvi*
Visitors, of the Spanish Customs, 741

Waade:
  Henry, 455, 497
  Sir William, 637, 641
Wadden, John, 647
Wainscots, 634
Wakeham, John, 652
Wakeman, Thomas, 228
Walcott, Gawen, 54, 641
Walker, Thomas, 23, 643, 664
Walrond(e):
  Henry, 649
  Osmond, 651
Walsingham, Norfolk, 400
Walsingham, *Sir* Thomas, *xiv, xxiv*
Walters, Thomas, 642
Waltham:
  Thomas, 230, 641
  Richard, 151, 641
  William, 289
Walton, William, 149, 641
Walweyne, Humphrey, 457
War, between England and Spain, *xvii, xix, xxii, xxiv, xxviii–xxx, xxxiii–xxxv, xxxvii*, 60, 96, 431, 438, 468, 620, 713, 740, 753
  prisoners-of-war, *xiv, xxxvii*
Warden, Thomas, 642
Warehouses, 78, 401, 628, 714
Warrants, 106, 180, 753
Warren, John, 652
Washer, Richard, 279, 330
Wastell (Wastle, Wasteele), William, 75, 641
Watkins, John, 643
Watson:
  John, 641
  Thomas, 447, 641
  William, 734
Watts:
  George, 644
  Jeffrey, 641
  John, 641
  Sir John, *xv, xxix–xxx*, 2–4, 11, 13, 16, 20–21, 28, 31, 36, 40, 64, 73, 119, 155, 641, 663
  John, jnr., 641
  Richard, 641
  Thomas, 641
  William, 641

Wax, *xlix*
Webbe, Christopher, 642
Weech, *see* Wych
Weight, *see* Wight
Welcham, Jeffrey, 643
Welden, William, 75
Wells, Norfolk, 400
Welsh merchants, *viii*
West(e), John, 649
West country, *xvii, xxxii, xliii, xlv, l*
West Indies, *xlix*
Westminster, *xxxii*, 321, 438, 468, 640, 704
Weymouth, Dorset, 47, 288–9, 448, 498
Whetenhall, Thomas, 641
White:
George, 642
George, of Corn Street, Bristol, 642
Whitehall, London, 96, 108
Whitehead(e), Thomas, 642
Whitmore:
George, 171
William, 171
Whitson, John, *xliii*, 119, 122, 124, 286, 318, 642, 664
Whitway, William, 330
Wich, *see* Wych
Widows, 672
Wight (Weight, Weighte), Ralph, 91, 641
Wilford(e):
James, 641
Thomas, *xi, xiv–xvi, xviii–xx, xxii, xxvi, xxix–xxx, xxxii–xxxvi, xxxix, xl, xliv–xlix, li*, 1, 3, 5, 10–11, 13, 16, 27, 35, 41, 45, 51, 57, 64–6, 68, 79–81, 84, 89, 92, 98, 100, 105, 110, 111, 113, 115–16, 118, 120–22, 124, 126, 130, 134, 139, 141, 144–6, 148, 151–2, 154, 156, 163, 165, 168, 174–5, 178, 180, 183, 186, 190, 200, 205, 207, 211, 223, 237, 239, 245, 250, 270, 282, 285, 305, 307, 317, 321–2, 324, 336, 338, 353, 356, 361, 367–8, 375, 377–8, 391, 394, 396, 402, 407, 411, 419, 421, 440, 443, 452, 459–60, 462, 464, 477, 479–80, 486, 492, 499, 501, 504, 507, 641, 661, 727
Thomas, jnr., 25
William, *xiv*, 641
William, jnr., 151, 641
Wilkins, George, 642
Williams, Edward, 642
Wilson:
Godfrey, 641
Thomas, *xxix*
Wincoll. Robert, 172
Winding, or winching, 376
Wines, *xxvi–xxvii, xxxii, xlvi*, 384, 459,
482, 484, 486, 631; *see also* Sherry-sack
Winter:
Richard, 642
William, *ix, xiv*
Wise:
Christopher, 652
Eustace, 652
John, 652
Nicholas, 652
Samuel, 652
William, 652
Witherall, Thomas, 242
Woder (Wodder), William, 75, 641
Wood(e), John, 642
Wootton, *see* Wotton
Worcester, earl of, *see* Somerset, Edward
Wormell:
Bartholomew, 228
John, 149
Worsupp (Worsopp), John, 54, 641
Wotton (Wootton):
Lord Edward, 97, 482, 485
Humphrey, *xliv*, 243, 351, 433, 474, 641
Wright(e), Thomas, 442
Writs, *xxxvi*, 690
Wych (Weech, Wich, Wiche, Wyche):
James, 43, 64, 347, 433, 472, 502, 641
James (? another), 641
Richard, *l*, 3–4, 6, 11, 18, 20, 31, 36, 39–40, 46, 69, 72, 81, 105, 110, 119, 122, 124, 141, 145, 155, 163, 168, 186, 188, 191, 193, 201, 205, 212, 225, 234, 253, 282, 325, 339, 353, 368, 403, 412, 420, 440, 453, 459, 465, 481, 493, 505, 641, 663
Richard, jnr., 188, 641
Thomas, 641
Wyms (Wymes, Wymies), Humphrey, 218, 641

Yarmouth, Norfolk, *xvii*, 158, 160, 225–8, 231–3, 276, 491, 493, 645, 665
Yelverton, *Sir* Henry, *l*
Yeoman, *xlv*, 478
Yong(e):
Augustine, 276
Gregory, 641
William, 276
York, 122, 124, 128

Zante, Greece, *xlix*
Zeeland, 81, 723–4, 748; *see also* Holland; United Provinces
Zouche, *Lord* Edward, 97
Zubiaur, Pedro de, *xxiv–xxv*

LONDON RECORD SOCIETY

The London Record Society was founded in December 1964 to publish transcripts, abstracts and lists of the primary sources for the history of London, and generally to stimulate interest in archives relating to London. Membership is open to any individual or institution, the annual subscription is £3·15, which entitles a member to receive one copy of each volume published during the year and to attend and vote at meetings of the Society. Prospective members should apply to the Hon. Secretary, Mr Brian Burch, c/o Leicester University Library, University Road, Leicester.

The following volumes have already been published:

1. *London possessory assizes: a calendar*, edited by Helena M. Chew (1965)
2. *London inhabitants within the Walls, 1695*, with an introduction by D. V. Glass (1966)
3. *London Consistory Court wills, 1492–1547*, edited by Ida Darlington (1967)
4. *Scriveners' Company Common Paper, 1357–1628, with a continuation to 1678*, edited by Francis W. Steer (1968)
5. *London Radicalism, 1830–1843: a selection from the papers of Francis Place*, edited by D. J. Rowe (1970)
6. *The London Eyre of 1244*, edited by Helena M. Chew and Martin Weinbaum (1970)
7. *The Cartulary of Holy Trinity Aldgate*, edited by Gerald A. J. Hodgett (1971)
8. *The Port and Trade of Early Elizabethan London: documents*, edited by Brian Dietz (1972)
   Price to members £3·15 each, and to non-members £4·50 each.

The following Occasional Publication is also available:
London and Middlesex Published Records, compiled by J. M. Sims (1970)
Price: free to members, and to non-members £1.

A leaflet describing some of the volumes in preparation may be obtained from the Hon. Secretary.